THE STORY OF
WALES

THE STORY OF
WALES

JON GOWER

With an introduction by Huw Edwards

First published in 2012 to accompany the television series entitled *The Story of Wales*, broadcast on BBC ONE Wales. The 6-part series was made by Green Bay Media for BBC Cymru Wales in partnership with The Open University in Wales. This accompanying book expands on the television series and, therefore, does not mirror the exact series structure. This paperback edition published 2013.

Executive Producer: Elis Owen
Series Producers: Phil George and John Geraint

1 3 5 7 9 10 8 6 4 2

Published in 2013 by BBC Books, an imprint of Ebury Publishing.
A Random House Group Company.

Introduction © Huw Edwards 2012
Text © Jon Gower 2012
Maps © Encompass Graphics 2012

Jon Gower has asserted his right to be identified as the author of this Work
in accordance with the Copyright, Designs and Patents Act 1988

The Random House Group Limited Reg. No. 954009

Addresses for companies within the Random House Group can be found at www.randomhouse.co.uk

A CIP catalogue record for this book is available from the British Library.

ISBN 978 1 849 90373 8

The Random House Group Limited supports the Forest Stewardship Council® (FSC®), the leading international forest-certification organisation. Our books carrying the FSC label are printed on FSC®-certified paper. FSC is the only forest-certification scheme supported by the leading environmental organisations, including Greenpeace. Our paper procurement policy can be found at www.randomhouse.co.uk/environment

Commissioning editor: Albert DePetrillo
Project editor: Laura Higginson
Copy-editor: Alison Sturgeon
Maps: Encompass Graphics
Typeset: Seagull Design
Production: David Brimble

Front cover image © Getty
Back cover main image © Billy Stock/Alamy
Smaller back cover images (from left to right) © Green Bay Media, © The Photolibrary Wales/ Alamy,
© Hulton Archive/ Getty Images, © Hulton Archive/ Getty Images

Printed and bound by CPI Group (UK) Ltd, Croydon, CR0 4YY

To buy books by your favourite authors and register for offers, visit www.randomhouse.co.uk

CONTENTS

LIST OF MAPS

INTRODUCTION

IT'S OUR STORY

My story of Wales is not your story of Wales, but your version is every bit as valid as mine.

My story is the sum of a singular set of circumstances and experiences. So is yours. Mine is the story of 'Cymru'. You may prefer 'Wales'. Both are equal entities; they are two sides of the same national coin.

My personal story is principally about Ceredigion, the Garw valley, and my native Llanelli. I am a product of these places. You may be a product of Pontrhydfendigaid, or Llantwit Major, or Llandudno, or Abergwyngregyn, or Amlwch, or Caerleon, or Port Eynon, or Swansea, or Pontypridd, or Wrexham, or Porthmadog, or Ton Pentre, or, indeed, any of the places we visited while filming *The Story of Wales*.

If you identify yourself as Welsh, maybe you are a Welsh speaker, like me. Or not. You may live in Wales. Or, like me, you may not. You may be proud of Wales, like me. Or you may not. Perhaps, like me, you have regrets about Wales. Or you may have none. So many permutations, so many potential divisions, so many differences for such a small nation – and yet all of us who claim a Welsh identity share one certain truth: each of us, regardless of our language or our region of origin, is part of the great story of Wales.

So it is perhaps no wonder that some thought I was unwise to take on a project of this magnitude. Great men and women have laboured in the field of Welsh history, and I follow in their footsteps with deep respect. While filming, we were always mindful of their achievements.

The Story of Wales packs 30,000 years of history into six hours of television. How was it possible to achieve this? We were helped in part by the memorable sights that abound in Wales. The site of Crawshay's immense iron furnaces in Merthyr is still impressive in scale and form, while the sadness and tranquillity evoked by Llyn Celyn in the early morning light is a very special experience. The ruins of Strata Florida Abbey near Pontrhydfendigaid offer a haunting glimpse of life in medieval Wales, and the vivid, lunar-like landscape of Parys Mountain in Ynys Môn, with its ancient copper workings, is unforgettable. Dinefwr castle, majestically sited above the Tywi, is probably my favourite castle in Wales. And who can resist the peace and beauty of St David's Cathedral, a prime site of Christian worship for the past 1,400 years?

The tracing of Welsh history led us to every region. We travelled to Wrexham in the northeast, where the Catholic martyr Richard Gwyn was executed in the beast market in 1584. In northwest Wales we toured the opulent Penrhyn castle, once home to the Douglas-Pennants who owned the vast Penrhyn slate quarry and who became one of the most despised families in the industrial history of Britain. We visited a section of Offa's Dyke, near Knighton in mid-Wales, where the landscape has remained unchanged over many centuries, and in the southeast we marvelled at the scale of the ruins of the Roman city Caerleon. We stood on the sands of Mill Bay on the Welsh southwest coast, the site of Henry Tudor's landing in 1485 on his way to claim the crown of England. And in the valleys of south Wales we paid our respects to Senghennydd, where 439 men and boys died in the Universal colliery disaster in 1913; there is surely no more potent reminder of the dominance of coal and the terrible price paid by thousands of families, including my own. These places, and many more, all play their part in the complex past of Wales.

This book adds depth to our television narrative: it is an ideal companion to the series. The author, Jon Gower, an old friend of mine from Llanelli Grammar School, has produced a stunning text.

Jon and I are among many of those who remember the major televised history of Wales, *The Dragon Has Two Tongues*, brilliantly fronted by Gwyn Alf Williams and Wynford Vaughan-Thomas for HTV more than a quarter-century ago. It mesmerized viewers: each presenter vigorously promoted his own story of Wales, engaging in endless argument about people, places and events. Their verbal sparring conveyed the volatility of that period; there was a palpable uncertainty about the very notion of Wales. The country seemed to be in flux as the political landscape was dominated by the year-long miners' strike of 1984–5. Gwyn Alf and Wynford taught viewers that the best history provokes debate and encourages reflection.

This series has been made 26 years later in a rather different climate. Wales is in many ways a new country, clearly energized and boasting its own government and law-making National Assembly. For the first time in the history of our nation, laws are being made by elected Welsh representatives, in Wales, for Wales. This is surely the glittering prize that eluded the revolutionary Owain Glyndŵr, whose vision of a cultured, educated, assertive Wales has inspired so many patriots over the centuries.

These recent developments suggest a temptingly neat storyline: we have a beginning (the birth of Wales and eventual union with

England); a middle (Wales transformed from rural backwater to industrial powerhouse); and an end (Wales starts to govern most of its own affairs). The narrative drive is compelling, but it ignores countless subtle layers of sense and significance.

Much of the story of Wales and its people is coloured by relations with neighbouring England. During our filming I visited the National History Museum in Cardiff. Tucked away in a corner of the main gallery was a prize exhibit: the Act of Union of England and Wales (the first of two, royally approved in 1536) was on Welsh soil for the very first time, on loan from the Parliamentary Archives at Westminster. This is the document that created the legal entity 'England and Wales' – a momentous event in Welsh history, which provoked not a murmur of protest, as Geraint H. Jenkins explains so lucidly in our series. The heroic failures of Owain Glyndŵr, Llywelyn the Great and Llywelyn the Last to create an independent Wales had sapped the people's morale, apart from which, there were certain economic benefits to be gained by the merging of Wales with England.

It is a powerful experience for any Welsh man or woman to handle the actual document that sets out the terms of the union (annexation is a more accurate description). That experience is even more intense for a Welsh speaker, given the explicit hostility to the language expressed in the legislation. But there is a powerful lesson in all of this: the Tudor authorities fully recognized that the Welsh language was easily the most powerful distinguishing feature of the people who lived beyond Offa's Dyke. It was a prime badge of nationhood.

It still is today – with one capital difference: what has changed beyond measure is the people's settled view of the language and its place in our national life. There has been a quantum shift during my lifetime, and certainly since Gwyn Alf and Wynford locked horns in the 1980s. When I arrived at Cardiff University in the late 1970s, we Welsh speakers were made to feel like outcasts in our own capital city; the language was a topic of poisonous debate. The venom even seeped into the exchanges on devolution in the referendum of 1979. That world has now gone – and good riddance. There are certainly some die-hard opponents whose crusade goes on, but they are fewer in number every year.

The roaring success of Welsh-medium schools, a solid base of new language legislation, and a healthy respect for different cultures in our mixed modern society have all been significant factors in the change of heart towards the Welsh language. The biggest challenge now is to make Welsh a relevant, natural medium in all walks of life for those who wish to use it. The current fear is that too many of the young people leaving Welsh-medium schools will be unable or reluctant to use the language in their working lives. There is more to be done, but the past 40 years have seen a profound transformation.

The shame felt by so many Welsh people after the 1847 publication of the notorious Blue Books (an official report on education in Wales, slamming most aspects of Welsh life) can nonetheless be perceived today in some quarters. I still meet people of a certain age whose lives appear to have been spent covering all traces of their Welshness; they seem to feel mortified by their true identity. My late father spent decades studying the psychological, social and literary impact of the Blue Books; he had no doubt that they caused a national trauma, the effects of which are still with us in the twenty-first century. Those effects are weakening, and the nation's view is, as I perceive it, more settled. But I feel it is essential to draw attention to this degrading episode highlighted in the television series.

The principal milestones of Welsh history are very familiar to most of us, and the challenge of any modern history project is to explore potential new perspectives, seek new significance, and dare to question some cherished interpretations where appropriate.

That said, there were some real surprises: I had not been aware that the prehistoric copper mines beneath the Great Orme in Llandudno are considered the most important in the world, and I was amazed that the laws passed by the English parliament after the revolt of Owain Glyndŵr had been so ferociously racist in their treatment of Welsh people. It was unexpected that the wise Welsh ruler Hywel Dda had made a pilgrimage to Rome in 928, and I was fascinated to learn that the church at Llantwit Major has a magnificent collection of ancient stone crosses.

There were plenty of questions too. Had Henry Tudor been such a good friend to Wales? Did the drowning of the village of Capel Celyn really kick-start the modern drive to devolution? Was the ancient land we now call Wales a backward, isolated place? How are global perceptions of Wales and the Welsh shaped by literature and film?

In considering the answers we are all forced to reflect, rethink and reappraise.

For someone who has been a London Welshman for the past quarter-century, the project has been doubly challenging. I have obtained an outsider's perspective to add to my insider's view. These perspectives overlap at times, creating an even more powerful understanding of some of the forces at work. I have a sense that my family represents some of the most salient themes in our story: farming, rural poverty, migration to London, emigration to the United States, coal mining, seafaring and Nonconformity. As the narrative of Wales's history unfolds, it is natural for all of us to work out how and where we and our families fit in. I found myself confronting episodes in my own family story – some of them happy, some tragic.

The Edwards family were tenant farmers in the wilds of Ceredigion in the eighteenth and nineteenth centuries. Theirs was a life of back-breaking poverty. Some of them fled this misery by emigrating to the United States, as did thousands of other Welsh people. The Edwards clan can still be found in Oak Hill, Ohio, today. Of those who stayed at home, two Edwards brothers left for London and set up in the dairy business. They were part of a great Welsh industry in the capital. My grandfather, John Daniel, was born in London, where his father was a dairyman's assistant. My grandmother, Olwen Myfanwy, was born in Llanbradach where her father was a miner.

On my mother's side, the Protheroe family were farm workers who came from Hereford and settled in the Garw valley, where they found work in the coal mines. My grandfather, Leo Price, was a miner who lost his life in a rock-fall at the age of 28. My grandmother, Elizabeth Muriel, was born in Cardiganshire, but spent most of her long life in the Garw valley.

That's the wide-angle view. But what of the close-up? My personal story of Wales starts in Llanelli, where I was raised, and leads to London via Cardiff and Neufchâteau, a town in eastern France, where I spent a year teaching. Llanelli is a town whose Welsh credentials are difficult to match. In its economic heyday, it was a heavily industrialized cauldron of working-class Welshness, truly one of the most remarkable towns in Wales. It has endured decades of economic hardship, but there are signs of renewal at last.

Renewal. That, in a word, is surely the dominant theme of our story of Wales.

For Gwyn Alf, the story of Wales was a series of ruptures and fractures. Wynford fancied a rather more fluid narrative. I am decidedly for Gwyn Alf's view, though I favour the theme of 'renewal' over his 'rupture'. Time and again, our country has shown its canny ability to change and adapt. It is still doing so today. Wales in the early twenty-first century is once more a country in the tumult of rejuvenation. The Welsh people, more culturally and ethnically diverse than ever before, are a nation in renewal.

A distinguished modern historian recently declared that there has never been a more exciting time to be Welsh. *The Story of Wales* has convinced me that he is right.

Huw Edwards

PART ONE

BEFORE WALES

CHAPTER ONE

THE RED LADY
OF PAVILAND

A DETECTIVE STORY

They had come to bury their dead: trudging across the permafrost, mantled in reindeer skins, they carried the corpse. On resting from their labours, they could see the huge mass of the glacier in the middle distance, the dense ice grey and glaucous. If you had inclination enough to stand there for a lifetime, you would see it moving, scraping slowly across the land. But at zero degrees it was too cold to linger long. This was Wales 29,000 years ago, in the Upper Palaeolithic era, and there was a lot more ice on the way.* A huge wall of it would cover the land as the climate chilled.

For now it was just possible to survive in this challenging world, and besides, they had a burial to perform. Their sacred cave filled with the sound of thin notes played on a bird-bone flute and the beat of a simple drum. They had been here before, as had others. That is how the cave had become a place of sanctity after all: by these simple acts,

---

* The most recent carbon dating work by a joint team from Oxford University and the British Museum in 2006 suggests that the corpse may have lived 29,000 years ago or 4,000 years earlier than previously thought.

which turned the cave into something else, something more than just a refuge for hunters from the cold threat outside.

The body, possibly a shaman or a medicine man, was laid to rest next to the skull of an adult mammoth. He was buried wearing red ochre-stained funeral clothes, and powdered, loose ochre found in rocks nearby was also scattered over the body in its cave-grave. On the chest of the deceased were placed fragments of ivory, as well as ivory bracelets and rings the size of teacups. Near his thigh were two handfuls of perforated periwinkle shells, objects used only for male burials. And at his head and feet were two small headstones, simple markers to indicate this was indeed a grave.

This was a small, intense, public ritual, conducted in a frozen land that would eventually thaw, and later become the country known as Wales. These primitive undertakers were among the earliest truly human occupants of this tough and rugged country, although not the first. Neanderthal man had dwelt here too, long before the cave dwellers of Paviland. These earliest inhabitants weren't *Homo sapiens*, not wise humans like us, but rather *Homo sapiens neanderthalensis*. But they were humans of a kind, nevertheless, with their hairy feet wrapped around a lower rung of the evolutionary ladder.

The earliest human remains known in Wales are about 230,000 years old and were discovered between 1978 and 1995 at Pontnewydd Cave in the Elwy valley near St Asaph, Denbighshire, during excavations by Amgueddfa Cymru, the National Museum of Wales. They date from deep into the ice age, when these Neanderthals had to cope with life in the fridge. This species, which pre-dated man and was, in a sense, a different branch of the same evolutionary tree, survived until about 36,000 years ago. At this point *Homo sapiens* would become the sole human occupants of this early world.

The short and stocky denizens of Pontnewydd would have possessed large, square jaws and heavy brow ridges. They would have used primitive tools such as rudimentary hand-held axes, scrapers and basic spear points. Their environment would have been shared with a menagerie of wild animals, including lions, bears, leopards and wolves, and their simple tools were used for defence, hunting and simple acts of butchery as they skinned and prepared their kills. The remains of people discovered in the Pontnewydd Cave ranged in age from young children to adults. The most complete discovery from the site is a fragment of an upper jaw belonging to a child aged around eight years old. In the jaw a very heavily worn milk tooth can be seen positioned alongside a newly erupted permanent molar. Had this child lived, this new tooth would eventually have pushed out the milk tooth. This is unusually rare and intimate evidence.

Questions remain as to whether these humans were originally buried in graves within the cave. The cave has since been washed through by the meltwater from the retreating ice sheets at the end of the last ice age. Unfortunately, the forces that led to the preservation of these teeth deep within Pontnewydd Cave coincidentally destroyed any traces of their original burial context.

But let us return to Paviland, where the real detective story began. This involved the finding of a skeleton – a skeleton that would later undergo the most famous 'sex change' in the country's history.

The original find at Paviland was commemorated in verse, albeit doggerel:

Have Ye Heard of the Woman So Long Under Ground
Have ye Heard of the Woman that Buckland has found
With her bones of empyreal Hues
O fair ones of modern days, hang down your head
The Antediluvians rouged when dead
*Only granted in life time to you**

The Buckland referred to in the verse was William Buckland, the first ever professor of geology at Oxford University, who is credited with the discovery of the famous skeleton. He had arrived at Goat's Hole Cave at Paviland on the south side of the Gower Peninsula on 18 January 1823 to begin an exploration. Excitement would have been coursing through his veins: after all, this was still the golden age of geology, when major discoveries and enormous leaps in human knowledge could be made.

Interestingly, this subterranean discovery happened in the same period that two geologists, Adam Sedgwick and R. I. Murchison, were exploring rock formations in Wales. Together, in the 1830s, they came up with a system for determining the relative ages of Lower Palaeozoic rocks, giving them the names of the ancient tribes of Wales, namely Silurian, Ordovician and, in the case of the oldest, Cambrian. Indirectly, it suggests that the ancient people of Wales were 'hard' – they had to be. The landmass of Wales is mainly mountainous, an unforgiving and thinly soiled terrain, with fertile valleys relatively few in number. Living off the land was far from easy.

---

* Buckland surmised that the poem was written by one of his undergraduates. In truth, its author was none other than Philip Bury Duncan, fellow of New College Oxford and Keeper of the Ashmolean Museum.

Buckland's explorations had been prompted by discoveries the previous year when a surgeon named Daniel Davies and a curate from Port Eynon, the Reverend John Davies, had ventured together into the pitch darkness of Goat's Hole. There they had found a scattering of animal bones, including a solitary mammoth tusk. They soon communicated the nature of their find to the Talbot family of nearby Penrice castle, prompting the redoubtable-sounding daughter, Miss Mary Theresa Talbot, to explore the cave for herself. There she discovered 'bones of elephants' on 27 December 1822.[1] A detailed letter from Miss Talbot was subsequently sent to Buckland at Oxford, and it proved sufficiently intriguing for him to visit Gower within a month.

During a week's work in the cave, this pioneering 'underground-ologist', who was also in his lifetime Dean of Westminster and a curate at Christchurch College, uncovered headless human remains. These he mistakenly presumed to be those of a young woman, picturing her as a shamanic figure, as a Romano-British priestess perhaps, and naming her the 'Red Lady of Paviland' because of the red ochre (naturally occurring iron oxide) that stained the ancient bones. Buckland had a ready explanation for the colour scheme as well, suggesting that the Red Lady may have been a relation or descendant of Adam, who was 'made of red Earth'. Buckland suggested that the Red Lady might even be Eve herself.[2]

As we know, there were objects in the cave other than bones: periwinkle shells and ivory rods. But the bones ... they were problematic. This was a period when intense debate raged about the history of humanity, when some questioned the belief that the whole of humanity was derived from survivors of the biblical flood, the children of Noah. The presence of animal bones, those of long-extinct species, might disprove the 'truth' of the biblical flood. Thus the Red Lady became fodder for Buckland's imaginative science, as he suggested various scenarios for her. At one stage he argued that this was the body of a customs officer, murdered by smugglers. Later he saw her as a Roman harlot, more scarlet woman than red lady, who serviced the sexual needs of soldiers from a nearby fort (which actually dated from the Iron Age). Buckland, sometimes known as the 'Ammon Knight' (a pun on 'ammonite', a common fossil) was a Romantic, drawn by the twilight glamour of his subterranean quests.

Modern science has since overturned his conclusions, showing that the skeleton was that of a young man, buried in the Goat's Hole Cave around 30,000 years ago. This makes his the oldest anatomically modern human skeleton found in Britain, and Paviland the site of the oldest ceremonial burial in western Europe.

As Stephen Aldhouse-Green, professor of human origins at the University of Wales, Newport, has pointed out, analysis of the carbon and nitrogen content of the bones has revealed a great deal of information about the young man's diet. He was partial to seafood, which would have been collected on the coast, then 100 kilometres (60 miles) away. There might have been salmon too, as evidence for this fish is present in the bones of bears that also used the caves at Paviland.

Aldhouse-Green has also given us some vital statistics, describing a 'healthy adult male, aged 25–30, about 1.74 metres (5 feet 8 inches) in height, and possibly weighing about 73 kg (11 stone)', but one who is less robust then might be expected for the period. Whilst the earliest anatomically modern humans in Europe were characterized by tropically adapted body proportions, arising from their African ancestry, this is not reflected in the Paviland skeleton, probably because this individual was a product of perhaps 10,000 years of evolution by modern humans within Europe.

The young man was buried in an area that would have looked very different back then. The cliffs of the Gower Peninsula were part of a ridge rising above a river plain that was located 113 kilometres (70 miles) from the sea. Even in warmer phases, the ice sheet was never far away, and mammoths made the ground quake as they lumbered by. On the great plain below the cliffs, rhinos would have grazed, as well as a plenitude of deer stalked by that designer carnivore, the sabre-toothed tiger. After dark, hyenas would startle the nights with their wild cries. The cave would have been a refuge from all this.

The Red Lady of Paviland lived in the distant past of the Wales we have come to know, but the story is a good metaphor for our journey: like the history of the Red Lady, the story of Wales is one worth revisiting with fresh eyes. And against the background of new historical evidence, it is a tale that might even need retelling, and the identity of the Welsh reappraised. The young man who lived and died so many thousands of years ago was shown to be resourceful, adaptable and intimately bound with the landscape around him – characteristics that we shall see displayed again and again by the people who lived on the landmass that came to be known as Wales.

CHAPTER TWO

THE STONE AGES

As the sun rises on Midsummer Day, the longest day of the year, fingers of light shaft thinly into the tomb. For thousands of years, at this precise time of year, the sun's first light has shone down the passageway into the burial chamber at Bryn Celli Ddu on Anglesey. There is only one other place in Britain where such a summer solstice alignment is to be found – although there are other sites that align with the low sun of the winter solstice – and that is Stonehenge, which was built several hundred years after the last stone tomb was completed. At both places, on Anglesey and in Wiltshire, the prehistoric folk of the Stone Age practised sun-worship that was backed up with a remarkable sense of celestial geometry.

The creators of tombs such as Bryn Celli Ddu were people mindful of death, and, quite possibly, respectful of a god. The tombs they erected were created without access to earth-moving vehicles or lengths of chain, or the benefit of precision instruments for measuring. Rather, they were built with the sweat of brows and a rudimentary but effective sense of how to set huge stone upon huge stone, employing nothing more sophisticated than timber levers, tree-trunk ramps and honeysuckle-vine ropes.

The exact reason for this once-a-year event is lost in the mists of time. Were the sun's rays meant to warm the bones in the chamber, nourishing the spirits of the dead on the longest day of the year? Or was it another demonstration of the ancient people's fascination with the appearing sun at the birth of the day – an event that, at its most basic, equates to life itself? Just as the Egyptian sun god, Re, crossed the sky in a ship each day, the sun above Wales was seen as the most powerful symbol of birth and rebirth. It seems natural that many tombs were aligned with the eastern edge of the horizon, as if scanning for their own sun gods.

In archaeological terms, Bryn Celli Ddu belongs to the New Stone Age, and dates from the period 4000–2000 BCE. The tomb is, in the formal taxonomy of archaeology, a 'passage grave' in the European Atlantic tradition, and is associated with similar constructions around the Irish Sea, and others as far north as the Orkneys. The tombs in Wales may be smaller than their great Irish counterparts – Bryn Celli Ddu is only 25 metres (85 feet) in diameter – but all usually display examples of simple decorative art.

Bryn Celli Ddu seems to have been erected circa 3500 BCE, and the inhumations, or burials, were made in a cross-shaped chamber that was set inside a circular retaining wall beneath a vast cairn. This was the age of great religious monuments that bore witness to cults of the dead and to fertility rituals. Constructed from stone, the tombs were built to last, although the people who raised the often-mighty capstones might not have guessed that they would last for 6,000 years and still be standing in the twenty-first century.

There are mysteries hidden even underneath the burial chamber at Bryn Celli Ddu. A carved stone was discovered buried below the chamber floor, its strange designs mystifying to the modern mind. Their meaning has been erased just as surely as the lines etched into the soft stone have lost their definition, blunted by time. Some have suggested that the inscribed pillar found on Anglesey was a phallic symbol, while others posit that the swirling marks on the stone reflected the trance-like states of those who participated in rituals in such tombs. No one can know for sure. But we do know with certainty that this style of carving was not confined to Anglesey – far from it. It was employed by tomb-builders in northern Spain and the Orkneys. Examples can also be found in the valley of the Boyne in Ireland, where three massive tombs at Knowth, Dowth and Newgrange were found. The last of these contained a staggering 43,000 cubic metres (56 cubic yards) of stone, mirroring the features of Bryn Celli Ddu and suggesting that the creation of such tombs helped connect these sea-facing communities in a common approach to death.

Eighteen kilometres (11 miles) from Bryn Celli Ddu is another, smaller site, Barclodiad y Gawres, the Giantess's Apron. Here excavations have unearthed evidence of the preparation of a strange, inexplicable ritual stew with ingredients such as wrasse, eel, whiting, frog, toad, grass snake and small rodents.[1] On encountering such a weird broth, it is hard not to think of the witches in Shakespeare's *Macbeth* and their 'double toil and trouble', as they added 'fillet of fenny snake', 'toe of frog' and 'lizard's leg' to their cauldron.

To add to the mystery of the 'Apron', excavators also found a fine series of carved stones – again with unmistakable French and Iberian connections. The meaning of the pecked geometric patterns is now lost to us. What are relegated today to being mysterious Stone Age hieroglyphs are, at the very least, signs of an early cultural unity, interchange and movement.

The setting of megalithic structures, such as tombs, in the landscape helped to mark meeting places, often utilizing the drama of a particular natural form. One such example is the tomb of Din Dryfol, which is set on a natural platform halfway up a hill on Anglesey. Other monuments seem erected simply to make a mark on the land. It was one way of changing the world, of establishing mastery over nature's mystery. Some tombs in coastal sites were easily spotted from the sea. Others marked former settlements, being built quite literally on the past. Sometimes the tomb was built because of happenstance, such as using the huge boulder deposited by a glacier on Cefn Bryn on the Gower Peninsula as reason enough to lever it into place as the basis of a striking tomb.

There were other figures in the landscape too. Many of the standing stones that punctuate the hills and valleys of Wales, such as those at Stackpole in Pembrokeshire, date from the Stone Age and suggest places of ceremony and congregation, while others mark established trackways. The existence of new tools also gave humans more control over the landscape. It was possible to fashion the land, mine it and eventually farm it. Humankind could suggest it was here for the duration by raising stones and monuments that could signal their existence over large distances. The circles of stones at places such as Gors Fawr in Pembrokeshire, and Cerrig Duon near the source of the river Tawe, seem to control the landscape, to gather the view around them.

We know very little about Stone Age people living in Wales during this period, but we know with certainty that before the advent of agriculture they would have had a tough time of it in the harsh and testing environment. Continuous human settlement began after the end of the last ice age, in about 9000 BCE. This was followed by a period of a rise in sea level, during which the country assumed the shape it has today. Temperatures rose and led to the spreading and thickening of a dense forest, which blanketed the landmass almost entirely. For Stone Age people, Wales was a huge, often-impenetrable wild wood, with the tree-line of oaks and birch extending almost to the mountaintops. This relatively swift change in environment would precipitate a change in the way Stone Age people lived. A more benign climate, coupled with new pastoral skills, meant they could keep their own animals close at hand, rather than hunt them over long distances.

From the Middle Stone Age, herding had started to replace hunting, and the peoples who lived between 9500 and 4000 BCE exchanged skills of tracking and spear-throwing for more sedentary ones, such as tending flocks of domesticated animals, erecting simple enclosures, and guarding their stock from the predations of wild animals. Deer grazed new clearings, created when man harnessed fire to burn the vegetation. Thus the erratic, literally hit-or-miss life of the ranging hunters – felling giant cattle known as aurochs with their simple spears, following the migratory treks of red deer though the wild Welsh woods, or managing to snag salmon in the surging rivers – slowly gave way to farming.

The hunter, with his newly domesticated dog – a descendant of the wolf – was still a gatherer of seeds, fruits and roots, but over time his mobile lifestyle evolved into that of settled man. Some of the first settlements might have been fairly temporary, such as the camp discovered on coastal mudflats at Goldcliff near Newport, dating from around 5600 BCE. This revealed evidence of pigs and red deer having been caught and butchered, of eels having been cooked, and hazelnuts gathered and shelled.[2] But although these settlements may have been only transient, they still indicated that the early dwellers did not feel compelled to be on the move all the time, and that some locales could be sustaining.

Agriculture itself seems to have arrived in western Britain after 4000 BCE. Farming had first developed in western Asia, then in the Middle East, after which it was introduced across Europe, community by community. Along with the early farming techniques from 6000 years ago came the tomb-building skills required to create Bryn Celli Ddu and Din Dryfol, not to mention the arrival of pottery and new flint tools.

New Stone Age findings reveal an existence with a sense of order or purpose, with possibilities even of high civilization. This manifests as memorials – such as those at Bryn Celli Ddu – that have much grandeur and dignity even today. These tombs for the dead bear witness to very early awe, and tell us where the awestruck people settled. They also demonstrate skills in logistics in transporting and erecting heavy, unhewn stones and in dry-walling too – the art of constructing a wall without the use of binding mortar. To give some indication of their relative antiquity, the laying and ordering of these megaliths, or huge stones, predate the pyramids by some 1,500 years and are 2,000 years older than the first Chinese dynasties.

In addition to the passage tombs, there are over a hundred chambered tombs or *cromlechi* in Wales. These massive stone chambers within stone or earth mounds are mainly to be found in lowland coastal areas, with the greatest concentrations on western promontories, such as Anglesey, Caernarfonshire and Pembrokeshire. These sitings suggest that their builders were a coastal people with connections via the seaways with other such people, although there are also *cromlechi* clustered along the valleys of rivers such as the Conwy and Wye. Some are located inland, on the highlands of Breconshire, and confound too much ready reckoning. Taken together, these tombs scattered around Wales are easily the oldest architecture to be found in our landscapes, and some date back to as early as *c.*3600–3000 BCE.

The *cromlechi*, simple as they were, were hubs of life and death for egalitarian clans, who, as communities, owned the land around them, with just five acres a head perhaps.[3] They were still mobile people, but the *cromlechi* anchored them. It gave them a place to honour the dead, and to preserve them. It allowed them to claim the land as their own, and, in so doing, claim it respectfully for their ancestors before them. The gradual rise of agriculturalism, and resulting increase in resources stemming from the growth of successful communities, enabled the strong and resourceful people to construct these *cromlechi*.

In the south of Wales, long cairns were built by peoples who came from western France to the Severn, and these simple edifices are collectively known as the Severn–Cotswold group. Even though the name derives from the fact that the greatest concentration of such tombs is between the Severn and the Cotswolds in Gloucestershire, there are also tombs of this kind in Glamorgan, even as far west as Gower. Further examples are also to be found in north Wales, such as Capel Garmon in Gwynedd, and Tyddyn Bleiddyn in Denbighshire. Like the *cromlechi*, long cairns were contructed by organized communities, and it took 200 people to put the capstone – the largest in Britain – on top of the Tinkinswood burial chamber in the Vale of Glamorgan, in which some 50 people are interred. The tomb interior was divided into various compartments and it has been suggested that different families took responsibility for building and filling their respective units. The area has a plentiful supply of the conglomerate rocks required to build it; these early builders often built near the source of their materials.

There is ample evidence that there were some relatively populous, settled areas in this period, with sufficient manpower to achieve considerable feats of very early civic building; a conservative estimate of the population of Wales at this time puts the figure at over 83,000.[4] Yet the wooden buildings they lived in have crumbled with time, suggesting that they were not built to last, a fact that distinguishes buildings with a domestic use from those with a ritual, higher purpose. In the same way that many people were involved in building these tombs, so too were many interred in them. The Parc-le-Breos tomb at Ilston on Gower, discovered in 1869, enshrined the remains of over 40 people, including men, women and children, in four side-chambers linked to a central passage. Interestingly, even though those discovered lived near the sea, there is surprisingly little evidence of seafood in their diets. Instead there is a preponderance of animal-based foodstuffs, such as meat, milk and possibly blood.

In general, time has tended to erode or totally diminish the mounds that enclosed and surmounted the New Stone Age tombs. An exception is the single survivor at Penywyrlod at Talgarth in Powys, where both mound and tomb have withstood the test of time. A man's skull exhumed from here is the basis for a computer-generated reconstruction at the National Museum. His face is revealed as long and slender, with sensitive features. However, the discovery at the same site of a human rib punctured by a flint weapon-tip – thus Wales's first murder evidence – suggests that they might not all have been sensitive folk. Science is able to tell us even more about the people buried at Talgarth: one elderly lady lived to such a ripe old age that she had no teeth left, while another had an inflammatory scalp disorder akin to psoriasis. Such intimate details serve to bring those long gone very much to life for us.

There are other striking testaments to the building prowess of the New Stone Age peoples, none more so than the portal dolmens, such as the one at Pentre Ifan on Carn Ingli, the Hill of Angels near Nevern. The massive capstone, at 3.12 metres (10 feet), is sufficiently high to ride a horse underneath and is set at a dramatic rakish angle atop an angled portal, or H-shaped stones. In this case, three earthfast uprights support the huge weight, and have done so for millennia. The dolmen's location is striking: the votary, walking towards the entrance during a burial ceremony, would have seen nothing beyond the great megaliths other than a remote vista, to the sea and beyond. Smaller portal dolmens exist at Coetan Arthur near Newport in Pembrokeshire, and there are half a dozen tombs in Dyffryn Ardudwy.

Other substantial structures from this period include the henges. These are circular earthen enclosures with an internal ditch. They were entered by single or double entrances, which suggest that they were sacred spaces. One of the best preserved and most impressive is that at Llandygái near Bangor, a natural place for trade and convention as it stands astride both sea and land routes.

When not constructing mighty feats of architecture, the people of the Stone Age would have spent their time farming. With all those trees to cut down to make way for farming enclosures, it is unsurprising that one of the hallmarks of the age was the polished stone axe. Evidence of manufactories has been found, such as Graig Lwyd, near Penmaen-mawr, a site discovered in June 1919. Axes were made here from a very particular kind of rock called augite granophyre, and this has been discovered as far afield as Wiltshire, southern Scotland and Northern Ireland. Each axe would have been made by chipping down a stone block into the rudimentary shape of an axe, then grinding and polishing it with sand and water. Southern England was a good source of high-quality flint, so it was worth making the long journey there to acquire the material. English flint could be exchanged for Welsh augite – the birth of an elementary trading system.

It was perhaps no coincidence that other such 'factories' were located near the sea-lanes, such as the one at Mynydd Rhiw on the tip of the Llŷn Peninsula, and at Carn Meini at Mynachlog-ddu in the Preselau Mountains of Pembrokeshire. Tools have been found in places right across southern, central and eastern England, confirming that this was a time of busy exchange and trade, of export and import, as evidenced by the fact that axes from places such as Cumbria, Cornwall, Northern Ireland and southeast England were in turn discovered in Wales. Towards the end of the New Stone Age artefacts such as axe hammers, battle-axes and mace heads were common, and suggested divisions in society according to rank or status. These could sometimes be sophisticated objects, such as the flint mace head, found in Maesmor in Denbighshire, on which 170 lozenge-shaped facets were carved most precisely.

The organizational abilities of people during the New Stone Age are evident in abundance: one has only to look at the gargantuan efforts involved in moving the huge slabs of Pembrokeshire bluestone from the Preselau Mountains to their stands at Stonehenge 4,500 years ago to realize the scale of their ingenuity. Just as these much-removed ancestors were adept at working with stone, so too were they able to harvest and utilize huge amounts of timber, although the wood used subsequently rotted away, leaving little evidence. But they did work with timber, and sometimes to an astonishing degree.

The discovery of an enormous palisaded enclosure near Hindwell Farm in the Walton Basin in Radnorshire, halfway between Llandrindod Wells and Hereford, enclosing an area of 34 hectares (84 acres) has shed light on the scale of timber erection in this era. With a circumference of over 2 kilometres (1¼ miles) it is by far the largest such enclosure in Britain.[5]

The Hindwell Palisade is likely to date from 2700 BCE, and in a European context its scale is dwarfed only by that at Urmitz on the Rhine, near Koblenz. The richness of the Walton soil and the sheltered location explains why people favoured this area, and there is evidence from the flint scatters (collections of worked flint) found on a central ridge overlooking the palisade that the settlers of the area practised mixed farming, planting crops, and raising sheep and cattle for both milk and meat.

The arc of a large ditch at the site was discovered as a result of aerial reconnaissance in 1994, and subsequent excavations in the area revealed the enclosure was made up of some 1,400 large, spaced posts, each up to a metre in diameter and up to six metres high. These had been set in holes some two metres deep. Each post would have weighed about four and a half tons and a total of 6,300 tons of timber would have been needed.

It would have required a colossal amount of manpower both to cut down the trees and dress the timber, as well as a considerable logistical effort to move the posts and then erect them. The purpose of the enclosure is shrouded in mystery. It might have been a tribal gathering place, a gargantuan cattle pen, or an enclosure for religious ritual. Whatever the case, it was probably not a defensive affair, but it certainly demonstrates teamwork to a sophisticated degree.

The Hindwell enclosure, taken together with the 100 tombs of Neolithic Wales and the manufacturing sites of axes at Graig Lwyd, are crucial to our understanding of Wales and its people during the Stone Age. Together they show an epic scale of ingenuity and creativity in stone and woodwork, born out of established and powerful spiritual beliefs. They also offer plentiful evidence of an evolving sedentary society based on farming over foraging.

Even as people put down tentative roots in early settlements, they maintained their links with other peoples and evolving societies. This region was clearly not an isolated one as there were trade links between Wales, Ireland and Western Europe. Peoples from the Iberian Peninsula and maritime France freely visited this western peninsula, where they shared building techniques and ideologies with its people.

Here were varied peoples with cultural and spiritual beliefs in common, demonstrating that Wales was both connected and visible to a wider world a very long time ago.

CHAPTER THREE

BRONZE AND IRON AGES

The people of the Stone Age readily made the move from a mobile life of hunting and fishing to herding, and eventually to the sedentary, settled life of early agriculture. They also dealt with profound changes in climate as the deep chill gave way to warmer times. Yet for all their respect for the dead and, presumably, for simple deities, and for all their skills in the building of structures in wood and stone, they were still relatively rudimentary makers of things, using primitive skills that never embraced elaborate art or decoration; as far as is known, there are no cave paintings under Welsh hills. But soon both art and decoration would enter their world, along with a more sophisticated sense of how to make things, when the age of metal-mining and metal-working dawned.

During the periods referred to as the Bronze and Iron Ages, the first intimations of a Celtic identity emerged through a shared set of aesthetic values, beliefs and respect for early gods, which would connect Wales with parts of England, Ireland and Scotland, and also with peoples across a large swathe of Western Europe.*

Trade and exchange really took off in the Bronze Age, which in Britain spanned the period from around 2000 to 1000 BCE. Metal, especially copper and then bronze, was now a sought-after commodity, and, even though discovering a variety of uses for metals didn't necessarily revolutionize early society, there were social and cultural changes that paralleled the spread of metal objects.

Copper was the first metal to be cast, which happened sometime around 2300 BCE. By 2000 BCE the far more useful alloy, bronze, was being created by the simple act of mixing copper with tin. This meant that the fashioning of basic objects, such as axes, was eventually followed by the making of more sophisticated tools, decorative objects and weapons, such as rapiers and slashing swords. Metalsmiths became important and respected members of society.

The Penard hoard of bronze tools, arrowheads and swords found in Glamorgan, gave its name to the Penard Period between 1300 and 1150 BCE, when bronze was traded both locally and overseas, with goods exchanged between England, Ireland, Wales, Scotland and western and northern France. There were links, discernible in a group of related domestic bronze instruments, between south Wales, and in particular Monmouthshire and Glamorganshire, with Devon, Cornwall and Somerset. This is known as the Llantwit-Stogursey tradition.

Occasional finds, such as a few hoards and some moulds for axes, suggest there was a trade along the Severn estuary and western sea approaches, with south Wales seemingly a principal destination.

---

* Academic work since the 1950s has overturned thinking about the Celts, suggesting that the Atlantic seaboard was connected by busy sea lanes, linking communities who chose to express themselves in a common culture. These places were later the focus points of the Celtic world. For more information on recent thinking, see research by Barry Cunliffe. John T. Koch's work on a very early Palaeohispanic language called Tartesssian suggests it may have been a prototype Celtic language. For more information on recent thinking, see Further Reading, pages 351 and 354.

Traders travelled in simple craft, and recently one of these was discovered during the laying of a new gas pipeline across south Wales. This Bronze Age canoe, found near Milford, weighed one ton and had been carved out of a single oak tree.

There were also many more complicated artefacts. The Parc-y-meirch hoard from Dinorben hillfort near Abergele, composed almost entirely of 100 horse-harness fittings, shows that exotic north-European objects were brought into even remote places, as well as highlighting the deep centrality of the horse in the culture.

Wales had several copper mines in this period, including ones on Parys Mountain on Anglesey, Nant-yr-arian in Ceredigion, and Gopa Hill in the upper Ystwyth valley, but these were simply dwarfed by the scale of the operation under the Great Orme or Pen y Gogarth, the colossal hump of rock that commands the western skyline above modern day Llandudno.

The massive scale of copper mining was a source of great wealth and extensive early mercantile opportunities for the Bronze Age people of north Wales.

A veritable catacomb of tunnels ran under the surface of the Orme, with no fewer than 6.4 kilometres (4 miles) having been surveyed since excavations began in 1987, the system having first been discovered by an amateur archaeologist in 1976. Some of the workings found are expansive caverns, while others are so small that only child miners could have squeezed through them.

The workings date back to 2000 BCE, when the workers would have had nothing more sophisticated than hammers fashioned from volcanic stones that they had picked up on the beach. Indeed, to date, no fewer than 2,500 of these tools have been found – simply rough stones shaped into hammer heads by scraping away at them with animal bones. These littered the floors of the caves in great numbers, mixed in with no fewer than 30,000 bones from sheep, goats, deer and wild boar.

The mines produced copper on a genuinely industrial scale, with an estimated 200 tons of metal produced here. Because of this grand scale, courtesy of this one site alone, Wales might have been considered a net exporter of copper at this time.

Too soft for any use other than ornamentation, copper required the addition of tin to make bronze, which was much tougher and suitable for manufacturing weapons and tools. The tin, remarkably, would have come from under the earth of Cornwall, some 400 kilometres (250 miles) away.

Stone axes were increasingly passé. Bronze ones would have been the most commonly produced artefacts, and the Orme mines would have made enough metal during the Bronze Age to make ten million of them. It was a veritable axe manufactory, a place at the cutting edge in so many ways.

The trading produced wealth, as well as advancing technological skills. The early metalsmiths of the Bronze Age – who also started to work in gold for the first time – produced a great many amazing artefacts in Britain. They were learning to roll and beat sheets of metal, allowing them to create objects as complicated and ornate as the Battersea Shield, and in quantities great enough to complete the Mildenhall Treasure and fill King Redwald's burial ship at Sutton Hoo. Taking its rightful place alongside these treasures are two objects from northeast Wales, namely the shale, tin and gold boat that decorates a bowl found near Caergwrle castle in Hope, and the astonishingly opulent Mold Cape. This short, golden poncho was discovered in 1833 by a gang of men digging for stone at the evocatively named Bryn-yr-ellyllon, which translates as Fairies' or Goblins' Hill, near Mold.

The workmen's picks opened up a stone-lined subterranean burial chamber that contained the cape. It was already tattered, but it was further damaged when its discoverers decided to share it out as spoils between them. They were hardly to know that this was one of the finest examples of prehistoric sheet-gold working, unique in both form and design.

Fortunately, the vicar of Mold decided to record the find, even though many things in the chamber, such as the skeletal remains, amber beads, several pieces of the cape and a pottery vessel containing human remains, were lost. Even more fortunate was that Mr Langford, the tenant of the land where the cape was found, decided to sell his part of the decorated gold ornament to the British Museum in 1836, with other small pieces coming to light later on.

Museum staff initially thought it part of a corselet, a garment made expressly for the chest. By the early twentieth century, it was mistakenly thought to be a decorative breastplate for a pony, even though no one had yet tried to piece the fragments together.

It wasn't until the 1950s that a distinguished academic from Liverpool University, Professor Terence Powell, came to the conclusion that what had been unearthed at Bryn-yr-ellyllon was a cape. In 1954 a reconstruction was drawn and attempts started to be made to fit the available metal pieces to this image of what the full, adorned cape could have looked like.

When work began in earnest in the 1960s the cape was fragmented. The pieces themselves were flat and the original contours were lost. There were cracks, splits and holes in the fragments, including the largest piece that came from the back of the cape. The detective work to reassemble it again would be laborious and painstaking.

As the object was repaired, many of the decorative elements began to make sense, with the embossed goldwork appearing like strings of beads draped over the shoulders, and the metal itself so finely shaped so that it resembled folds of cloth. Perforations in the gold suggest that it might once have been attached to a lining, perhaps of leather.

Recent research work has overturned the idea that the cape was initially designed to be worn by a man. It would also have fitted any woman of a slim and athletic build. It was undoubtedly an impressive garment, which gives rise to the belief that it had a ceremonial function. It restricted movement of the arms, suggesting that the wearer might have been required to do nothing more than lead a ceremony, or take part in it. And it displayed wealth, as so much gold was used to make it. As one expert put it: 'It must have come from the centre of great wealth and power, perhaps comparable to the contemporary courts of the pharaohs of Egypt or the palaces of Minoan Crete, for the cape must have been made around 1700 BCE.'[1]

The cape was not at all robust, despite the bronze framework on which the gold was hung. Scientific evaluation has improved since the initial examination of the find, and by analysing both the gold and the bronze in the cape straps, it has now been established that the cape dates to between 1950 and 1550 BCE. Made by the 'Tiffanys or Cartiers of the Bronze Age', it is a supreme example of the deft and detailed way in which the people of that time were able to work and fashion metal.[2]

The Mold Cape was decorated with small amber beads that must have come from the Baltic, which in itself places Wales within a web of trade and exchange that connected it to the Mediterranean and Scandinavia. Meanwhile, the decoration on the side of the Caergwrle Bowl, showing a ship at sea, serves to underline the importance of sea trade at this time, an exchange of ideas as much as goods. Elsewhere in Wales, gold was worked into wire, a technique imported from Ireland.

There have been many other discoveries in northeast Wales, such as the twisted gold neck ornament known as the Westminster Torc; the Rossett Hoard, which included two pieces of knife and a socketed axe containing cut pieces of a gold bracelet; the Burton Hoard of axes and finely fashioned gold jewellery; and the collection of bronze axes known as the Acton Hoard. Singly and severally, they all underline the strength of the bronze-working tradition in the area.

The Bronze Age people may have been prehistoric, but they were far from primitive. As the copper workings of the Orme and the ornate complexity of the gold Mold Cape attest, such people did not work in isolation. Rather they thrived on connectivity and commerce.

* * *

The Iron Age can be marked out from the Bronze Age, not just for the evolution in metalwork it denotes, but also by the change in climate. Professor Geraint H. Jenkins in *A Concise History of Wales* described an age of:

Heavy rain and strong winds impoverished the soil, peat bogs proliferated, deforestation was rife and upland farms were deserted with alarming swiftness. This potentially lethal cocktail of environmental problems caused a general mood of fretfulness and insecurity during the Late Bronze Age and throughout the Iron Age.[3]

As climate change caused a significant reduction in available arable ground, it was little wonder that the people of the Late Bronze Age and the Iron Age took to fortifying themselves against the hostile world around them, protecting their land which had now become a precious commodity. Following the seemingly free exchange of materials, techniques and ideas during the Early Bronze Age, the Late Bronze Age and Iron Age are marked, in Wales most notably, by a proliferation of hillforts – around 600 from the Iron Age alone – over a fifth of the British total. Some of them were as populous as villages: Tre'r Ceiri, for example, had 150 stone dwellings in a stunning setting high above the Llŷn Peninsula, and there was very substantial construction at Llanymynech in Powys. These forts were built not to repel foreign invaders, but simply to defend precious land resources from the neighbours.

Recent explorations on north Wales hillforts, such as Dinorben, Breiddin and Moel-y-gaer, have shown that some of these were occupied for a long time, from about 1000 BCE and into the first millennium CE.

Some, such as those on St David's Head and St Brides in Pembrokeshire, were simple collections of stone huts protected by a basic rampart. Many of the Welsh forts were individually defendable homesteads that could often house not only the owner and his family, but a substantial entourage as well.

This period was characterized not just by fortification, but also, of course, by the advent of the use of iron, and this move from bronze to iron required the use of new techniques by metal-workers. Elsewhere in Wales we have glimpses of how the iron was actually made, such as the two bowl furnaces found in the small defended enclosure of Bryn-y-castell in Ffestiniog, along with piles of slag, the by-product from smelting the ore. One of the furnaces is oval in shape and measures about 20cm by 30cms and was probably used to reheat raw blooms (a mix of iron and slag) during the early stage of the forging process.

Evidence from the Iron Age Coygan camp in Carmarthenshire, on a site that dates back to the Early Stone Age and is located on a limestone bluff overlooking Carmarthen Bay, gives us an insight into the way these Iron Age dwellers farmed the land.[4] Analysis of the bones found at Coygan show that 64 per cent of the animals were cattle, with sheep and goats a mere 16 per cent, while pigs made up some 15 per cent of the total. Because a cow would give seven times the meat yield of a sheep, it is unsurprising that beef was the main component of the diet. There is little evidence of stones having been used for grinding grain, though grain can't be entirely ruled out as a component of the diet. Nearby, at Pen-y-coed, near Llangynog was a simple grain store, little more than four posts and a roof, set against a hillside, while on Pembrey Mountain overlooking Carmarthen Bay was some evidence of cereals. In the main, though, Coygan was a centre for pastoralists, who grazed their animals on the estuarine salt marshes beneath the camp. The sea also provided its bounty, with shellfish gathered in great quantities from the estuary of the river Taf and from rocky pools at the base of Pendine's cliffs.

As the forts were built, the land was cleared, and huge areas of woodland were felled from the Stone Age onwards. The historian John

Davies cites a possible reference to this practice in the early medieval tale *Culhwch ac Olwen*: 'Do you see that great thicket out there? I want it uprooted and burned on the ground down to cinders and ashes for manure; I want it ploughed and sown.'[5] The resulting fields and field patterns are still visible today in places such as Skomer island off the Pembrokeshire coast.

In north Wales encampments ranged widely in their configuration: the settlement at Castell Odo near Aberdaron had several circular timber houses and a corral for stock, whereas that at Llwyn Du Bach in Caernarfonshire was based on concentric circles. Bryn-y-castell in Snowdonia was a simple stone-walled enclosure, where iron smelting and forging would have been a major activity. Elsewhere, groups of huts, near enough in proximity to suggest they were related to each other, clustered and huddled together on mountainsides, such as the one at Cwmystradllyn in Caernarfonshire.

Easily the most striking developments in this part of the world were the large hilltop settlements, big enough to house up to several hundred people and defended by stone walls. Those on Conwy Mountain and Garn Boduan, were each home to 400 people. One of the most dramatic locations for these settlements is Tre'r Ceiri, the aptly named 'Town of Giants', with its densely occupied interiors and large number of enclosed farmsteads. Here, as in the rest of Wales, round-houses were the order of the day, other than for rare exceptions, such as the encampment on the south Wales coast at Goldcliff, where the houses were rectangular in shape.

As in the Stone Age, what happened to the dead had significance. During the Bronze Age, the so-called Beaker Folk (named after their distinctive pottery and style of burial) made an appearance. The

Beaker Folk would bury their dead in individual graves, as opposed to communally in tombs, and good examples are found at Tinkinswood and Parc-le-Breos. In these graves, also known as barrows, objects were placed near the corpse to denote the status of the deceased, and often these would be pottery beakers. This was an idea imported from the Rhineland and Iberia.**

It used to be commonly held that early Welsh history was shaped by a series of invasions from Celtic war bands sweeping in from central Europe in one wave after another, originating from parts of present-day Germany, France and Switzerland. But the latest research tells a different story. It was an altogether more gradual encounter between Wales and a wider world. Discrete, small migrations and exchanges, rather than sweeping population movements and militaristic invasions, gave us the three triumphs of Celtic technology, mythology and metalwork. This process, the slow, steady introduction of influences, has been described as 'culminative Celticity'.

This reversal of previous theories about the arrival of the 'Celts' is supported by the evidence that the first axis of the trading movement came from the edges of 'Celtic' central Europe's expansion into Iberia (an area including modern-day Spain, Portugal and Andorra), and from there to the coasts of Wales. Indeed, the Celts were expert expansionists, and they moved as far as Anatolia in Turkey to the east, and Ireland to the west.

As we know, there had been some interaction and exchange of ideas between England, Wales, France and the Iberian coast since the

---

** In truth, there are very few examples from the Early Bronze Age in Wales, although sites at Brymbo and Llanharry do have the typical stone cists featuring a small collection of grave goods.

New Stone Age just over 3,000 years earlier. A common language with features we can call Celtic seems to have functioned widely in western Europe from 4000 BCE because people needed to sell each other things or exchange ideas, or simply talk. By the Iron Age, this language had developed into Celtic, along with a recognizable people called the Celts that, by 500 BCE, spanned from Ireland to Turkey.

The ancient Greeks called these peoples Keltoi. Some referred to the Celtae. The Romans named them Galli. Others Galatae. Many writers of the ancient world, such as Caesar, Herodotus and Strabo, used versions of the word 'Celtic' to describe the peoples of central Europe and Gaul, but it is nowadays used largely to describe a rich and complicated material culture shared by people across great swathes of Europe. They had a glorious, complicated art in common, evident from numerous archaeological finds.

The art is astounding, with never-ending lines that twist and knot into eternity like early versions of Moebius strips, and spiral shapes that turn in like bracken fronds. Leaf crowns sprout and fantastic creatures form mythical menageries. The art is some of the most sophisticated outside the classical world. Taken together, these are outward manifestations of a shared sensibility and sense of the world, or rather worlds: this one and the next.

The Celts also had their gods – although their actual names are lost into the mists of time – and we know how they often appeased them, by throwing objects of great worth into standing waters. Often these were made of iron, a material from which weapons of such value were forged that warriors took them to their graves. These sacrifices suggested a relationship with nature and a real sense of an otherworld, a world lying almost within reach.

Archaeology is full of serendipitous moments, of stumbling upon unexpected treasures. One such find was a rich trove dating from 600 BCE, which came to light in 1913 – a discovery suggesting that Celtic beliefs in an otherworld had spread and were upheld in Wales. Workmen had been removing peat from the drained lake at Llyn Fawr on the Rhigos Mountain overlooking Hirwaun in Rhondda Cynon Taf as they were deepening it for use as a reservoir. They had to down tools because they had found some tools.

The objects they found date from the beginning of the Iron Age – indeed, these are some of the earliest iron objects in Britain – and included a sword, a spearhead, a razor, sickles, socketed axes, chisels and horse-harnessing equipment. The prize among the findings was a cauldron made of bronze, weighing 7.5 kilograms. The Llyn Fawr Hoard was an extremely important discovery, because it not only illustrates the crossover between the Bronze and Iron Ages (the iron sickle being modelled on an earlier bronze version), but also shows an unusual mix of styles among the objects, a diversity that suggests a wide range of origins, including Celtic influences from central Europe (namely Austria and Switzerland).

The beautifully wrought cauldron was an impressive example of a vessel that played an important role in the life of the Bronze and Iron Age peoples. Cauldrons were used for cooking food, especially during feasts. They were also regarded as ceremonial possessions, invested with symbolic powers of regeneration and fertility. These artefacts were buried in a complete rather than a broken state, and many were items of the highest quality. Could this material have been a gift to the deities of the Celtic otherworld?

There is a story that originates not far from Llyn Fawr, which suggests that Celtic spirituality has permeated and been retained in Welsh folklore: 'The Maiden of Llyn y Fan' concerns a glacial lake. It tells of a beautiful maiden who appeared from the depths of the lake, bringing with her a herd of magical cattle. A local farmer fell in love with her at first sight and he was granted permission by her father to marry her on one condition: should he hit his wife three times, she would return to the lake, along with the animals. The love-struck man, seeing no earthly reason why he would ever harm his beloved in any way whatsoever, happily agreed. But, by accident, he did strike her on two occasions, and then, after the third and final blow, the beautiful maiden and her magical herd disappeared forever into the deep, deep waters. The husband followed her and drowned.

Iron, cauldrons, and iron cauldrons recur in later Welsh literature and folk tales. *Preiddeu Annwn*, 'The Spoils of Annwn' collected in the fourteenth-century *Book of Taliesin*, contains an account of a raid made by Arthur on Annwn, or the otherworld, to plunder a magical cauldron that held secrets of both wisdom and inspiration. The stories mirror reality: a fine find in the peaty edges of Llyn Cerrig Bach, a lake on the island of Anglesey in the 1940s, brought to light an impressive tally of 177 iron and bronze artefacts. These included farmers' tools, slave chains and unadorned bars of metal.

Items similar to the ones chanced upon at Llyn Fawr were identified elsewhere in Wales and are signs of the absorption and assimilation of Celtic beliefs through trade and peaceful migration, rather than military invasion. The landscape was not strewn with military hardware, but with domestic and spiritual artefacts.

The Bronze and Iron Ages saw huge advances in complicated metalworking, social organization and art. It was a period when Wales became increasingly Celtic as it readily embraced the new foreign culture, its language and beliefs. Trade links started in the Stone Age had consolidated and deepened through peaceful migration and voluntary assimilation. Wales was not an outpost of a Celtic empire, but rather a realm of ongoing influence.

The Celts 'ruled' Europe, including Wales, for approximately 750 years, but despite the longevity of the reign, and because of the deep-rooted tribal culture led by chieftains, rather than one leader presiding over one Celtic people, they did not stand a chance when the imperial might of Rome turned its attention west.

CHAPTER FOUR

EDGE OF EMPIRE

When the military juggernaut of the imperial Roman army rolled across Europe and beyond, little could stand in its way. Its colossal, hyper-efficient land grab was eventually to include, and often enslave, a huge swathe of the world. At its height this included territories in Europe south of the rivers Rhine and Danube, much of Asia Minor, the whole of Egypt, and an enormous ribbon along the north African coast. If war is a competition between opposing technologies, then the native tribes' equipment was equivalent to training pea-shooters against Panzer divisions.

Well before the invasion of Britain in 43 CE, the Romans had known about the Iron Age society in Wales through trade. They knew there was ready plunder in the hills and ample resources to appropriate. Five years after Emperor Claudius ordered the Roman army to Britain in 48 CE – sending no fewer than 40,000 highly trained men across the sea – it was to be found encamped on what would become the borders of Wales. Wales had not yet defined itself from the rest of Britain, but Roman rule would certainly help form what was to become a Welsh identity.

Five principal tribes lived in Wales at the time: the Silures, Demetae, Ordovices, Cornovii and Deceangli. The warlike Silures commanded the southeast, in an area covering Glamorgan, Monmouthshire and southern Breconshire. We know what they looked like because the historian Tacitus describes them as *colorati*, suggesting they were ruddy and swarthy, not to mention the fact that their hair was unusually curly, leading him to conclude that they had migrated from Spain.

Elsewhere, the peaceable Demetae dwelt in the southwest and would give their name to modern Dyfed. The Ordovices operated in the northwest, and the Cornovii occupied the central highlands of what are today known as the Cambrian Mountains in Powys. The Deceangli territory extended across a small swathe of land in the northeast. The Deceangli – commemorated, if only in name, in the district later known as Tegeingl – were the first to confront the might of Rome. They were to find that resistance was futile as the killing machine of the Roman army trundled ever onwards.

The invading army, marching under the eagle standard, ended up fighting on many fronts in Britain. The Romans met serious resistance in Scotland. They never got as far as Ireland, but Wales was soon deep in the hurly-burly of battle, facing opposition that was armour-plated, supremely well disciplined and equipped with sharp-edged and much-bloodied swords, and javelins that could accurately find their target.

Some of the earliest attacks were across the river Dee, which borders on present-day Wales and England. Not only was this an easier entry point for the legions, who could march in phalanx if need be across the marshy flatlands rather than crossing the Clwydian Hills to the south, but the legionaries also had use of special landing craft, which could ferry cavalry across open water.

Attacking the tribes of the northeast was a means of driving a wedge between the people of highland Wales and those who dwelt

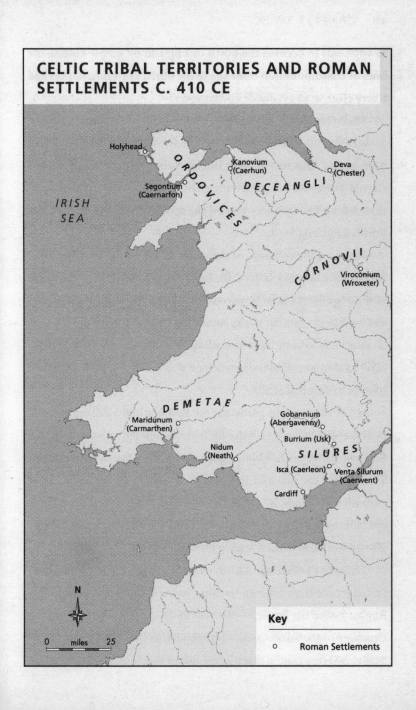

CELTIC TRIBAL TERRITORIES AND ROMAN SETTLEMENTS C. 410 CE

Holyhead

ORDOVICES

Kanovium
(Caerhun)

Deva
(Chester)

Segontium
(Caernarfon)

DECEANGLI

IRISH
SEA

CORNOVII

Viroconium
(Wroxeter)

DEMETAE

Maridunum
(Carmarthen)

Gobannium
(Abergavenny)

Burrium (Usk)

Nidum
(Neath)

SILURES

Isca (Caerleon)

Venta Silurum
(Caerwent)

Cardiff

N

0   miles   25

Key

○   Roman Settlements

in what was to become the north of England by simply cutting the lines of communication from one to the other. The Romans thus had a very clear strategy: divide and conquer.

The state-of-the-art soldiery, under Ostorius Scapula, marched arrogantly and swiftly into Wales and, by 48 CE, the Deceangli had been forced into submission. Roman mine managers had already started to extract lead in Deceanglian territory, even in advance of that defeat. The invaders wanted the spoils of war before they had finished fighting for it.

However, the conquest of the whole of Wales was anything but a stroll for the Romans. Indeed, the fiercest opposition during the whole of their invasion was to be encountered here, where the native tribes were willing to face up to the advancing troops. It took the Romans 30 long years to tame the tribes, whose disunity was one of their principal weaknesses. Had they presented a united front, they might not have been defeated at all.

In the southeast in particular the Romans had a difficult time of it, as the Silures put up a fierce fight and concerted resistance. In fact, they were to wage a full-blown guerrilla war for a quarter of a century. Their leader for much of this period of regular skirmish and clever ambush was Caratacus (son of Cunobelinus, King of the Catuvellauni, the basis of Shakespeare's character Cymbeline), who would eventually transmute into the Caradog of Welsh legend.

This brave soldier was actually an early refugee. Caratacus had been forced to flee from his own territory in the southeast of present-day England after the Battle of Medway in 43 CE, possibly to avoid the treachery of the Trinovantes, whom his father had subjugated. Caratacus was to be a painful thorn in the side of the Roman administration as he ranged freely, attacking forts and Roman convoys alike. Tacitus, the Roman historian, describes one pivotal battle, possibly Caratacus's last, as follows:

> ... *[His] many battles against the Romans ... had raised him to a position of pre-eminence amongst the other British chieftains. Since his strength lay not in military superiority but in the tactical advantages to be gained from knowing difficult terrain, he transferred the scene of the conflict to the territory of the Ordovices. He recruited from those who dreaded the establishment of a Roman peace and staked his fate on one last confrontation. He chose a place in mid-Wales for the battle, where the entrances and exits were to our disadvantage but favourable to his own troops. On one side there was a precipitously steep gradient, and where there were gentler approach routes, he piled up stones to form a kind of embankment. There was also a river of uncertain depth flowing past and here bands of fighters were stationed to provide defence.*[1]

The Roman leader Ostorius Scapula did finally achieve victory over Caratacus. His family was captured and he was forced to retreat to the hills, seeking refuge with Cartimandua, the Queen of the Brigantes, who betrayed him and offered him up for capture. As a consequence of his stubborn and steely-eyed guerrilla resistance, Caratacus's fame had already spread far and wide. The captured tribal leader made a good trophy. He was therefore taken to Rome in about 54 CE to be displayed before the emperor Claudius. Addressing the Roman senate, Caratacus made an eloquent and impassioned speech, recorded by Tacitus:

Had my moderation in prosperity been equal to my noble birth and fortune, I should have entered this city as your friend rather than as your captive; and you would not have disdained to receive, under a treaty of peace, a king descended from illustrious ancestors and ruling many nations. My present lot is as glorious to you as it is degrading to myself. I had men and horses, arms and wealth. What wonder if I parted with them reluctantly? If you Romans choose to lord it over the world, does it follow that the world is to accept slavery...[2]

His speech elevated him not only to the status of a hero: it also made him a free man, and he and his family were released to live in Rome. Over the centuries Caratacus was to transmute into a pan-Celtic hero, one especially beloved by the Welsh, who claimed him as their hero Caradog, helped in no small part by the works of Iolo Morganwg, the eighteenth-century polymath. Caratacus's reputation accreted like a pearl around grit, in this case heroic grit. An eighteenth-century society, the 'Caradogion', was named in his honour, and paintings of him filled many a canvas, while the quintessentially English composer Edward Elgar penned a cantata for soloists, chorus and orchestra called *Caractacus*. This Caradog can be properly considered as the first national hero of Wales.[3]

Even after the defeat of Caratacus, the Silures managed to defeat a legion, the Twentieth, in 52 CE, and two successive governors of what was now called Britannia fretted themselves into an early grave because of the shame of it, not to mention the ignominy of failing to vanquish the poorly equipped barbarians of the hills. It took until 74–8 CE, and a determined campaign under Julius Frontinus, for the Silures finally to succumb.

The bountiful island of Anglesey was next on the Roman hit list. The island was a renowned centre for Druidical activity, focused around the settlement of Penmon and the lake at Llyn Cerrig Bach, where a class of Celtic priests taught others in an age before writing. The Druidic stronghold fell to the imperial stormtroopers led by Suetonius Paulinus in 61 CE. Somewhere not far from Bangor, at an undefined spot on the Menai Straits, the flat-bottomed landing craft took the cavalry across. We owe one of the earliest descriptions of the inhabitants of Wales, specifically the islanders of Anglesey, to this deadly incursion. Tacitus describes the Druids of Anglesey invoking terrible curses amid the scene of battle, or rather, massacre, as the Romans took on hordes of screaming women dressed in black and gangs of fierce warriors:

> Urged on by their general's appeals and mutual encouragements not to quail before a troop of frenzied women, they bore the standards onward, smote down all resistance, and wrapped the foe in the flames of its own brands. A force was next set over the conquered, and their groves, devoted to human superstitions, were destroyed. They deemed it, indeed, a religious duty to cover the altars with the blood of their captives and to consult the deities by inspecting human entrails.[4]

Once the Druidic oak groves had been felled, a garrison was established on Anglesey, but that was soon commandeered to tackle the Queen of the Iceni, Boudicca, and her rebellion, and the Romans would not penetrate Anglesey again until 78 CE, when they followed up the massacre of the Ordovician Druids by reconquering the island.

At this point the rule of Rome was finally imposed in both England and Wales.

The ferocity of the resistance in Wales, coupled with the richness of some of the natural resources the invaders found here, helped to explain the incredible complexity of the Roman infrastructure that developed throughout the territory. Those famously straight roads, totalling 1,025 kilometres (637 miles), linked forts to marching camps across the new territory. In the south they linked Nidum (or Neath) with Moridunum (or Carmarthen). In the north the roads ran from Deva, present-day Chester, to the western stronghold at Segontium (or Caernarfon). Roads helped tame the place, gain passage through wild, wooded countryside, and accelerate the pace of exploitation. Conquerors need spoils, and the coupling of convict labour and engineering ingenuity allowed the Romans to exploit the very earth over which they marched. The conquest might have been a personal triumph for Claudius and an aid in the perennial power struggles that typified Rome, but Welsh gold was a very tangible reward too. Victory also brought ample food, as the climate was conducive to agriculture, even suitable for vineyards on sunny slopes. There was also a ready supply of slaves: human booty to take home.

In Dolaucothi, in Carmarthenshire, the Romans found plentiful gold bullion for the imperial mints. The newcomers used a range of techniques to acquire the soft metal, such as hushing, which involved releasing large quantities of water from tanks to sweep away soil, revealing the bedrock underneath. They created an extensive system of hydraulics and reservoirs, using water carried along lengthy chutes or conduits. They also employed open-cast mining (simply digging for gold in open pits). They went deep too, digging tunnels and adits down which they pushed their enslaved-miners ever further, and newer and more complicated tools, such as water-powered trip hammers, were also used.

Mining here was determined and on a large scale. Indeed, gold, silver and lead might have been some of the principal attractions that led to the conquest of Britain in the first place. The autocratic emperors of Rome also knew Britain to be a good source of slaves, hunting dogs and grain. Their representatives in Britain displayed their usual rapacity after they arrived. Parys Mountain on Anglesey was mined for copper, as was the hump of rock that is the Great Orme.

Acting as cornerstones of the colonialist push were two fortresses, one just outside the Welsh border at Chester, and the other within the confines of Wales at Caerleon. These two centres, together with the fortress at York, oversaw the new province of Britannia, providing a linked chain of command for the army in the west.

The Britannic highlands were essentially militarized zones, and each fort could house many men. In Wales, a spider's web of up to 30 auxiliary forts was created, linked by roads that cut across the terrain, each fort no more than a day's march from the next. These forts were not in themselves insubstantial: two of the biggest, at Hindwell in Radnorshire and Arosfa Garreg, south of the Upper Usk, could house 12–13,000 men. At its peak, around 70 CE, perhaps as many as 30,000 Roman troops were stationed in Wales. They came from all over the empire, as demonstrated by fragments of building inscriptions, with Vettones from Spain based in Brecon, Nervii from northeast France at Caergai near Bala and Asturians from the corner of northwest Spain at Llanio in Ceredigion.

In south Wales, Caerleon, known as Isca by the Romans, was the base of the Second Augustan Legion. It is said that an army marches on its stomach, and to keep the legion amply supplied with bread, corn from Wessex was transported in bulk to grain stores on the banks of the river Usk. Isca was equipped for warfare, plus rest and relaxation, with a palace and impressive baths, as well as extensive barracks to accommodate the men, a hospital and a commanding amphitheatre complete with tiers of stone seats. This amphitheatre was a late addition to the buildings in the area and is unusual because it is situated inside the town, not outside it. Here ceremonial meetings were held, as well as plays.

And, of course, there were the gladiator contests that have proved such enduring subjects in popular cinema, from *Ben Hur* through *Spartacus* to the more recent *Gladiator*. At Isca, up to 6,000 baying spectators enjoyed the sight of bloody spectacles. In the absence of a ready local supply of lions, some featured bouts in which men were pitted against brown bears, packs of wolves, or snarling wildcats.

A major new discovery at the site might alter our view of this Roman settlement. A complex of monumental buildings has recently been located at Caerleon by archaeologists from Cardiff University. A combination of archaeology and geophysics has started to reveal huge civic buildings outside the fortress. These might have included markets, administrative buildings, such as town halls, bath-houses and temples. The biggest edifice within the recent discoveries is among the largest building remains found in Roman Britain. These civic buildings were connected to a port with wharves and warehouses on a scale never before realized. The Romans may have planned to link Wales, via the main connection of Caerleon, to the port serving Rome. It certainly looks as if the Romans intended Caerleon to become a great city.[5]

The archaeologists' work at Caerleon has brought into relief the story of one man: Roman veteran Flavius Rufus, of the Second Augustan Legion, who fought his way through the wars to subdue the Silures. He left his official mark on buildings in Wales and survived to return to Rome as a discharged man. He married a slave woman he had freed and, tragically, had to record her death in childbirth on her gravestone in the great city where his career began.

The inhabitants of Wales swiftly adapted to life under the Roman thumb – complying with a new civic order, learning Latin alongside their native Brythonic tongue, and taking luxurious steam baths. This was a chameleon people, able to blend in perfectly when necessary or expedient, or when they were ordered to. So a Silurian tribal leader was able to change without too much fuss into a local notable, learning how to live a Mediterranean lifestyle in a rainy outpost of a mighty empire.

As the native tribes were increasingly pacified, large civil settlements sprang up around the legionary fortresses. Little wonder that buildings around Caerwent mushroomed as traders, soldiers' families and some of the natives settled there.

Caerwent, or Venta Silurum, the 'market of the Silures', had created a tribal senate by as early as 120 CE and used Roman law, coinage and literacy, which gave locals access to all the economic might of the empire. Caerwent was the fully developed administrative centre of Silurian territory, with some 3,000 inhabitants enjoying fine living, including works of art and the benefits of heating and bathing facilities. It was a *civitas,* or form of city-state, complete with its own forum and basilica, or marketplace and civic hall, while Carmarthen, or Moridunum Demetarum, formed the civic centre for the Demetae lands.

Some of the fertile lowlands of the southeast saw the erection of grand villas. In places such as Llandough, Ely in Cardiff and Cowbridge in the Vale of Glamorgan large farmsteads, some of them up to 2,428 hectares (6000 acres), grew new crops, such as leeks, carrots and oats. At Llanfrynach near Brecon a villa was discovered with a very substantial bath-house, complete with elaborate fish mosaics. Small civilian settlements, or *vici*, sprang up as more and more people saw the advantages of a Roman way of life and the benefits of a coinage system.

By the third and fourth centuries many of the forts in Wales were ungarrisoned, with the exception of Ordovician territory, where resistance was stubborn and persistent. In fact, you can still see a mosaic map of the Roman Empire in the Forum in Rome from which the land of the Ordovices is conspicuously absent.

The resigned air of compliance in Wales meant that Roman troops could be sent to the heavily fortified border to be known as Hadrian's Wall in present-day northern England, where there was serious building work to be done from 122 CE. Curiously, this area has inscriptions and place names commemorating a character familiar from the collection of medieval Welsh folk tales, the *Mabinogion*, namely Mabon, or Maponus. It might have been a not so subtle way of saying to the Roman legionaries 'We were here first'.

Stability in society led to a melding of cultures, with the advent of the hybrid known as Romano-British culture. It all happened quickly, taking only a generation for savage fighters to turn into aspiring citizens. And new quasi-citizens emerged, for as the Romans developed the province of Britannia Prima (comprising Wales and the West Country), with its capital in Cirencester, subdued peoples were given increasing rights, leading to a proclamation in 212 CE that stated that henceforth every free man in the empire had equal rights to that of a Roman citizen.

Worship during this period was directed at a *mélange* of native and imported gods, with Celtic deities rooted in the natural world taking their places alongside Roman gods such as Mercury. In fact, at a curative spring at Llys Awel near Abergele, archaeologists found a figurine of Mercury, along with two bronze dogs and votive plaques; dogs in both the Celtic and the classical world were associated with healing. Elsewhere in Wales, such ritualistic animals were connected with death and burial, such as the funerary lion from Cowbridge in the Vale of Glamorgan, and the iron firedog unearthed at Welshpool.

Evidence of the melding of religions in Wales is clear from the existence of a temple to Mars-Oculus at Caerwent, while oriental deities, such as Mithra, attracted followers to shrines at Caerleon and Caernarfon. The former was described in the Chronicle of Kings, *Brut y Brenhinedd,* as 'the second city to Rome in the beauty of her houses, her wealth of gold and silver, and her pride'.

Christianity started to make an appearance here too. Roman Britain's first martyrs, Julius and Aaron, were put to death in Caerleon for disturbing the 'peace of the gods', during the religious persecutions by Emperor Diocletian in 304 CE. However, things were very different later in the century, and Christianity was increasingly imposed on the land that was to become a crucial part of its dissemination. The fact that the emperor Constantine had himself become a Christian accelerated the spread of the faith and towards the end of the fourth century Christians were worshipping in Caerwent.

Roman Britain later increasingly saw troops stationed along the coast when the empire became riven by internal dissent and suffered external threats from assorted barbarians. It isn't clear when the legionary garrison at Caerleon was finally withdrawn, possibly by the end of the fourth century, although a skeleton force might have remained there until the middle of the fifth century.

Ireland had been left untouched by the Romans, and over the following 300 years it had emerged a very different place from romanized Wales. The growing threat of Irish bands in the fourth century saw new fortified development at Cardiff, Caernarfon, Holyhead and Caerhun. Forden, in present day Montgomeryshire, was also redesigned in 364–78 CE as a response to an unrecorded crisis inland. By around 393 CE, soldiers were needed on a new front in Gaul, so Wales was gradually demilitarized by the Romans, although some troops were probably left to guard the towns of Carmarthen and Caerwent into the fifth century.

Roman legions finally left Britain in 410 CE, and not all mourned their going. One crucial source chronicling the period after their departure comes from a sixth-century Celtic monk named Gildas. His Latin work, which translates as *On the Ruin of Britain*, gives us the perspective of a romanized Celt on Rome's retreat from Britain, and the arrival of the next invaders and occupiers:

> *The Romans, therefore, having slain many of the rebels, and reserved others for slaves, that the land might not be entirely reduced to desolation, left the island, destitute as it was of wine and oil, and returned to Italy, leaving behind them taskmasters, to scourge the shoulders of the natives, to reduce their necks to the yoke, and their soil to the vassalage of a Roman province; to chastize the crafty race, not with warlike weapons, but with rods, and if necessary to gird upon their sides the naked sword, so that it*

was no longer thought to be Britain, but a Roman island; and all
their money, whether of copper, gold or silver, was stamped with
Caesar's image.[6]

Although the Romans had left, their legacy continued. It is to be seen to this day in the Welsh language, peppered as it is with Latinate words, such as *pont* for 'bridge', derived from *pontus* and *eglwys* for 'church', from *ecclesia*.

It is also evident in the legends of Arthur and Macsen Wledig, a character based on an authentic figure, Magnus Maximus. Gildas helped cement the reputation of Maximus, a Roman Spaniard, who became one of the first heroes of British, and Welsh, history. He commanded the Roman army in Britain from 380 CE. In 383 he was proclaimed emperor by his troops and at this point he decided to lead an assault on the emperor Gratian. Magnus Maximus became emperor for five years, ruling Britain, Gaul, Spain and Africa before being defeated in battle and executed in 388. His fame, as glorified by Gildas, came from his deal-making with tribes, such as the Votadini (based in northeast England) and the Dumnonii (from southwest England), who were deputized to keep control of land north of Hadrian's Wall. He also supposedly married British royalty – 'Elen of the Hosts', or Elen, the Princess of Segontium (now Caernarfon). He later became a heroic character in a number of Welsh and English folktales, including in the *Mabinogion*, namely *Breuddwyd Macsen*, or 'The Dream of Macsen Wledig'.

His transmutation into Macsen has been seen by Gwyn A. Williams as a pivotal point: 'In a very real sense, Wales can be said to begin with the British hero Maximus. Wales is born in 383 CE with Macsen Wledig.'[7] Most historians disagree with this assertion. But there is no doubt that he is a figure of enduring appeal, featured in popular songs, such as the perennial favourite, Dafydd Iwan's crowd-rousing *Yma O Hyd*, 'we're still here', and in a recent version of *Breuddwyd Macsen* in *The Dream of Max and Ronnie* by the novelist Niall Griffiths.

The lasting impact of Roman occupation can also be detected in the sense of common culture and identity amongst the different tribes of the west. After nearly 400 years of occupation, Wales, like England, had become Roman, although it retained a lot of its Celtic heritage and tribal divisions headed up by chieftains. The people of Wales had absorbed Latin, mixing it in with their evolving Brythonic language. They had also embraced Roman custom and culture, blending it with Celtic traditions and legends, as well as the vestiges of their surviving tribal identities.* At this point they could be described as 'Britons'; romanized peoples with a shared culture and beliefs, living at the edge of the Roman Empire.

However, in Wales change and discontinuities are also important to note. The Roman towns were largely abandoned and a new world of kingdoms emerged, replacing the old tribal territories with head-quarters in small hill forts or mound castles. The seeds of a new order had been planted in the rubble of a once-mighty empire.

As the Romans retreated, the external threats its empire had battled against along Britain's coasts pressed in. The Britons were left to deal with these threats as best they could. Gildas concluded that the decline and ruin of Britain, caused by its debauched and decadent rulers, and the rise of subsequent pagan invaders was God's revenge for Rome's spectacular fall from grace.

---

* The transition from Brythonic to early Welsh occurred sometime between 400 and 700 CE.

PART TWO

INVASION AND ASSIMILIATION

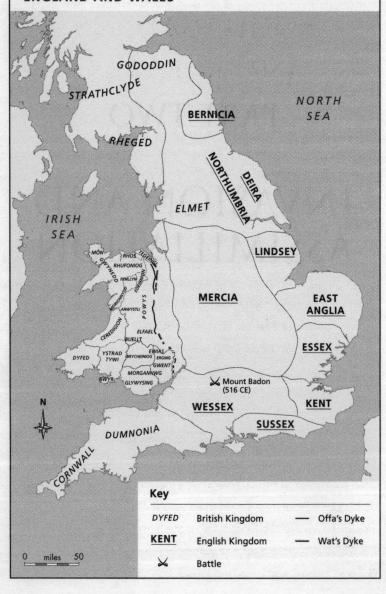

EARLY BRITON AND ANGLO-SAXON KINGDOMS OF ENGLAND AND WALES

GODODDIN

STRATHCLYDE

RHEGED

BERNICIA

NORTH SEA

NORTHUMBRIA

DEIRA

IRISH SEA

ELMET

LINDSEY

MÔN
RHOS
TEGEINGL
GWYNEDD
RHUFONIOG
PENLLYN
MEIRIONYDD
ARWYSTLI
POWYS
CEREDIGION
ELFAEL
BUELLT
YSTRAD TYWI
BRYCHEINIOG
DYFED
EWIAS
ERGING
GWENT
GWYR
MORGANNWG
GLYWYSING

MERCIA

EAST ANGLIA

ESSEX

Mount Badon
(516 CE)

KENT

WESSEX

SUSSEX

N

DUMNONIA

CORNWALL

Key

DYFED   British Kingdom   —— Offa's Dyke

KENT   English Kingdom   ······ Wat's Dyke

✂   Battle

0   miles   50

CHAPTER FIVE

ANGLO-SAXONS AND BRITONS

The dismantling of Roman Britain happened as a consequence of a three-pronged attack: the Irish streamed in from the west, the Picts attacked from the north, and the Angles, Saxons and Jutes from the east.

The Picts or Picti, meaning 'painted ones', controlled the largest kingdom in Scotland and had systematically repelled the Romans, thus creating a true north–south divide in the British Isles. It did not, however, ensure their longevity, as they had disappeared from history entirely by the end of the first millennium – swallowed whole by another group, the Gaels, from Ireland.

The Angles, Saxons and Jutes – who would enjoy a longer history – attacked from their home bases in northern Germany and southern Denmark. For an already overstretched empire battling barbarians on many fronts, this was an overwhelming onslaught. In 410 CE Emperor Honorius sent word that he had no reinforcements to spare, leaving the local authorities in Britain to deal with these threats as best they could. This post-Roman age, once known as the Dark Ages, is now more usually referred as the Heroic Age or the Early Christian Age.

This was also the Anglo-Saxon age in Britain, which began around the fifth century and lasted for 400 years. The invaders brought their own religion and a language that would form the basis for English. Their kingdoms – Northumbria, Mercia, East Anglia and Wessex – were not only soon established, but also soon at odds with each other, creating a shifting map of power. This was most clearly seen in the shape of eastern borders of Wales, which was determined in the main by the annexations and colonization by the Anglo-Saxons of British lands. But if the first influences were made through sword and blood, there followed periods of intermarriage and settlement too.

In the aftermath of empire, Wales started to create its own hierarchies, dividing the land into new political units that would see the emergence of new royal houses. The new powers would envy each other's adjoining lands in a way that mirrored the jostling for territory in the areas under Anglo-Saxon control. New kingdoms such as Dyfed, Gwynedd, Morgannwg, Brycheiniog and Ceredigion came into being, their rulers carving up the land and vying for further control. Their neighbours to the east had a name for the people of these Welsh kingdoms – 'Wealhas' – the Anglo-Saxon term for those who had lived in a romanized world. But the Welsh lived in that world no longer.

This is the period when one might expect to hear the 'true story' of King Arthur, the 'once and future' king who defended Christian Britain against the invading pagan hordes. This was the time of kingdoms, and fragments of fact do exist to fuel the myth: Gildas, who had previously commented on the passing of the Roman world, recorded a big battle at Mount Badon between the Britons and the Saxons in southwest England in 516 CE. Although the battle at Badon was won by the Britons, Gildas considered the victory marred by the fact that Brythonic military men went on to steal civic authority as a consequence of it. The Briton leader of this battle has been identified as Arthur by later writers.

One such writer was Nennius, an early ninth-century Welsh monk, who gathered a jumble of tales and fragments under the umbrella of his *Historia Brittonum,* which is the only source for information, however fanciful, about this time. The *Historia* thus includes the story of Cunedda (a warrior king who travelled from Scotland to claim lands in north Wales), which lists Brutus as an ancestor of the Welsh. Nennius's ragtag assortment of stories also includes the first ones about Arthur, usually featuring his magical accomplice Merlin, long associated with Carmarthen, or Caerfyrddin, which means Merlin's Fort. It is Merlin, the wild, Druidic, wise man of the woods, who prophesizes that the Red Dragon, or the native Britons, will eventually defeat the White Dragon, the invading Saxons.

The whole paraphernalia of the Arthurian legend – the sword in the stone, the knights of the Round Table and the fairytale court of Camelot – are much later medieval inventions, but there are within it tantalizing true fragments from this post-Roman age in which the Britons fought against the invading hordes. Six centuries later, the 'heroic liar', or pseudo-historian, Geoffrey of Monmouth compiled his *Historia Regum Britanniae,* a book that wove a Celtic history using the accounts of Gildas, Nennius, the *Mabinogion,* Bede (another chronicler) and other sources of half-remembered events. It was then that Arthurian splendour really became British history.

The famous routing of the Anglo-Saxons at Mount Badon by the Britons was only a temporary setback, and the invaders kept up their relentless expansion towards the west and into Wales. Another battle, at Dyrham near Bristol in 577 CE led to the conquest of Cornwall, separating the Britons in Wales from their brethren and sisters in the southwest. But just as Cornwall was defeated by the Saxons, so the northern kingdoms of Rheged and Gododdin eventually succumbed, leaving Strathclyde alone to maintain and defend its independence, at least until the late eleventh century.

One of the key moments in the conquest of the northern kingdom Gododdin was captured in a piece of very early and dramatic reportage, the great poem *Y Gododdin*, preserved in a thirteenth-century manuscript kept in Cardiff Central Library. This details conflicts with Angles in Yorkshire and Northumbria in the 590s. It is written in haunting Old Welsh by the poet Aneirin, who lived in the settlement we now call Edinburgh, in what the Welsh still refer to as *Yr Hen Ogledd*, or Old North.

Y Gododdin opens with a powerful, marching rhyme:

Gwyr a aeth Gatraeth oedd ffraeth eu llu
Glasfeydd eu hancwyn a gwenwyn fu
Trichant mewn peiriant yn catau
Ac wedi elwch tawelwch fu…

It all sounds much more prosaic in English, 'The men marched to Catterick…' but it is a moving work, a heroic, long poem about a war band selected from among the tribe known as the Gododdin, who died after this disastrous attack in Yorkshire. This tribe ranged across a territory known as Manaw Gododdin, which hugged the shores of the Firth of Forth. Its capital was at a place called Din Eidyn, which might have been the Rock of Edinburgh, or Caeredin in modern Welsh.

The men marched a 240 kilometres (150 miles) to the scene of battle at Catterick, which demarcated the western boundaries of two separate Anglian kingdoms, namely Bernicia and Deira. The Gododdin might have been trying to drive a wedge between the two realms to scupper their unification.

Slaughter might best describe what then ensued on the field of battle, as at most three men were left alive after the fighting stopped. The bare facts in the poem are scant. The leader of the Britons was Mynyddawg Mwynfawr, who had a *gosgordd*, or retinue of 300 hand-picked men, some of whom joined him from other British kingdoms, including a contingent from Gwynedd, a lone warrior from Elmet near Leeds, and one who had travelled all the way from Devon to join the fray.[1] These leaders rode on horses, but the exact number of men under their command is not given, though we know they feasted well for a whole year by way of preparation – a fact that suggests this battle was planned in meticulous and deadly earnest. The poem praises ferocity in battle and lays out the values of a warrior aristocracy, resounding down through the centuries of Welsh literature in a rhythmic tale of valour and sacrifice.

When the Romans had been located to the south and east, it had been easier for the Britons to safeguard their northern frontiers against the Picts, and their western borders from the encroachments of the Irish. The Irish were most certainly in expansionist mode and they made landfall all along the western coast of Britain, establishing communities at intervals along that coast from Cornwall to Argyll in Scotland. Sometime between 350 and 400 CE, Irish raids into Wales had similarly given rise to Irish settlements: the Déisi (or Old Irish) had made their home in southwest Wales. Not only did they settle parts of modern-day Pembrokeshire, but these early immigrants might well have progressed east right the way across to the Severn estuary, as there is evidence at Lydney of the worship of Nodens, an Irish deity associated with hunting and the sea, who equates to the Welsh Nudd.

Waves of settlers from Ireland followed through the fourth, fifth and sixth centuries and there were parallel settlements by the Scotti – the Roman term for those who sallied forth from Ireland to attack Roman lands – on the Llŷn Peninsula of northwest Wales, possibly filling the vacuum left when Magnus Maximus removed his troops in 383 CE.

One of the heroes to emerge at this time, and who fought to expel the Irish, was Cunedda, who came from near the Firth of Forth in southeastern Scotland sometime in the fifth century. He brought eight of his sons and one grandson to fight alongside his force of Votandini and they successfully drove out the Irish. He may have travelled by boat from Scotland to northwest Wales, as the sea route across the Celtic pond of Morecambe Bay would have been more expeditious. Many Welsh families in Gwynedd today trace their lineage back to Cunedda.

Many subsequent leaders had links to one of Cunedda's sons, but there were other heroic figures too, such as Vortigern, another fifth-century Briton leader from whom subsequent kings in the valley of the river Wye traced their line.

We get a glimpse of what life might have been like at the seats of one of these rulers in a description by John Davies of a settlement at Dinas Powys, near Cardiff, excavated in the 1950s:

> ...The ruler of Dinas Powys was able to provide his followers with feasts of beef and pork, no doubt tribute taken from the peasantry

in return for his 'protection'. He and his retainers enjoyed the
contents of amphorae filled with wine and olive oil brought
through Mediterranean and Atlantic trading networks from
Asia Minor and the Aegean. At feasts, the chieftain was able to
use tableware from what is now the west coast of Turkey, from
Tunisia and from western France, together with glass beakers also
imported from France. His jeweller produced fine metalwork,
including brooches decorated with enamel and millefiori glass.[2]

Despite these trappings of comfort and wealth, and connections with
the Continent that echoed Roman times, Wales was a chessboard: all
the sinuous borders between the small kingdoms were porous,
unwalled and subject to takeover. Some of the dominant families who
ruled in this period held sway for 500 years, yet change and continu-
ity also seemed to apply in equal measure, and there was violence as
rights of succession were challenged and defended with blades and
blood. In the *Annales Cambriae* ('Annals of Wales') there are glimpses
of an often savage world, with the ruling families blinding, castrating
and executing as effective ways of quashing or eliminating rivals.* As
tradition held that a king should be without blemish, mutilation was
as good as murder in preventing an heir from taking the throne.

But one thing helped bind the Britons: Brythonic, one of the two
branches of Insular Celtic, which would evolve into the language
we now know as Welsh (as well as Cornish, Manx and Breton), was

---

* The *Annales Cambriae* were compiled no later than the tenth century and form a record
of earlier events in the country and further afield. A synopsis of the endemic violence
and ugly deeds of the medieval period can be found in David Walker, see Further Reading, page 356.

spoken throughout the whole of southern Scotland, western England, Wales and Cornwall in what would turn out to be a relatively brief interlude between Roman might and Saxon show of strength.

In Roman times Latin had been the language of law and administration. Nevertheless, the majority of people spoke Brythonic, even if the cities tended to be bilingual. After the collapse of the empire it would have been possible to travel through the Brythonic kingdoms from Cornwall to Scotland speaking nothing other than Brythonic. And as their neighbours to the east, in the new Anglo-Saxon kingdoms, grew in strength and piled on the pressure, this had the effect of fostering a sense of identity, of 'them and us'. Eventually the incomers proved too powerful for the speakers of two of the other languages that succeeded the British language, namely the Cumbric speakers of the northwest who were overwhelmed by English settlers in Northumbria, and the Cornish speakers of the southwest, who would see their kingdom succumb around 950 CE. In this way an Anglo-Saxon wedge was driven through the communal language of the people of the west.

As the Anglo-Saxons established themselves in places such as Cumbria – then known as Rheged – the Britons retreated into Wales. Here smaller kingdoms, such as Ewias, Penllyn and Tegeingl, jostled with larger ones, such as Ystrad Tywi, which followed the fertile river plains of modern day Carmarthenshire and Gwynedd in the mountainous northwest. By the eighth century a front line was to be found between the kingdoms of Briton Powys and Anglo-Saxon Mercia. Wales and England did not exist yet as single entities, but were still divided into Brythonic and Anglo-Saxon kingdoms. These independent kingdoms were ruled by rapacious warlords, but it was the kingdom of Mercia that was to exert the greatest supremacy. And it was the expansion of Mercia, pushing ever westward into Briton power, that kickstarted the struggle for these early kingdoms.

Central Wales, in particular, was under assault from Mercia. The royal line of Powys, descendants of Brochwel Ysgythrog, bore the brunt of repeated attacks, and just to add to their woes, invaders also sallied forth from Northumbria. In the year 716 or 717 CE Aethelfrith, the King of Northumbria, attacked Chester and in the battle the then King of Powys, Selyf, son of Cynan Garwyn, was killed, and the monastery at nearby Bangor-on-Dee became a bloodbath. This massacre was reported in many later records, each bearing testament to the ferocity and merciless nature of the attack.

The Mercians, because their lands adjoined Powys, proved the more persistent attackers, however, fixated as they were on the Briton wealth and rich lands. There had been moments of peace between these kingdoms, when there was free trade and ready intermarriage, but from 640 CE onwards Mercia had tried to seize control, putting a punishing squeeze on their neighbour's economy.

Yet Powys remained unbroken, and we have a remarkable record of its subsequent struggle for survival. Near Llangollen stands a large early ninth-century cross called the Pillar of Eliseg. An inscription on it records that King Eliseg freed Powys from Mercia: 'It is Eliseg who annexed the heritage of Powys … from the power of the Angles which he made into a sword-land by fire.' Cyngen (d. 855 CE), who set up this fine war memorial, seemed to be claiming, or reclaiming, the territory of Powys, as well as reminding people of the success of his great-great grandfather, a descendant of Brochwel, in defeating those threatening his patch of earth.

Mercia was ruled from 757 to 796 CE by King Offa. He exerted massive force to control the Britons of Wales, above all in the construction of the titanic dyke earthwork to keep out raiding warriors from Powys, the northeastern kingdom. It was up to three metres high in places, and at the time of its construction, was the biggest engineering project in Wales. Offa's Dyke was longer than Hadrian's Wall, and so vast that no comparable building work on this scale was undertaken until the great canal schemes of the late eighteenth century.

Offa wasn't the first King of Mercia to build a dyke to separate his lands from those of the Britons of Wales. Offa's predecessor, King Aethelbald, who reigned from 716 to 757 CE, erected what became known as Wat's Dyke. Running between Basingwerk in Flintshire and a point on the river Severn near Welshpool, Wat's Dyke was a far less ambitious undertaking than Offa's stupendous earthwork. Like Offa's Dyke, it had a deep ditch on the west side and a shallower one on the eastern side.

Like the later castles of Edward I, Offa's gargantuan earthwork was testimony to the continuing threat posed by the Britons of Wales, and it was also a very physical means of trade control. It was this defensive barrier that crucially helped to define the 'Welsh': they became known as the troublesome people beyond the dyke. Geographically and culturally, it physically marked out two domains on either side of the barrier. Psychologically it defined two peoples: to the east were the people *beyond* the dyke, while to the west, the Britons were the people *behind* it.

While it's difficult, in the absence of documentation, to know much about the people behind the dyke, there is one site that has shed a great deal of light on how they built their settlements. Excavations between 1989 and 1993 at Llangorse Lake, which was once the centre of the kingdom of Brycheiniog, revealed one of the most spectacular archaeological finds to experts from the National Museum and Cardiff University. A *crannog* (artificial island) settlement in a lake was a familiar find in various sites in Ireland and Scotland, but had previously been unknown in Wales. The one at Llangorse was constructed in the 890s and razed by fire in 916 CE.

The small island, possibly 30 x 30 metres (100 x 100 feet), was constructed from many layers. Wicker fences lay under rafts of brush-wood, pinned down vertically by oak timbers that would have been driven through the structure, into the submerged ground using some kind of primitive pile driver. Some of these pieces of oak – measuring up to 15 metres (50 feet) high – were assembled in the form of palisades to aid the defence of the site. On top of these was a large deposit of stone that had been brought in by boat from some distance away.

There was also evidence not only of *where* the King of Brychein-iog and his war band (of 20 or 30 warriors) lived but also *how* they lived. The *crannog* was probably a hunting lodge because bone remains of wild boar and deer have been uncovered, probably given as gifts to the king. There was also evidence of meat from domestic livestock such as beef, and pork and lamb, as well as the plentiful fish and wildfowl for which the lake was renowned.

The *crannog* was painstakingly investigated to reveal patterns of stylized grapes and vegetation, not to mention lions, such as those found on similar textiles from the Mediterranean, Persia and central Asia. Dr Alan Lane was one of the team on the dig who discovered the *crannog*, and he was stunned by the links with the eastern Mediterranean:

The patterns themselves have parallels with textiles known from Persia and central Asia, which were then brought into the Mediterranean. People from this area would have had connections through trade routes back to France. Some of the churchmen and some of the kings are known to have visited Jerusalem, so it's not surprising to find these long-distance connections. But it's nevertheless exciting to have the concrete proof of it.[3]

An unusual feature of the *crannog* is that its destruction can be accurately dated to the Viking Wars, which spanned the ninth and tenth centuries. *The Anglo Saxon Chronicle* details how, in 916 CE, Aethelflaed, the Queen of Mercia and daughter of King Alfred of Wessex, sent her army into Wales to destroy the royal residence known as Brycheiniog and capture its inhabitants.

While the Briton kingdoms of Wales and the Anglo-Saxon kingdoms of England were battling it out, new and terrifying sea-borne raiders, the Vikings, arrived on British shores in their longboats from Norway, Sweden and Denmark. They would pose problems for both the kingdoms in Wales and England, but would also prove helpful allies for the Britons against their troublesome rivals on the other side of the dyke.

CHAPTER SIX

THE VIKINGS AND RHODRI THE GREAT

Bitter is the wind tonight
It tosses the ocean's white hair
Tonight I fear not the fierce warriors of Norway
Coursing on the Irish Sea.[1]

They would shark in from the open water, their early location finders fixed on monastic plunder. Driven by overpopulation and dwindling resources in their native Scandinavia – like thrushes driven south to feed on bloody berries – the Vikings were hungry and desperate marauders. Well-honed nautical skills and exceptional know-how when it came to ship building meant they could traverse huge sea distances, crossing cold and wind-whipped waters to places as far-flung as Greenland and Iceland, even extending the range of their shallow longboats to the edges of Newfoundland.

The Vikings, named from the Old Norse term for 'sea-borne robbers', became a byword for rapacity and berserk behaviour. The terrifying fact that their agile craft would barely register as events on the horizon, and that they could appear and disappear so very quickly, made it hard to plan against them, or marshal any kind of defence other than to run and hide. The heathen Northmen from coastal Norway, and the Danes from Denmark were particularly successful in locating and attacking rich and defenceless monasteries full of plentiful golden and silver booty.

The Vikings made their first attack on western Europe in 789, reaching the coast of England in their longboats to raid Portland, Dorset, and later the Northumbrian island of Lindisfarne in 793. In the face of these raids, people living along the crenellated coastline of Britain were placed on high alert. Even in an age when mass communication meant telling the people next door, news of the Viking speed and rapacity spread panic rapidly from one coastal community to the next. A nervousness bordering on the paranoid was described in the ninth-century *Anglo-Saxon Chronicle*, which also detailed attendant phenomena, such as the rise of a blood-red moon and an unseasonal and heavy snowfall after Easter. One of the Viking emblems was the raven, and its wings spread dark shadows of fear. Little wonder, then, that the sighting of a raven was considered an ill omen.

The Vikings may not have had an empire in the Roman, Mongolian or British sense, offering permanence and civilization, but the people who rowed in open longboats to settle in North America and Russia, Iceland and Byzantium had expansionist aims. Having sought out coastal monasteries, they set up trading posts in their wake, introducing both commerce and coinage. In England, Scotland and Ireland, the Vikings established settlements and even brief kingdoms. Initially they were summer plunderers, returning north with their spoils in the winter. Then the Vikings started to stay throughout the year, encamped in northern Scotland. In Ireland too they settled in

Dublin. They would, from the 780s until 1100, be a significant factor in the politics of all three countries.

Some experts maintain that Wales never had a Viking age, and that is largely true: the Vikings established few permanent settlements here, other than perhaps in the southwest. There were semi-permanent trading posts at places such as Tenby and Swansea, and there are almost 60 Viking place names, such as Milford and Fishguard, along the coast.

Viking place names are also to be found off the coast, with a clutch of places called Sker (rock), as well as all the principal Welsh islands: Grassholm, the 'cold island' of Caldey, Ramsey, Skomer, Skokholm, and Bardsey. Tusker Rock, an island in the Bristol Channel just off the coast at Ogmore-by-Sea, took its name from Tuska, a Danish Viking who inhabited the fertile Vale of Glamorgan with his fellow warriors. Tusker is not far as the raven flies from another place with obvious Viking connections, namely Ulfs Well. The island of Anglesey, which formed a third of the territory of Bretland – the Viking name for Welsh territory – saw repeated attacks, and had lost its name Ynys Môn by the late eleventh century, when it was known as Ongul's Isle. Swansea is said to have been founded by Sweyne Forkbeard, who was shipwrecked in the open bay there, while Worm's Head, on the tip of the Gower Peninsula was so named because the Vikings thought it resembled a sleeping dragon.

Although Wales may not have undergone much in the way of settlement by Vikings, it was still very much a target for attack. Vikings were often known as 'Gentiles', with those based in Dublin known as 'Black Gentiles', and these were the Northmen who attacked Wales from many compass points between 852 and 877. Their modus operandi was neat and simple: surprise, raid and loot. In 878 a Viking force overwintered in Dyfed, Wales, for the first time, an act subsequently repeated.

In 896 the Welsh kingdoms of both Gwent and Brycheiniog suffered at the hands of an army of Danes and pirates led by Viking chieftain Haesten. His army had been ranging and ravaging freely throughout England for almost 15 years. In 903 the Black Gentiles reappeared for another surprise raid, and again in 914 when they sortied up the Severn and captured sets of slaves.

Sometimes their slave-raids were on a much grander scale: in 987 the Vikings captured 2,000 people on Anglesey, which, given the levels of population at the time, can't have left that many people behind. They harried other stretches of coast: Maredudd, the ruler of Dyfed, agreed to pay tribute in 989, a bribe both to release captives and save themselves from further attacks. But the Vikings continued their murderous raids in the northwest and the southwest. Later on, Maredudd found a use for his attackers when he employed the Vikings as mercenaries to attack rival Glamorgan.

So wave upon wave of attacks punctuated this period of Viking marauding, with St David's and Anglesey taking the brunt of them. In Anglesey, archaeological digs during the past few years have unearthed a refortification of a low-lying coastal settlement during the ninth century. The massive enclosure wall at Llanbedr-goch not only reflects the prosperity of the owner but may have been constructed in the time of Rhodri the Great in response to Viking pressure.

At the same site five dismembered, roughly buried skeletons have been discovered and may represent victims of the ninth-century Viking attacks. The remains belong to three adults and two children, all of whom were dumped in a shallow grave outside the defensive wall, and covered by large stones. All the bodies lay at different angles. One was pushed up against the side of the grave; another lay on top of an infant with its feet by the infant's chin, and seems to have been buried with hands tied behind the back. Although disease followed by hasty burial to avoid contagion cannot be ruled out, a violent death is thought more likely.

If this settlement's initial contact with the Vikings was violent, friendlier trading contacts soon developed. Evidence from further excavations here has shown an increase in Viking-style metalwork and other artefacts at the site during the tenth century.

It was during the late ninth century, as the Vikings attacked Wales and the Anglo-Saxons and Britons of Wales battled it out over the border and across Offa's Dyke, that one of Wales's first military national heroes was forged: Rhodri Mawr (Rhodri the Great).

The course of history is studded with kingly epithets, or more accurately cognomens – extended names that sum up an essential quality or aspect of character. From Edward the Confessor to Alfonso the Chaste, from Basil the Bulgur Slayer to the fear-inducing Mehmed the Executioner, assigning nicknames has been history's way of passing long-term judgement. Not that it has always proved accurate. Mistranslation might leave some wrongly judged, such as in the case of the Saxon king Ethelred II, remembered for being 'Unready', though in fact he was 'without counsel'. But in Rhodri Mawr's case, 'Great' was spot on.

Rhodri the Great is the only major Welsh ruler to have this epithet applied to him, joining other 'greats' in history, such as Charlemagne, Alfred and Peter. Rhodri's greatness lay in his ability to be a unifying force, a creator of a sense of statehood, bringing large swathes of Wales under the control of a single political leader for the first time. He also proved himself a skilled military tactician, as he repelled successive waves of Viking attacks and Anglo-Saxon invasions in the east.

Rhodri became the leader of the kingdom of Gwynedd from 844. The House of Gwynedd had been established by Cunedda, head of the Gododdin tribe, after he travelled from the Firth of Forth to displace the Irish who had settled in northwest Wales. Cunedda's eight sons gave their names to many parts of west and north Wales, such as Ceredigion. They were the traditional forebears of the House of Gwynedd, the heads of which would include Merfyn Frych, who became ruler around 825. Merfyn was the father of a long line of distinguished leaders who came to play important roles in changing the political map of Wales in the period up to the conquest by Edward I. Rhodri was Merfyn's eldest son.

In 844, Powys came under Rhodri's rule after the death of his uncle. Rhodri revealed his diplomatic foresight and enlarged his domain further by arranging his marriage to Angharad, the sister of the last King of Ceredigion. Marrying Angharad brought substantial tracts of west Wales under Rhodri's control, including Ceredigion and Ystrad Tywi (Carmarthenshire), so the marriage created the wide kingdom of Seisyllwg, which separated Dyfed (Pembrokeshire) from other southern kingdoms. Rhodri now ruled a great swathe of Wales covering the northwest, centre and southwest.

Rhodri was also the first ruler to consider the international dimension of his reign, bringing his court into contact with foreign powers while also developing it as a centre of native culture. His court was polyglot: Welsh, Irish and Latin were spoken, not to mention a couple of other continental tongues. Visitors to the court might be entertained by having to solve word games, the answers to which would only be revealed if one could transpose the letters from Latin into Greek.

As the Saxons pushed westward over the shared and still-contested border with Mercia – even after the building of Offa's Dyke – and the Vikings threatened, permanently intent on plunder, Rhodri's containment of the dual menace bore ample testimony to his powers, diplomatic nous and energy at a time when foreign threat had to compete with the domestic agenda for the king's attention.

Reports of Rhodri's fame as a warrior offer us some of the scanty information about his life. He is mentioned in *The Ulster Chronicle* and also by an Irish scholar who served the Frankish king Charles the Bald. In a famous battle in 856 he killed Gorm, the leader of the Viking fleet, leaving them 'gormless', as it were. News of this victory was relayed to Charles the Bald, who was mightily pleased to hear of it as he had been suffering severely at the hands of the Vikings. In a subsequent skirmish in 877, however, the Danes forced Rhodri to flee to Ireland. He returned to Wales the following year to reclaim his kingdom, only to be killed in battle against the Anglo-Saxons.

Until Rhodri's day, Wales was completely unused to any sense of unity. After his death, his lands were divided between his several sons, as was the way in Wales at this time, and the land became fractured by squabbles and dissent.

Meanwhile, the Anglo-Saxon peoples living in England were uniting, coming together under a succession of kings. In what can now be seen as an early nation-building project, small kingdoms were being subsumed into a single larger, dominant one, that would, crucially, be passed on through primogeniture (the right of the first-born son to inherit the land). Alfred the Great (r. 871–99 CE) had defeated the Danes and made an agreement with them that extended the powers of the kingdom of Wessex to include Mercia and Kent, while Danelaw ruled in the north and east of England. His son Edward the Elder expanded the kingdom further and Athelstan (r. 925–39 CE), Alfred the Great's grandson, was the first king to rule all of England. Meanwhile, Rhodri's land was being carved up amongst his successors. Had he lived, Rhodri might have overseen a Welsh project to both mirror and eventually contest this burgeoning Anglo-Saxon domination.

Meanwhile, the Viking marauders who had so terrifyingly emerged towards the end of the eighth century had in some places stayed long enough to establish proper, albeit temporary, commercial centres or trading posts, such as in Swansea and Milford Haven, and there were some who thought they could more easily do business with the Vikings and Danes than with the Anglo-Saxons. Some of the peoples living in Wales cut deals and sealed informal treaties. In the time of Anarawd, son of Rhodri Mawr, alliances were forged with the Viking headquarters at York.

Rhodri's heirs formed a dynasty of kings that ruled Gwynedd for four generations. But one among them was to stand proud from the rest, a man forever connected with an act of law-making that was uniquely Welsh, equable, fair and enduring. If Rhodri was great, his grandson Hywel Dda was most certainly good.

CHAPTER SEVEN

LAW AND ORDER

Three indispensibles of a king: his priest to celebrate mass and to bless his food and drink; his bodyguard to execute his commands; his court judge to determine sentences. Three things which a king does not share with anyone: his treasurer, his hawk and his thief.[1]

The great Welsh leader Hywel ap Cadell (r. 910–50), otherwise known as Hywel Dda or Hywel the Good, had a more successful relationship with the Anglo-Saxons of Wessex than his predecessors. He was the well-travelled grandson of Rhodri Mawr, having visited Rome, and was also well-acquainted with the Vikings. He saw that his best interests lay in an alliance with King Aethelstan of Wessex, and the relationship was mutually beneficial: Wessex also needed to defend its borders against Viking attacks from the north and east of England and against invasions from Scotland.

Under King Aethelstan, law codes were largely put in place to strengthen royal control over Wessex; currency was regulated to control silver's weight and to penalize fraudsters; buying and selling was largely confined to the *burhs* (fortified towns), encouraging town life; and areas of settlement in the Midlands and Viking towns were consolidated into shires. Overseas, Aethelstan built alliances by marrying off four of his half-sisters to various rulers in western Europe.

Aethelstan was an effective and forceful king. The very fact that Wessex was able to extend its boundaries even as it resisted Viking expansion was testament enough to Aethelstan's political and military skills. Wisely, Hywel saw that he could better safeguard his own lands by choosing alignment rather than armament, by opting for partnership rather than a punishing war.

When Aethelstan summoned the Welsh princes to Hereford in 926 and demanded a tribute in gold, silver, cattle, dogs and hawks, Hywel was happy to oblige. It was a not inconsiderable tribute, comprising 20 pounds of gold, 300 pounds of silver and 25,000 oxen. He frequently attended the English king's council, the *witan,* and was one of its most important members. He even called his son by the Anglo-Saxon name of Edwin. Of course, he was the junior partner in this relationship, but the deal was mutually beneficial for the two leaders.

Hywel inherited the southern part of Seisyllwg and carried on the fruitful family tradition of strategic marriage. In 904 he married Elen, daughter of Llywarch ap Hyfaidd of Dyfed (Pembrokeshire), a small kingdom established originally by the Deisi tribe from Ireland. This gained Hywel another part of Wales to add to his domain, which he called Deheubarth. This meant that he had control of the whole of west Wales, from the Dyfi to the Tawe. Restless for further acquisitions, he claimed Brycheiniog around 930 and went on to seize Gwynedd and Powys when its bald king, Idwal Foel, was killed 12 years later. This left only Morgannwg independent of Hywel's will.

Hywel favoured diplomacy over warfare and his way of dealing with the ongoing scourge that was the Vikings was to deepen an allegiance with Wessex, thus becoming subservient to England. Some have even gone so far as to describe him as an Anglophile. It is note-worthy, though, that his name took precedence over other Welsh kings on contemporary charters.

A defining moment for Hywel and the Welsh kingdoms came in 937, when an anonymous Welsh poet in the tenth-century prophetic poem *Armes Prydain* urged the Vikings, Picts, Scots, Irish and Welsh to rise up in revolt against the Anglo-Saxons and drive them out of Britain once and for all. The poet was buoyed up by incredible confi-dence, claiming that 'heads would split open without brains' and 'wives would be widows and horses riderless'. But Hywel decided not to enter the fray. The Anglo-Saxons were not driven out and, on the contrary, in the Battle of Brunanburh in 937, King Aethelstan defeated an alliance of Scots and Vikings with his own alliance of the Welsh and the Danes from Dublin. Whether the relationship Hywel courted with the English king was cowardice or diplomatic strategy, it not only bought him time, but also marked him out as having a certain inde-pendence; he was no longer automatically linked to the actions of the peoples of northern and western Britain.

Hywel, described in *Brut y Brenhinedd* as 'the chief and most praiseworthy of all the Britons', was also the only king in Wales to mint his own coins, which carried the inscription 'Hywel Rex'. In a thirteenth-century manuscript there is an image of Hywel in iconic posture: seated on a throne, he appears as a bearded man with long tresses of hair sprouting from beneath his crown. He is dressed in clas-sic green robes, holds a sceptre in one hand, and points an abnormally long finger into the middle distance – perhaps a reference to his status as visionary. Hywel's greatest contribution to nation-building was his alleged creation of Welsh Law, which was essentially a codification of custom and practice in Wales, intended to assist the unification of the Welsh kingdoms.

The Laws of Hywel (Cyfraith Hywel) show us the components of social class at the time, with the king claiming the top tier, followed by the *breyr*, or free landowners, and the bottom tier occupied by the *taeogion*, or serfs. The laws were shot through with common sense, mercy, and an unusual fairness in matters relating to the rights of women and children. The laws are also rich sources of information about the age: for example, we can learn about the nine buildings for the king stipulated necessary by law; these were the great hall, chambers, kitchens, chapel, barn, kiln-house, privy, stables and dog kennels.

There are interesting aspects of native law, such as the *galanas*, which means murder or manslaughter. There was no capital punishment for murder. Instead the murderer's family, as far forward as the seventh generation, had to pay a murder price to the family of the deceased. This price varied according to the status of the deceased. Thieves also faced a sliding scale of fines, so stealing a property would result in the thief being hanged, while the taking of an oak tree warranted a fine of 120 pence, and the theft of a fox-skin eight pence.

The laws were nothing if not detailed and meticulous, and there was a law for every occasion. The guide to a fair 'divorce' settlement, for example, divided everything:

If anyone send away his wife without lawful cause, and take another in her place, by judgment the woman who has been put out is entitled to come to her home, and be in her home until the ninth day. And if on that day she is sent away, first let all things which are hers go out from the house, and after the last of the

number, let her herself go out of the house. The husband shall
have all of the pigs, the wife the sheep. The husband shall have
all the horses and mares, the oxen, and cows, bullocks and heifers:
the wife shall have the goats. Next the household equipment shall
be divided as follows: all the vessels of milk, except one baeol
[pitcher] are the wife's and all the dishes, except one meat dish,
that is cigddysgl *[meat dish] are the husband's...* [2]

Some 70 manuscript law books have survived, the majority of them in Welsh and some in Latin, housed in an array of great libraries. About half of these are late copies, made by and for scholars in the sixteenth, seventeenth and eighteenth centuries. The others come from an earlier period, between 1200 and 1500, when the laws, sometimes called codes, were active, and were therefore set down for use by lawyers. An author of one of the books, one Iorwerth ap Madog, had compiled the volume from four other books, which accounts for its patchwork quality. Another author included *A Book of the Rudiments of the Law of Hywel Dda*, an ABC of its day, while a further author has couched some of the information in the form of a catechism, testing the reader with both questions and answers. Over the years these manuscript accounts tended to overplay the role of the Church in the compiling of the laws, an understandable tendency since they were written by clerics.

Whether Hywel actually orchestrated the compilation of Welsh law, with obvious echoes of the laws passed by Aethelstan in England, we cannot tell, but this set of rules, claimed to be devised during his reign, were used in Wales until they were replaced by English Law in 1536–43. Hywel is certainly very strongly associated with the laws, even if they first appeared only some 200 years after his death. It is the case that all the Welsh law books that survived start with a preface that includes versions of the same story, namely that Hywel summoned an assembly consisting of the chief ecclesiastics of Wales, together with six men from each of the local subdivisions of the country; that the assembly examined and discussed the laws of the period for 40 days; that as a result of their deliberations, they made various changes and improvements in the law; and that the revised laws were set down in an authoritative book.

The period after the death of Hywel the Good was typified by chaos, insecurity and bloodshed, and no fewer than 35 Welsh rulers died between 950 and 1063, as leaders grabbed land and carved Wales up into smaller kingdoms once again. One name emerged during this period of bloodshed, and that was Gruffudd ap Llywelyn.

The son of a Danish princess, Gruffudd ap Llywelyn was a supreme opportunist and completely ruthless. In 1039 he had seized Gwynedd and Powys, and by 1055, with the death of Gruffydd ap Rhydderch, he controlled Deheubarth. He then swiftly turned his attention to Mercia, looking east for extensions to his domain, and terrorizing the Anglo-Saxons at the Battle of Rhyd-y-groes near Welshpool in the same year. Aelfgar was the Mercian heir and a man Gruffudd needed to influence.

His intriguing alliance with Aelfgar, Anglo-Saxon Earl of Mercia, bolstered the position of both men, which meant that Gruffudd was an ever-present thorn in the side of the kingdom of Wessex. In 1055, to aid the Earl of Mercia, Gruffudd sortied well beyond his court at Rhuddlan, and over Offa's Dyke, taking Anglo-Saxon land and having the arrogance and confidence to loot and burn the cathedral city of

Hereford. In response, the Earl of Wessex, later to become King Harold I, attempted a counter-attack on him, which failed.

Meanwhile, around 1057, Gruffudd drove out the ruler of Morgannwg, Cadwgan ap Meurig, meaning that for the first time, one man had brought all the kingdoms of Wales under one leader.

Tension continued for another seven years, with Gruffudd supporting the Earl of Mercia, until Harold launched another attack on Gruffudd at his court in Rhuddlan in the winter of 1062. Gruffudd escaped, but Harold launched a second attack in the summer of 1063, which pushed Gruffudd into central Wales, where he was killed by his Welsh rivals – a high price for a rather one-sided deal with the Mercians.

His epitaph, recorded in the chronicles known as *Brenhinedd y Saeson*, summed him up thus:

> *Gruffudd ap Llywelyn, golden-torqued king of the Welsh and their defender, died after many plunderings and victorious battles against his foes, after many feasts and delights, and great gifts of gold and silver and costly raiment, he who was sword and shield over the fate of all Wales.*[3]

Gruffudd had been murdered and his head sent to Harold. It is unclear who killed him – some say he was killed by his own men, while the *Ulster Chronicle* suggests it was Cynan ap Iago, the son of Iago ab Idwal, the leader of Gwynedd put to death by Gruffudd in 1039. While the perpetrator's identity is a mystery, the reason for the slaying is perhaps a little clearer: it was probably an action that resulted from festering resentments about the method in which

Gruffudd had united Wales, and one that took advantage of the fact that Harold's attacks had weakened him. Yet before his death, Gruffudd had united disparate parts of the country, created a loose alliance of Welsh leaders, formed an alliance with an Anglo-Saxon earl, and maintained Viking connections. He was certainly an extraordinarily brutal man, but he had also sown seeds of future nationhood and one later assessment of him, by Walter Map in his *Trifles of Courtiers*, compared him with Alexander the Great. Things were shaping up on the Welsh side of the dyke, and its inhabitants were moulding into a more unified entity.

CHAPTER EIGHT

NORMAN WALES

Alas! That life hath led us to such time as this, wherein a cruel power threatens to oust from their rights those who walk justly. Free necks submit to the yoke. Things once lofty lie despised. Both people and priest are scorned by every motion of the French. They increase our burdens and consume our goods. The youth no more delight in jests, nor pay they any heed to the poet's verse. A stupor has fallen upon the people. Righteous hands are branded with hot iron. Prison and slavery are our lot, with lack of ease.[1]

Six hundred years after the ruthlessly systematic Romans retreated from Britain and the Anglo-Saxons arrived, and 300 years after the first harrying raids of the Vikings, Wales had another more oppressive foe – the Normans – and they would dictate the future identity of England and Wales.

Not only did the Normans subjugate the native people, they also introduced new names to describe them and the land where they lived: *Wales* and the *Welsh*, from the Old English for 'foreign land' and 'foreigners'. The Welsh had their own name for themselves, the *Cymry*, a noun that came from the Celtic *Cambrogi*, meaning 'fellow countrymen', but it was the Norman label that stuck in the end.

The Norman conquest had, of course, started with William of Normandy's invasion from the Continent. In 1066, the year Harold inherited the Anglo-Saxon crown from Edward the Confessor, a strange apparition, namely Halley's Comet, appeared in the night skies, which the new king took to be a fearful portent. The Battle of Hastings, in which Harold's men were outnumbered three to one by those of William, ushered in an age when a new aristocracy came to rule England, and the ambitious Norman who had battled at Hastings became William the Conqueror.

During William's reign, earldoms were swiftly created in Chester, Hereford and Shrewsbury, and the annexation of Wales should have been a mere formality. After all, England was effectively subdued in a mere four years, and on the eve of the Norman conquest Wales had lost its greatest leader, but even after 25 years, there were still parts of Wales that eluded Norman rule. The wide power of Gruffudd ap Llywelyn, who died three years before the arrival of the Normans, affected English polity as it suggested that Wales was a home of powerful and dangerous kings who could challenge the authority of England.

When the scholar-poet Rhygyfarch, who wrote the biographical work *Life of Saint David* during the late eleventh century, penned his 'Lament' he was writing a sort of news analysis of its day, describing a country tamed and traumatized by the Normans. Rhys ap Tewdwr, the Welsh king of Deheubarth, had previously had his rights to Deheubarth sanctioned by William the Conqueror, who had travelled through south Wales to visit St David's in 1081. This was both a show of force and a demonstration of the good relations between the two rulers. These good terms remained in place until William's death in 1087. Under his son William II, the patronage had come to

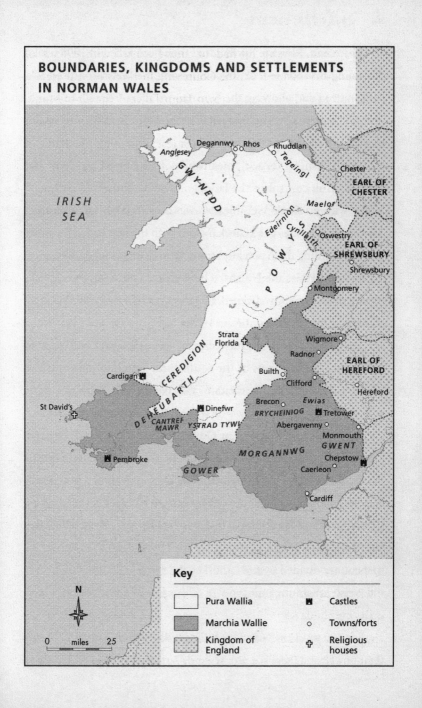

BOUNDARIES, KINGDOMS AND SETTLEMENTS IN NORMAN WALES

IRISH SEA

Anglesey

Degannwy
Rhos
Rhuddlan
Tegeingl

GWYNEDD

Chester

EARL OF CHESTER

Maelor

Edeirnion
Cynllaith
P O W Y S

Oswestry

EARL OF SHREWSBURY

Shrewsbury

Montgomery

Strata Florida

Wigmore

Radnor

EARL OF HEREFORD

Builth

Clifford

Hereford

CEREDIGION

Cardigan

DEHEUBARTH

Dinefwr

Brecon
Ewias
BRYCHEINIOG

Tretower

Abergavenny

CANTREF MAWR

YSTRAD TYWI

St David's

Pembroke

MORGANNWG

Monmouth
GWENT

Chepstow

Caerleon

GOWER

Cardiff

Key

Pura Wallia	Castles
Marchia Wallie	Towns/forts
Kingdom of England	Religious houses

N

0   miles   25

an abrupt end. Rhys ap Tewdwr had then been killed in 1093 whilst defending Brycheiniog, or Brecon, leaving the Welsh confused and demoralized and allowing the Norman invaders free rein to brand, mutilate and yoke those free necks. Resistance would come again, though not for a time.

The Welsh landscape, meanwhile, had helped to deny the Normans full control of the land, and the decentralized nature of Wales, with no single Welsh leader, was also arguably an advantage. The Welsh dynasties lived cheek by jowl with the new order, the most powerful among them actually strengthening their kingdoms.

In south Wales the Normans built their castle complexes, creating a territory collectively known as the March or *Marchia Wallie*, in contrast to Welsh Wales or *Pura Wallia*.

Anglo-Saxon peasants moved in, as well as knights, and in some of the most fertile lands of the south there were too many for the Welsh to assimilate. To contain the Welsh, the Normans used 'enforced displacement', by which they allowed settlers to displace the natives in south Gower, or Gower Anglicana. In 1105, Henry I granted Flemish settlers permission to take over land in south Pembrokeshire; it was a linguistic takeover, as well as a land grab, because eventually only seven of the 50 or so parishes in the area had Welsh names. Welsh attempts to expel the Flemish colony failed, not least because of special patronage of the Crown, and in so doing, led to a county divided by the Landsker, a linguistic dividing line, with the Welsh inhabiting points north of this line of demarcation, which exists even today.

For 200 years the Normans built garrisons and castles to enforce their power, and these got progressively larger and more forbidding as time went by. They also established civic arrangements known as boroughs and lordships.

Chepstow, Tretower and the gargantuan great keep of Pembroke were meant to be frightening symbols of authority and repression. Historian Jan Morris considers Chepstow castle to be the most brutal in Wales, 'like a huge fist of rock at the very gate of Wales'.[2]

Viewed from the English side of the Severn, Chepstow castle is the very epitome of impregnability. The *Domesday Book* records that the builder of the first castle at Chepstow was William FitzOsbern, who was created Earl of Hereford by William the Conqueror shortly after the Battle of Hastings in 1066. Building began from 1067 and carried on until 1075.

FitzOsbern chose the spur of rocky land that forms the last cliff on the Welsh side of the river Wye for obvious reasons. The river, flowing languorously to meet the Severn estuary, was itself a formidable natural defence. Coupled with an unscalable cliff to the north and a militarily controllable little valley to the south, it made the logistics of defence all the more manageable. This gave FitzOsbern command over the main route from England into south Wales, and a military launch pad for incursions into the fertile lands of Gwent.

FitzOsbern died in 1071 and his son, Roger, had to forfeit the place to the king four years later. The castle was subsequently added to by its new owner, William Marshal, who introduced the drum tower, and later by his sons, and then altered again by Roger Bigod III, Earl of Norfolk.

From border bases such as Chepstow and Hereford the Norman soldiers radiated out. In Wales it wasn't so much conquest as incursion, as the lords of the March sent out closely ordered troops of mailed knights and men-at-arms crashing through the wooded country. The Earl of Shrewsbury sent soldiers along the Severn valley and down as far as Pembroke, while the Earl of Chester claimed parts of Tegeingl, sweeping out towards the Dee estuary just as the Earl of Hereford launched his attacks on Brecon. The Normans' ruthlessly efficient assaults were helped by having a network of Roman roads to follow.

As they gained territory, the Norman soldiers would often pause to group around mottes and baileys. These were simple wooden towers defended by palisades, which were rapidly erected on top of conical mounds. In due course some of these structures became stone castles, built both to withstand attack and command respect.

By the eve of the twelfth century the Normans had crossed south Wales as far as Pembroke, and the boundaries between the Welsh March and Welsh Wales were more or less established, but Wales would not accept Norman supremacy. The Welsh revolted against William II, and by 1100 the Normans had lost control of large swathes of land in Gwynedd, Ceredigion and large parts of Powys.

The Normans had followed the valleys of mid-Wales to the coast and taken their army as far as Anglesey, but had failed to commandeer the mountainous interior and northern highlands of Wales. Norman rule was then concentrated in *Marchia Wallie*, the lordships of the borderlands, and parts of the south that were under the control of strong castles. These lords were not subject to the law of England, giving them the right to run their fiefdoms as they chose, be it holding court or waging war: the March was to exist for 450 years and prove an important element in Welsh history.

While the Normans built castles from stone, the natives saw their mountains as castles. From here they organized their opposition, which in Gwynedd came in the shape of Gruffudd ap Cynan.

Gruffudd ap Cynan, son of Cynan ap Iago, was born in exile in Ireland, among his mother's Norse friends. From the end of the eleventh century, he attempted to win back his inheritance. On the third attempt, he was successful, and by the time he died in 1137 he had reclaimed most of Gwynedd. Gruffudd's son Owain not only consolidated his father's power, but built on it by threatening adjoining Powys and beating the Normans when annexing Ceredigion to territory in Gwynedd.

This success by the kingdom of Gwynedd, which was to extend from the Dyfi estuary to the mouth of the Dee, and which remained stubbornly defiant, was part of what has been described as the 'Welsh resurgence', providing resistance through the reigns of William II (1087–1100) and Henry I (1100–35). A Welsh kingdom was also restored in lowland Gwent during the reign of Stephen I (1135–54), after military successes by Iorwerth and Morgan, the grandsons of Gruffudd. Stephen I was a weak king who was unwilling to support the Marcher lords after many of them had supported his rival for the throne, Henry I's daughter, Matilda.

But it was not only a story of battle and confrontation. The Welsh also adopted many of the Norman ways, absorbing the Continental influence and, in particular, buying into an urban way of life. The Normans refined feudalism and developed trade. Towns meant trade and trade meant money. Coinage proved popular, and towns such as Cydweli were built around the castles. The Welsh also appropriated Norman castle-building techniques for themselves, either against the enemy or each other, and motte and bailey-style forts were gradually replaced by rectangular stone keeps, those such as the ones in centres like Dynevor and Dolbadarn, where kings enjoyed sitting in ceremonial state. Even in Welsh Wales, the Norman ways proved attractive, at least to the upper classes, and the Welsh learned from foreign settlers, such as the Flemish weavers of Pembrokeshire.

New lands were cultivated and older, bonded holdings were seized, and a system known as *gwely* came into being. This was a system of mixed arable and pasture land that was held by free men whose bond was a common ancestor. At the same time new administrative divisions sprouted, including the *cwmwd* and the *cantref*.

The Normans also brought in new names, which soon became popular, such as Richard, Robert and William. French words were also soon assimilated into Welsh, and Welsh literature began to be influenced by French conventions and forms. Also, a handful of French place names appeared on the map, such as Beaumaris and Hay, from Haie Taillée.

There was political as well as linguistic assimilation too. In contrast to Gruffudd ap Cynan and Owain ap Gruffudd in the north, other Welsh leaders found alternative ways to deal the Normans.

One of these was Rhys ap Gruffudd, the grandson of Rhys ap Tewdwr, who had been the last of the Welsh kings of Deheubarth before they were overthrown by the Normans in 1093. Rhys was fluent in French, the language of the aristocracy in England and Wales during the Norman period, and also in Welsh (though he spoke no English).

He was to use both diplomatic and military skills as he restored much of southwest Wales to its ancient dynasty by wresting Ceredigion and Ystrad Tywi from the control of the Normans. This left the Normans in charge of places such as Pembroke, with lordships spread sporadically along the south coast.

Rhys faced opposition from his contemporary Owain Gwynedd, who wanted to expand his own domain south. Owain was a powerful figure who ruled Gwynedd from 1137 until his death in 1170. To thwart Owain's encroachments, Rhys began building a castle on the Dyfi. Meanwhile, Stephen I had died and England had a new king, Henry II (r. 1154–89), the first of the House of Plantagenet (a noble Frankish family). More powerful and resourceful than Stephen, Henry was keen to bring Wales back under the control of the English Crown.

Drawing on his resources, Henry II entered Wales and imposed his power on the Welsh leaders. Madog ap Maredudd, the ruler of Powys at this time, capitulated to Henry in 1156. Manipulating the long-standing rivalry between Powys and Gwynedd, Henry used the King of Powys's support to force Owain Gwynedd to yield to the Crown once more in 1157.

In the early years of Henry II's reign, Rhys ap Gruffudd defended his territory from the Norman lords, harrying them constantly but also entering into negotiations if it would protect his position. On one occasion, Rhys took Lord Robert Fitzstephen hostage during an assault on Cardigan. One condition of his releasing was that Fitzstephen should turn his attention to Ireland and invade there instead, leaving Rhys in peace.

But Rhys's predations and attacks whittled away at the king's patience and by 1163 he had become sufficiently troublesome for Henry to muster a force against him. Henry II's campaign of that year pushed Rhys back to his native Cantref Mawr.

After his retreat back to Cantref Maw, Rhys swore an oath of allegiance to the king in 1163 at Woodstock, where all the native princes had been summoned by Henry. For a couple of decades, Rhys made peace with the king, despite 1164 being the year of widespread insurrection by the other princes in Wales.

But Rhys had local matters to attend to; his enemies were set on claiming Cantref Mawr, and Rhys had his work cut out to reclaim the castle of Dinefwr and the surrounding lands. His Marcher foes had also paid a servant, Walter ap Llywarch, to murder Rhys's nephew Einion ab Anarawd as he slept, before fleeing for sanctuary with Earl Roger at Ceredigion. Further brutality came when Rhys's nemesis Walter Clifford, owner of Llandovery castle, raided Rhys's lands.

Rhys, along with other Welsh leaders, had joined forces with Owain Gwynedd in 1163 to challenge English rule. An expeditionary force sent by Henry foolishly decided against approaching along the coast, and they found themselves pitted against a combined Welsh army, led by Owain Gwynedd in the Berwyn Mountains, which were not easy to reach on foot, let alone fight on after a very long slog.

Torrential rain helped the Welsh cause, and later attempts by the English king to raid Gwynedd by sea failed because the Irish mercenary fleet employed for the task proved wholly inadequate. Incensed, Henry took out his rage on 22 of his hostages, including Rhys's son Maredudd, who was summarily blinded.

Owain Gwynedd died in November 1170, thereby creating a power vacuum. In September 1171 Rhys met King Henry II, who had since been weakened by his disputes with the powerful Archbishop Becket in December 1170 at Newnham, on the margin of the Forest of Dean.

Henry wanted a trouble-free Wales so that he would not have to add to his existing problems with Norman lords who sought to rule independently in Ireland. He also needed safe passage for his army to Milford Haven, on their journey to Ireland. Rhys could help ensure both. The two men met a few times subsequently, and a truce between them allowed Rhys to turn his ragtag of scattered territories into something resembling a kingdom. Even when Rhys failed to raise the money necessary to pay tribute to the king, Henry turned a blind eye, and even released another of Rhys's sons, Hywel, who had also been held hostage.

In 1172, Henry appointed Rhys justice in all south Wales. The new appellation recognized Rhys's right to rule, not only over his own territories but, after 1172, other Welsh rulers in places such as Elfael, Brycheiniog and Gwent had to deal with Lord Rhys in all matters regarding the king. In that sense he was a powerful deputy – the sword had been replaced by the diplomat's skill. Appointing Rhys as justice for south Wales served to underline the friendship between the two men, which remained until Henry's early death on 6 July 1189. It was a détente that lasted despite Rhys facing constant problems from the Marcher lords.

In his later years, Lord Rhys was actually allowed to live a life of some splendour. He developed his seat of power at Dinefwr castle, an ancient site with roots in antiquity. But he had other castles too, and they were places of culture as well as defence. In 1176, for instance, Lord Rhys was able to preside over an impressive eisteddfod at Cardigan castle, where poets and musicians from all over the country convened, and the 'chair' for poetry was awarded to a poet from Gwynedd, while a harpist from Deheubarth kept the home crowd happy by winning the chair for music. The eisteddfod had been proclaimed 12 months in advance, in Ireland and Scotland, as well as in Wales. It was an international cultural event.

Lord Rhys died in 1197. After his death several elegies were written bemoaning the loss of this leader and cultural patron. In the history *Brut y Tywysogyon*, or Chronicle of Princes, he was compared to an array of classical heroes, and one anguished poet claimed that 'the glory of Wales has passed away, Rhys is dead'. Another lavished his memory with praise:

> If its source is sought, there is great majesty in that place;
> If one asks what is its end, behold there are ashes;
> One who loved a fair name, one fragrant with distinction,
>   a fount of gentleness,
> Rhys is buried in this small tomb;
> The Prince's hair, like a mass of the sun's rays,
> And his face is turned to ashes.
> Here he lies hidden, but because his fame is revealed and is
>   ever fresh,
> It does not allow the ruler, famed for his words, to lie concealed,
> His ashes are collected in this tomb but his nobility flies
>   beyond it
> Refusing to be confined by a short rope while
> Wales now bereft and doomed to be destroyed by her grief,
>   mourns.[3]

Lord Rhys had ruled south Wales for what was, in those times, a substantial span, between 1155 and 1197, during which he had managed to make Deheubarth the premier Welsh kingdom. Rhys had been active in war and politics for 60 years, and for 40 of these had been the most dominant among the princes of Wales.

The piecemeal Norman conquest of Wales had created new lordships independent of the English Crown in the March, mirrored by the evolution and consolidation of the principal Welsh kingdoms such as Gwynedd, Deheubarth and Powys.

Despite the arrival of substantial numbers of French and English speakers under the Normans, Wales remained Welsh-speaking in the main. The majority of people in such places as Brecon and Abergavenny remained monoglot Welsh speakers, despite the ethnic diversity that followed in the wake of the 'conquest' and subsequent settlement, so when Henry I drew up his charter for Carmarthen Priory he included greetings to 'the French, English, Flemings and Welsh'. In other parts of the country, such as Gower, Pembrokeshire and the Vale of Glamorgan, the linguistic character was permanently changed, as local folk became Anglicized.

Not only did Wales change in terms of ethnicity, it also saw the growth of towns, the use of coins for trade, and a European sense of chivalry, not to mention the new and striking architecture of abbeys and castles. But there was another change too: a sense of Welsh identity developed. A people linked and nurtured by a particular territory and language began to cohere, partly as a reaction against the conquest, and partly developed by native writings used by native rulers to underline their rights.

Poets too rose to the challenge, and the Gogynfeirdd, the early court poets, sang songs that celebrated the past even as they praised their present lords, such as Lord Rhys. Histories, such as *Brut y*

Tywysogyon, detailed events in Wales from 682 to 1282 and held up a new mirror to both past and present, using the former to shore up the latter. The Welsh no longer saw themselves as Britons, or as the *weallas,* the 'foreigners' they had been dubbed by the Anglo-Saxons, but rather as *Cymry* – 'fellow countrymen'. It was a sea change.

CHAPTER NINE

RELIGIOUS AWAKENING

The remarkable and swift Christian development of Wales in the fifth and sixth centuries, between 450 and 700 CE, occurred in a period that is often called the 'Age of the Saints'. Even before St Augustine's germinal mission in 597, Christianity was relatively well established in Wales and other parts of western Britain, such as Cumbria and Cornwall, thanks to the Roman occupation, which spanned 400 years. The later poems of the sixth-century poets Taliesin and Aneirin both attest to the fact that Christianity was, by this period, well established among the Britons.

Myths abound about saintly men who weren't necessarily canonized, so weren't strictly saints. But the light of their religious conviction, fervour and missionary zeal seems to shine down through the centuries. From the first saint onwards, namely St Dyfrig, these men – for they were mainly men, with rare exceptions such as Non, Gwenffrewi, Melangell and Dwynwen – set shining examples and were to lend their names to myriad churches. The map of Wales is peppered with place names beginning with the prefix 'Llan', meaning 'religious enclosure': from Llanelli in the south through Llanbedr and Llanbadarn, and from Llangollen to

Llanfairpwllgwyngyllgogerychwyrndrobwllllantysiliogogogoch in the north, on Anglesey.

There is plentiful evidence of the sheer industry of these early Christians in the proliferation of standing stones decorated with Christian-related carvings or inscriptions. Some carry bilingual inscriptions in Latin and Ogham (an early Celtic alphabet that arrived in Wales courtesy of Irish settlers at the end of the Roman Empire). There was heavy traffic in religious ideas and artefacts. Other stones have intricate carvings that have become characteristic of the Celtic identity, such as the cross at St Brynach's Church in Nevern, Pembrokeshire.

It is possible to argue that Wales was pivotal in the Christianization of the British Isles and Brittany, and part of the story revolves around the remarkable monastic centre of Llanilltud Fawr, or Llantwit Major. Llanilltud had its heyday in the sixth century, at which time it was a place of committed learning and a busy training centre for monks who would eventually become religious leaders and missionaries.

The monastery was established in the fifth century by Abbot Illtud, a rare figure because we do have some contemporary facts and details about him. Many of the lives of the saints weren't written until the eleventh century, meaning that a gap of five or six hundred years had passed between the actual life and the recorded life. although In Illtud's case there is also a gloriously fanciful medieval 'Life', or sycophantic biography.

A European figure, Illtud is said to have been a disciple of the great Germanus of Auxerre, to whom two churches in Wales are dedicated, one at St Issells near Tenby, and the other tucked away in the middle reaches of the Tywi valley.

Illtud, educated by the influential early saint and bishop Dyfrig (425–505), was the most 'renowned master of the Britons',[1] learned in the teachings of the Church, the culture of the Latins, and in the traditions of his own people. The hundreds of monks and students in his care included St Samson, who later set up his own monastery in Dol in Brittany. On a late sixth-century cross in the church at Llantwit, there is an inscription declaring that Samson erected it for his soul and the soul of Illtud and others.

Samson is considered one of the main founders of the Church in Brittany. After being ordained by Dyfrig, or Bishop Dubricius at Llanilltud, he became Abbott of Piro (present-day Caldey island), before travelling to Ireland. Subsequently, Samson apparently embraced a hermit's life on the banks of the Severn, before moving to Brittany, where he busied himself establishing churches and playing an active role in the politics of the day.

In north Wales, the sixth-century cult of St Beuno based at Clynnog Fawr was sufficiently well rooted and resilient (and remote) enough to survive the Reformation of the sixteenth century. Later saints of the sixth century, such as Teilo, Padarn and Deiniol seem to have favoured a more ascetic life than that of Illtud, improving the depth of their conversation with God by deprivation and meditation, starving the flesh in order to enrich the spirit. St Deiniol, the first Bishop of Bangor, who lived in the middle of the sixth century, founded significant monasteries at Bangor Fawr and Bangor Is Coed, the latter housing 2,000 monks.

This Christian flowering in Wales blossomed into missionary activity in Ireland, Scotland, Cornwall and Brittany, giving rise to images of holy men in small boats, possibly coracles, crossing wild seas to spread the gospel.

Arguably the most famous 'Welsh' missionary is the patron saint of Ireland, St Patrick, who initiated the Christianization of the Emerald Isle, from whence, in turn, waves of subsequent missionaries would travel across choppy seas to all parts of western Europe. The southwest of Wales also saw the celebration of Irish saints, such as St Brynach, known in Welsh as Brynach Wyddel, or Brynach the Irishman. A small necklace of churches named after him connects north Pembrokeshire with places in Carmarthenshire and southeast Wales.

The key figure in this export trade in saints, carrying their simple cargos of conviction across those perilous seas was, of course, St David, or Dewi Sant who died *c.*589, and became the patron saint of Wales. He is the only patron saint in Great Britain who was native-born to the country of his patronage. His cult spread far beyond the southwestern corner of Wales where he settled, and there are no fewer than 60 Welsh churches dedicated to him.

What facts we know about St David are sketchy in the main, as the key source for his biography, the *Vita Davidis* (Life of David), is a literary masterpiece that reads like very early magic realism. It was composed by Rhygyfarch ap Sulien, the son of Bishop Sulien in Llanbadarn Fawr, near Aberystwyth, in about 1095.

Rhygyfarch tells the mythical account of David's life and describes how David was born to his mother, Non, who had been raped by the then King of Ceredigion, ironically enough named Sant, which means 'saint'. This story is allegedly based on a much earlier documentary source, now lost, that had allegedly survived time's decay. The *Vita* is an extraordinary account right from the start, beginning with a vivid description of what was expected of David's father by way of preparation for his birth:

When you wake up tomorrow, you will go hunting: having killed
a stag near the river, you will find there beside the river Teifi three
gifts; namely the stag that you will pursue, a fish, and a swarm
of bees situated in a tree, in a place called Llyn Henllan. You
should set aside, out of these three, the honeycomb, and a portion
of the fish and the stag; and you should deliver them to the
monastery of Meugan, keeping them for the son who is going to
be born to you.[2]

The rest of Rhygyfarch's fanciful life of David is equally vivid and
action-packed: numerous further angelic visitations, prophesies, great
storms attendant on birth, appearance of magical springs – and, at
that pivotal moment when he established his own monastery, 'a fire
was lit in the name of the Lord, the smoke rose on high, and it seemed
to fill the whole island, also swirling around Ireland too'.

St David also studied under Illtud at Llanilltud Fawr before his
life's journey took him to the secluded village he chose for his
monastery, Vallis Rosina or the Valley of the Rose, which was most
likely located near to where the great cathedral of St David's stands
today in Pembrokeshire. Like many other semi-hermitic saints who
gravitated toward these western coasts, such as St Carannog at Llan-
grannog, St David had chosen a secluded spot, but it was also very
well placed to access the sea lanes.

The sea routes echoed those used in much earlier times, when
people shared knowledge about how to bury their dead in tombs such
as Bryn Celli Ddu. From Dublin Bay, sea routes reached across present-day St George's Channel to Anglesey and the Menai Straits. There
they connected to trackways across north Wales to continue along the

borderlands. There were also maritime routes from southern Ireland into northern Pembrokeshire and south Wales, and then on to the softly rolling lands of the Cotswolds.

Armes Prydein, 'The Great Prophecy of Britain', contains the earliest reference to St David in Welsh literature. Written in c.930, it mentions David's 'holy banner' and that his church was a magnet for pilgrims. The fifteenth-century Welsh bard Lewys Glyn Cothi depicted David as a 'waterman' who 'took bread and water cress, or the water from cold rivers'. Some thought this referred to the fact that nothing other than water passed his lips, but experts now suggest this referred to the fact that he was given to testing his faith by standing for hours in ice-cold pools.

The 'biography' of this 'Aquaticus' was consolidated by Giraldus Cambrensis in Norman times, as he added another version of the events. Giraldus Cambrensis, Gerald of Wales, was one of Wales's earliest travel writers. His father was a Norman knight and his mother a Welsh princess, and Gerald was destined to be clergyman. As a boy he built sand churches when his brothers built sand castles. His writing is wonderfully colourful and contains deep insight into the character of the Welsh, even if it was often shaped by his own agenda. Gerald had his eye on the bishop's seat at St David's Cathedral, and his account of St David amplified the success story of this early holy man. He informs us that David established no fewer than 12 monasteries, although he catalogues only nine of these: Glastonbury, Bath, Crowland, Repton, Colva, Glas-cwm, Leominster, Raglan and Llangyfelach.

Although David was only really known in the southwest of Wales during his lifetime, his presence in literature as far as Brittany is testament to how significantly his influence grew in the centuries after his death, as is the number of churches dedicated to him. Before the literary canonization of David, courtesy of the appearance of the *Vita*, the saint's ecclesiastical stock was already seemingly high: he appears in lists of early saints and was held in esteem in Ireland and in Rome, where he was canonized in 1120.

St David deserves his place as a national figurehead as it was under his guidance that a distinctive Welsh form of the Christian faith emerged – one that tried to keep hold of its independence for the next five centuries. Even when the pope later sent missionaries, such as St Augustine, from Rome in 597 to convert Britain to Roman Christianity, planting the missionary ethos within the Celtic churches of Scotland, Ireland, Cornwall and Brittany, Wales managed to keep its own version of the faith, marking the country as a land particularly open to religious spirituality. Besides, the Welsh bishops of the time saw no reason for acceding to the wishes of Canterbury, a fledgling archbishopric that had been in existence for less than a decade.

One of the key men in ensuring as great a degree of separation as possible between Canterbury and St David's was Gerald of Wales. As well as being an energetic writer, he was a zealous ecclesiastical reformer and, coincidentally, was also related to Lord Rhys, whom he described as 'a man of excellent wit and quick in repartee'. Gerald long nursed his ambitions of becoming archbishop of St David's, which suggests the role held a status equal to that of Canterbury. Gerald was nominated to be its bishop on two occasions, only to be twice rejected by the Norman king. His frustrated attempts to become Bishop of St David's are insightful of the new relationship that was being forged between politics and the Church.

Until the Normans, the Welsh Church operated under the *clas* structure, not dissimilar to the traditional tribal organization of Welsh society. It meant that the Welsh Church was decentralized, instead made up of a number of 'mother' churches, headed by either a bishop or abbot, which exerted influence through the smaller houses. This resulted in religious practices varying widely throughout Wales. Under the Normans, Norman practices and the parish structure replaced the *clas* system. The Welsh Church came increasingly under secular control, and the king had final approval of all elected bishops. To keep closer control of the Church, the king ensured that all successful candidates were also political nominees (this often meant that a number of Marcher lords were also made bishops).

The papal missionaries were not the only visitors seeking to influence Welsh Christianity. The Normans also sought to impose their brand of Christianity on the Welsh only a few years after their conquest by setting up Benedictine houses. These institutions failed to make much impact on the Welsh, but a more ascetic offshoot of the Benedictines, the Order of the Cistercians or 'White Monks' (named after their habit), were more welcome.

The Cistercians built their monasteries in remote positions, far from Norman settlements and, during the twelfth century, the Welsh embraced this hugely influential monastic order from France, drawing the country closer to Latin Europe. The establishment of the Cistercians in Wales was greatly aided by the Welsh lords, among them Lord Rhys, who was a great religious patron of Cistercian monastic houses at Strata Florida and Whitland.

Rhys supported many other religious institutions during his lifetime, helping these orders to establish and thrive in Wales, including the Order of St Benedict and the Order of Premonstratensians. He built a new abbey at Talley, along with the convent at Llan-llŷr. But it was his involvement with the Cistercians that was to be of paramount significance to the culture and economy of Wales. The Cistercian monasteries were places of learning and culture as well as contemplation, and they were places with strong links to writing and writers, welcoming poets such as Guto'r Glyn and Gutun Owain.

Strata Florida, or Ystrad Fflur, was particularly important among the baker's dozen of Cistercian monasteries in Wales. The Cistercian monastery at Strata Florida was first established on the banks of the river Fflur in the upper reaches of the Teifi valley, an offshoot of the house in Whitland. Lord Rhys lent it his patronage just as the majority of Deheubarth was coming under his command, so both houses became part of the life of Welsh Wales, and Ystrad-fflur became 'the premier abbey in Wales.'[3]

The Cistercian scribes helped to assemble and record the native literary tradition of poetry, not least by writing down folk tales, as well as books of history and law. At the beginning of the fourteenth century the monks at Strata Florida probably compiled the *Hendregadredd* manuscript,* which was an anthology of the work of past princes' poets. They also played a formative role in compiling the lost Latin version of *Brut y Tywysogyon*, the Chronicle of the Princes, sometime towards the end of the thirteenth century. The Welsh now had a written history, and the library at Strata Florida became the first national archive.

---

* Fortuitously, this ancient manuscript was discovered in a cupboard at Hendregadredd mansion near Pentrefelin in Gwynedd in 1910.

Among the most important texts probably transcribed at Strata Florida was the *White Book of Rhydderch*, written on vellum parchment about the middle of the fourteenth century, and containing the 11 folk tales known as the *Mabinogion*, also captured in *The Red Book of Hergest*. These 'wonder tales' of Celtic superheroes are among the most enthralling and magical in the canon of European folk literature. The stories, handed along from generation to generation, and from storyteller to storyteller, are vivid and vital even now: a woman is made out of flowers, sorcerers weave complicated spells, dead men are brought back from the dead – Lazarus-like – by being thrown into a special cauldron, while others go hunting for magical boars, and pregnant mice are hanged. The *Mabinogion* meld Celtic mythology with Arthurian romance, and chivalry with history – with the emphasis clearly more on fancy than on fact.

Of the 600 or so Cistercian monasteries established by the thirteenth century, 15 were to be found in Wales. The Welsh were thereby opened to cultural influences from the Continent and encountered translations of major European texts. The abbeys and granges of the Cistercians also excelled at agriculture and developed a major trade in wool that was crucial to the Welsh economy. The monks proliferated, and there were several hundred Cistercians in Welsh Wales by the early thirteenth century.

Meanwhile, the Norman influence slowly but steadily changed the ecclesiastical map, with Norman appointments in Llandaff, St David's, Bangor and St Asaph. The new appointees worked with vigour to progress further change, not least the eradication of Celtic practices, such as allowing the clergy to marry.

Yet real pockets of resistance had persisted. In the 1160s, feeling secure with the support of Owain Gwynedd, the clergy of Bangor had steadfastly rejected the dictat of the then Archbishop of Canterbury, Thomas Becket, that required the new Bishop of Canterbury to swear fealty to him. It was an act of defiance and definition, suggesting that the process of Norman-driven reformation had not quite been fully realized.

The separatism Wales had largely maintained from the arrival of Christianity under Roman occupation to the turn of the thirteenth century led to a degree of isolation. The Welsh Church was seemingly removed from the larger politics of Christianity. But the work of a quiet legion of saints and their followers had planted fertile seeds in a bedrock of faith, which was then nurtured under Norman rule. These early holy men and women, and their fervent supporters, had fashioned one simple thing: they had created a Christian Wales.

The trumpet of that faith would sound even louder centuries later in this western peninsula, and Wales would become one of the most religious places on Earth. But that holy transformation lay many centuries into the future.

A COMPARISON OF TERRITORIES AMASSED BY WELSH LEADERS, 878–1240

RHODRI THE GREAT'S TERRITORY BY 878

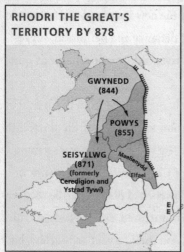

GWYNEDD (844)

POWYS (855)

SEISYLLWG (871) (formerly Ceredigion and Ystrad Tywi)

Maelienydd

Elfael

E E

HYWEL THE GOOD'S TERRITORY BY 950

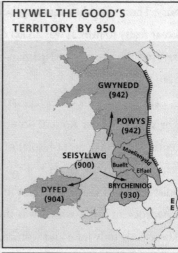

GWYNEDD (942)

POWYS (942)

SEISYLLWG (900)

Buellt

Maelienydd

Elfael

DYFED (904)

BRYCHEINIOG (930)

E E

GRUFFUDD AP LLYWELYN'S TERRITORY BY 1063

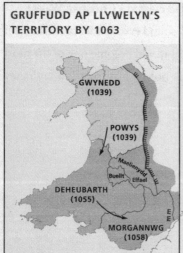

GWYNEDD (1039)

POWYS (1039)

Maelienydd

Buellt

Elfael

DEHEUBARTH (1055)

MORGANNWG (1058)

E E

LLYWELYN THE GREAT'S TERRITORY BY 1240

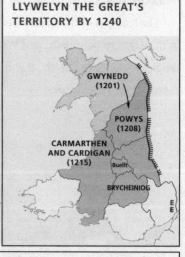

GWYNEDD (1201)

POWYS (1208)

CARMARTHEN AND CARDIGAN (1215)

Buellt

BRYCHEINIOG

E E

Original territories of the ruler

Additional territories brought under rule

Offa's Dyke

CHAPTER TEN

LLYWELYN THE GREAT AND LLYWELYN THE LAST

In the first decade of the thirteenth century, power in Wales was set to migrate, shifting from the south to the north. At the death of Henry II in 1189, followed by the accession of Richard I, Lord Rhys's special relationship with the English Crown broke down. Rhys had also left too many sons, both legitimate and bastards, and after his death in 1197, Deheubarth disintegrated into squabble and division as sons jostled for supremacy. There was also trouble in Gwynedd, as Owain Gwynedd's descendents also rivalled each other for land, leaving Powys Wenwynwyn the most unified domain in Wales. The ruler of Powys, Gwenwynwyn, however, could not rally enough support to ascend to Rhys's vacated role of Prince of Wales, and he was crushed at the Battle of Painscastle by the Marcher lords in 1198.

From 1194, politics in Gwynedd were reordered and as Gwenwynwyn's power declined following his 1198 defeat, Gwynedd emerged as the political centre of Wales.

Llywelyn ab Iorwerth (Llywelyn the Great, 1200–40) was to dominate Gwynedd and the rest of Wales for well-nigh half a century and become one of the greatest rulers of independent Wales. He came within a sniff of creating a unified, recognized principality. He was a gifted military leader and he also drew on legal authority and propaganda to consolidate his rule: one legend manufactured during his reign named his ancestor, Maelgwn Gwynedd, the chief King of Wales. Llywelyn encouraged the Gogynfeirdd, the poets of the princes, who penned effective propaganda as well as courtly verse. One of them, Dafydd Benfras, had this to say about Llywelyn:

> *Llywelyn, the ruler of rulers,*
> *A gentle advocate in the council of the wise.*

Here was a king who acted as protector and patriarch, and many native rulers acknowledged him as their lord. His claim to rule was further shored up by specially constructed legal texts, which referred to a special insult-payment owed to the Prince of Gwynedd. Eventually all the kings of Wales were to pay Llywelyn a relief and accept their lands from him as *mechteyrn dyled*, an overlord. As the laws of the time put it, 'His word shall be a command to all the kings of Wales, but no other king's word shall be a command to him.'[1]

Llywelyn, the son of Iorwerth Drwyndwn and the grandson of Owain Gwynedd, had been a troublesome young man, challenging the authority of his two uncles Rhodri and Dafydd. Between 1194 and 1197 he had expelled them from their respective territories. By 1201 he had taken control of the whole of Gwynedd and assumed the title 'prince of the whole of north Wales'.

His status was not just nominal. This was the year he made a treaty with King John – the first-ever such agreement between a Welsh ruler and an English king – which, into the bargain, served to recognize the unitary and distinct character of Welsh law.

To deepen the link between himself and the King of England, Llywelyn married John's illegitimate daughter Joan, or Siwan, and gained the Manor of Ellesmere in Shropshire. This marriage was unashamedly strategic, especially as Llywelyn already had a partner, Tangwystl, daughter of Llywarch Goch, with whom he had two children.

Later Llywelyn was to marry off his daughters to Marcher lords, thus creating new alliances with powerful leaders who often opposed the king. Such power-consolidating marriages were very much the order of the day, and for a brief while Llywelyn entertained the idea of himself marrying the daughter of the King of Man, from the Isle of Man. This would have helped him take control of the sea-approaches to his territory, where sporadic Viking raids still made the people of the coasts edgy.

He was also generous to the Church. Like Lord Rhys, he could look to the past and support and develop the new Cistercian abbeys at Cymer and Aberconwy, as well as establishing the first Franciscan house in north Wales.

In castle construction too he showed a readiness to learn from the Anglo-Normans, as evidenced by the round tower at Dolbadarn in the lee of Snowdon, and the gateway at Cricieth. Castell y Bere, which guards the southern flank of Snowdonia from its position on a promontory overlooking the Dysynni valley, has a mix of Welsh and foreign features, and the whole of the building shows the level of ambition within Llywelyn.

In 1208, Llywelyn marched into Ceredigion, rebuilt Aberystwyth castle and annexed Powys, before joining his father-in-law John I on a Scottish campaign. John already had plenty on his mind as war against France had resumed and the cost of it had led to spiralling taxes and subsequent discontentment, but Llywelyn's dealings at the time with the Marcher lord, William de Breos, nevertheless upset the king. In response, John invaded Gwynedd in 1211.

While John fought against France, the papacy (which had excommunicated John after a dispute) encouraged Augustus, then King of France, to offer Llywelyn an alliance. This gave Llywelyn sufficient confidence to reclaim lands, and in 1215 he sojourned south. Mild weather in the depths of December blessed a ferocious three-week campaign in which no fewer than seven castles were seized, including those at Carmarthen and Cardigan. Meanwhile, John I died of dysentery in 1216 and was succeeded by Henry III (r. 1216–72).

In 1217 Llywelyn arranged a military excursion into the south, marching down the Wye valley, threatening Brecon and crossing the mountains into Swansea, which promptly surrendered to him. The campaign also netted him protection money of a thousand marks of silver when the men of Rhos and Pembroke, fearful of a raid, paid him off.

His military mastery drove the English government to recognize his pre-eminence and they asked him, in 1218, to 'persuade all the magnates of the whole of Wales to come to the king [Henry III] to do homage'.[2]

That same year a ceasefire came in the shape of the Peace of Worcester, which was agreed with the Earl of Chester. It recognized Llywelyn's status and he was given custody of two key castles, at Carmarthen and Cardigan. Llywelyn was later to bind himself further to this powerful earl, when he married one of his daughters to the earl's heir, while Llywelyn himself married one of Henry III's sisters, though that did not entirely sweeten relations between the two men.

After 1218, one of the areas that commanded much of Llywelyn's attention was that which stretched from Ceri to Brecon. It was important politically and geographically as a far outer rim of his defences, and an important channel for communications with upland Gwent and Glamorgan. Supporting the native leaders who lived there would show how far his authority radiated from the mountains of the north. Llywelyn could range over most of Wales, though he made little effort to move the southern lords, apart from some forays in 1220, 1231 and 1232.

It was also in this period that Llywelyn gave himself a new title: Prince of Aberffraw and Lord of Snowdon. He was at the same time trying to reach an accommodation with Henry and seeking recognition of the full extent of his domain.

A treaty between Llywelyn and Henry III, signed in Middle in Shropshire in 1234, meant the end of hostilities with the king for the rest of Llywelyn's days. In 1237 Llywelyn suffered a stroke, which coincided with his son-in-law, the Earl of Chester, dying without an heir. This caused the earl's lands to revert to the Crown, leaving Llywelyn's eastern border exposed. He was swift to transfer powers to his son Dafydd and in 1238 the other rulers were summoned to Strata Florida to pay homage to him as Prince of Wales. Llywelyn died on 11 April 1240 and was buried at the Cistercian abbey in Aberconwy.

His son Dafydd was swiftly summoned to Henry III to do homage, and his half-brother Gruffydd, whom Dafydd had been keeping prisoner, had to be handed over to be locked up in the confines of the Tower of London. Trying to escape on St David's Day in 1244, Gruffydd fell to his death when his makeshift rope snapped. Dafydd was sufficiently incensed to take up arms against the king, but he died prematurely from natural causes in 1246. This left a land without an heir, and ushered in a new period of great insecurity in Gwynedd, on which the English king was swift to capitalize.

Llywelyn ap Gruffudd, or Llywelyn the Last, was the grandson of Llywelyn the Great. He was shrewd and canny, and even at a young age, he was gathering his grandfather's advisers around him, attentive to the wisdom of others. After the death of his uncle Dafydd, it seemed inevitable that Llywelyn would be a suitable successor. But his brother Owain ap Gruffudd returned from England to claim his share and, as per Welsh law, Gwynedd had to be carved up among them and a third brother, Dafydd ap Gruffudd (a division that was covered by the Treaty of Woodstock, sealed in April 1247). This did not serve any of them particularly well. They also had to hand back to the king the area known as Perfeddwlad (also known as Gwynedd Is Conwy), the land between the rivers Conwy and Dee, which had briefly been owned by the Crown in 1211. In addition, they had to offer men for military service.

Llywelyn was determined to unify Gwynedd under one leader once more, so started to make deals with the leaders of Powys and Deheubarth. With the support of these other domains, Llywelyn went to battle against his brothers Owain and Dafydd, and defeated and captured them both after a short but significant battle at Bryn Derwin in 1255. On his victory, Llywelyn became the only ruler of Gwynedd Uwch Conwy (the land west of the river Conwy not given over to the

Crown) and thwarted Henry III's hopes for the disintegration of Gwynedd.

In the summer of 1256, Henry III's son, Prince Edward, visited northeast Wales in an attempt to grapple with growing Welsh feelings of disaffection. Llywelyn translated Edward's visit as a military manoeuvre. He sent out his soldiers and they once again claimed the Perfeddwlad, reducing the English holdings to just two isolated fortresses at Diserth and Deganwy.

Between 1256 and 1258 Llywelyn took control of almost all of Welsh Wales, the *Pura Wallia*. In 1256 he forced out the native ruler of Meirionnydd and returned northern Ceredigion, and then both south and north Powys, to native rule. He met little resistance from the English. Llywelyn's men used guerrilla tactics, classic hit-and-run pillaging, or sometimes tactical retreats to avoid heavy English cavalry. Llywelyn focused on rallying local support in each area he entered by instilling a sense of nationhood.

By 1258 Llywelyn assumed the title of Prince of Wales, suggesting that most, if not all, of the Welsh princes were paying homage to him. This year was described by the historian R. R. Davies as Llywelyn's *annus mirabilis*, and one contemporary commentator, Matthew Paris, marvelled at the remarkable union between south and north, which 'had never previously been seen, since the men of north and south Wales had always been opposed to each other'.[3] For the first time, the regions of Wales were not just unified politically, but united with a national spirit against the English.

Llywelyn the Last, like his grandfather, was a confirmed patron of Cistercian abbeys. He developed towns and castles, had university-trained clerks at his court and maintained contact with the pope, who was sympathetic to his royal claim. His military prowess provoked the building of the massive Caerphilly castle by the Marcher lords. He was a leader of energy and vision.

After 1258 it was time for reflection and consolidation. Military gains were expensive to hold, and it was prudent to offer peace deals. He offered Henry 4,500 marks by way of surety, and a year later increased the sum to 16,500 for a definitive peace, or a discounted 700 for a truce lasting seven years. Llywelyn also wanted territories back and recognition of his feudal overlordship. The deal resulted in a four-year truce.

In the early 1260s Llywelyn broke the truce, making more gains in the March, where large tracts of eastern and central Wales were surrendered to him. These stretched from the Severn to the Brecon Beacons, right up to the frontier with England. In January 1260 he marched into Builth, and by the summer had wrestled the castle there from the grip of Roger Mortimer, before promptly razing it to the ground.

In November 1262, Llywelyn seized Roger Mortimer's new castle at Cefnllys, ending the truce once and for all. With land from the Severn to the Wye now under his control, Llywelyn could train an ambitious eye on places such as upper Gwent and Brecon. Alarm bells were certainly ringing in Abergavenny, where the royal commander, warning about the Welsh, said, 'If they are not stopped, they will destroy all the lands of the king as far as the Severn and the Wye; they will ask for nothing less than the whole of Gwent.'[4] A paranoid Bishop of Hereford reported that 'the whole March is in terror'.

When civil war broke out again in England in 1264, drawing the king's attention away from Wales, Llywelyn pursued status and recognition through alliances with Roger Mortimer and Simon de Montfort, arranging a marriage by proxy to Simon's daughter Eleanor.

At the end of the civil war, Henry III officially recognized Llywelyn as Prince of Wales and all his successors, in the Treaty of Montgomery of 1267, which also gave him control of the March. The document, issued by Cardinal Ottobuono, the papal legate in England, was designed to produce a lasting peace between the two countries and it was a key moment in the story of Welsh autonomy.

For a while, political compromise and royal recognition offered stability and a respite from battle. In return, Llywelyn agreed to pay 25,000 marks over a period of ten years and give homage to the Crown. The first payment alone, of 5,000 marks, was probably as much as the prince's annual income. The fact that he failed to keep up the payments due under the Treaty of Montgomery was quite possibly not an act of defiance on his part, but simply because he didn't have the cash.

After the death of Henry III, Llywelyn did not pay homage to his successor Edward I; neither did he attend his coronation. The same year, Llywelyn's brother Dafydd reappeared on the political scene, aligned with Gruffudd ap Gwenwynwyn of Powys Wenwynwyn, and took part in a failed plot to assassinate Llywelyn. The pair fled to England, and Llywelyn refused to recognize Edward until he had returned the would-be assassins. The plot had highlighted the vulnerability of Llywelyn's line, so the heirless Prince of Wales revived his plan to marry Eleanor.

This marriage to a Plantagenet princess was thoroughly opposed by Edward I, and English sailors captured and imprisoned her on her way to join Llywelyn. Both sides appealed to the pope, but ultimately Edward declared he was at war with Llywelyn and branded him a rebel.

Edward's campaign against Llywelyn, launched in 1277, lasted a year. A well-orchestrated invasion began with incursions by the Marcher lords. Then military command centres were established by Edward in Chester, Carmarthen and Montgomery, from whence they could squeeze Llywelyn at the very edges of his power. The avowed aim was that of relegating him to the mountains and containing him there, before finally hunting him down.

Edward I defeated the Welsh prince after the grain larder of Anglesey was seized by the royal fleet and Llywelyn was starved into submission. He was forced to sign the Treaty of Aberconwy, which took back most of the gains recognized in the Treaty of Montgomery. He did keep the title Prince of Wales, although it would have a hollow ring, and his territories shrank back to include only the lands of Gwynedd Uwch Conwy. He also lost the homage of most of the major Welsh lords and was fined the huge sum of 50,000 marks for his disobedience. Meanwhile, Edward constructed castles, such as those at Flint, Rhuddlan and Aberystwyth, and repaired some of the native castles, such as Dinefwr and Carreg Cennen.

Eventually, Llywelyn was allowed to marry Eleanor in 1278 at Worcester Cathedral, and a window commemorating the wedding of the 'Prince of Wales and the Lady Eleanor' can still be seen there. At times Eleanor was a skilled and patient go-between between her husband and the English king, and Edward paid not only for the wedding feast, but also gave the newlyweds lavish gifts. But the real price was high, as Edward forced homage and other concessions from Llywelyn.

Relations between Llywelyn and Edward deteriorated during the Arwystli dispute, in which Llywelyn claimed possession of an area in what is today the southwest of Montgomeryshire from his would-be assassin Gruffydd ap Gwenwynwyn. It was left to Edward to adjudicate, but he allowed the dispute to drag on, fuelling Llywelyn's growing resentment. Other princes felt a similar sense of frustration in their own territories, as they were unfairly taxed and Welsh laws and customs were overruled.

In March 1282 rebellion broke out, beginning with Llywelyn's brother Dafydd's attack on the English-owned Hawarden castle. Several Welsh rulers followed suit and Llywelyn became embroiled in the rebellion, this time coming to the aid of his brother. Support was widespread: Welsh anger at the way alien officials rode roughshod over native customs, and a general resentment of English rule, was given the means for violent expression.

Edward's reaction was very definite: he announced that he intended 'to repress the rebellion and the malice of the Welsh'. Edward then paid attention to Perfeddwlad, a gateway to Snowdonia, as his forces replicated their success story in gaining Anglesey and its crops. In this way Llywelyn found himself the victim of the classic pincer movement, and not only squeezed but starved into the bargain.

Llywelyn refused Edward's offer of an estate in England as the price of surrender. Instead Llywelyn's council chose to detail a full list of Welsh grievances by way of reply, and to defend the revolt as a defence of a people's national identity. This strongly suggests that the revolt was more than just a political power struggle between a few – it was the action of a frustrated people.

When some of Edward's men drowned while trying to reach Anglesey, Llywelyn took the opportunity to march into the Wye valley. At Builth he was separated from his army and killed at Cilmeri, on the bank of the river Irfon by either Robert Body or Stephen Frankton. Whoever killed him, it was an inglorious ambush and an unheroic ending.

In *Brenhinedd y Saeson*, a chronicle listing events in Wales from the seventh to the thirteenth century, the entry for 1282 describes the effect of the death, summarizing vividly how it traumatized an entire country. Poets lamented Llywelyn's death with great outpourings of grief. His own poet, Gruffudd ab yr Ynad Goch, penned the most passionate, heart-wrenching elegy, seeing the event as one of cosmic significance, a truly shattering moment. Thus, on a winter's day the House of Gwynedd was crushed.

Edward I wasn't satisfied with just the death of Llywelyn; he wanted to extinguish his very memory, so in the months that followed his death, he arranged to have his seals of office melted down, and took away *Y Groes Naid*, the treasured crown-shaped reliquary so that it could have no symbolic power. It would be deposited eventually in Windsor castle. In raising his iron ring of castles in north Wales, including the stupendous symbol that is Caernarfon castle, and the eight round towers and barbicans of Conwy, Edward gave physical expression to his adamant determination not to let the Welsh 'snake lying in the grass' have any opportunity whatsoever to bite or strike back.

The year 1282 was a bitter watershed in the story of Wales – the country was now an English colony. The Welsh, a group of people starting to resemble a nation much more clearly, were left bereft of their prince: they were destined to become subjects and underlings once more.

PART THREE

COLONIZATION AND REBELLION

CHAPTER ELEVEN

TREASON
AND PLAGUE

For some, the plague years marked the end of the medieval age, an ecological upheaval as devastating as the two world wars of the twentieth century. The impact would be economic as well as social, and would come at a time when the English Crown had just consolidated its hold over Wales.

After the death of the last of the native princes, Edward I reigned supreme, and, as befits a conqueror, he toured the country in triumph, even following William I's example by visiting St David's.

The conquering king spent most of 1283 and 1284 in the country – a period when three princely dynasties in Gwynedd, northern Powys and Deheubarth were entirely extinguished or dispossessed. Even as the Welsh bards proclaimed their sense of loss – one asking whether it was the end of the world, another for the sea to simply drown the land – Edward revelled in his victory, quite literally. He held an 'Arthurian' tournament in Nefyn, in which knights from Europe and England jousted; he took over Llywelyn's halls or otherwise razed them to the ground; and, symbolically, he transferred Llywelyn's coronet to Westminster.

Life in Wales, be it political, legal or fiscal, was now determined by outside forces, forces most tangible in the castles built by Edward to underpin his dominion. Money was no object, and by 1301 the king had spent some £80,000 on eight castles, including hugely impressive ones at Caernarfon, Harlech and Conwy.

The castles were followed by boroughs, which brought administration in the wake of domination. Institutions, such as the shires and sheriffs, formed the civilian arm of military rule, along with new officials, such as the justice and chamberlain. Among these shires were Anglesey, Caernarfon and Merioneth, all under the aegis of the newly created justice of north Wales, based in Caernarfon.

Legally, these changes were all bundled together into the grand-sounding Statute of Rhuddlan, also referred to as the Statute of Wales, in which Edward set out his stall for the governance of the conquered country. The document is a bit of a misnomer: even though its preamble discussed 'the land of Wales with its inhabitants', in truth it only concerned the king's lands, those royal counties of Flint, Merioneth and Anglesey which formed only a small share of the land.[1]

While he created new Marcher lordships in the northwest, Edward I also created new titles in the Marches, taxed them and recruited the military from their ranks as subtle forms of control, and controlled *Pura Wallia* outright. Furthermore, he introduced English criminal law to Wales to replace the Law of Hywel.

Edward also brought in new measures to control the Welsh: ordinances from 1295 denied them the right to buy property within the walled towns, or even to live in such places. They were not allowed to sell produce other than in official markets, or gather in public.

The king also had new costs to defray, such as those of building castles, so taxes had to be raised. The lower classes were those most affected by tax rises (a punishing 600 per cent increase). This pressure was compounded by a change in the way taxes were demanded, as these were now expected as cash, whereas previously produce had sufficed. In 1294 the Church of Wales was taxed for the first time.

Meanwhile, English families were given lands in Wales at the expense of Welsh families – even though many of these were being assimilated – and tension was building. The English in Wales also enjoyed better tax and rent terms than the natives. It was not a recipe for harmony.

While English rule appeared to dominate in Wales, the Welsh spirit of rebellion had not been entirely quashed. Welsh soldiers made up a significant part of Edward's army and were crucial in a number of his campaigns against Scotland and France. But they were a law unto themselves. On one occasion a large number of them refused to go to France to fight on behalf of the Crown, and this sparked a revolt in 1294. It was led by members of old Welsh royal houses, including Madog ap Llywelyn, son of the last Lord of Merioneth and a descendent of Owain Gwynedd, who also railed against royal administrators and the burden of new taxes. A second revolt in 1295 spread more widely, during which Madog assumed the title Prince of Wales, but this uprising was swiftly quelled, not least by Madog's defeat at the Battle of Maes Meidog in Caereinion in March 1295.

After Edward's death in 1307, Edward II (r. 1307–27) took the throne and granted Wales some distinction from England. He had

had a closer affinity with the country after being officially invested as Prince of Wales in 1301.

Edward II's reign was marked by discontent between him and his nobles, namely the Marcher barons. The king was unpopular from early on and chose unpopular favourites. First there was Piers Gaveston, executed in 1312 after disregarding an order of exile, and then Hugh Despenser, lord of Glamorgan, and his son. Despenser carved out a domain for himself in south Wales, much to the annoyance of the Marcher lords. This sparked off a revolt in March 1320, which resulted in Hugh being exiled. The Welsh, meanwhile, were still revolting, even as English identity was consolidating. In 1316, Llywelyn Bren, Lord of Senghennydd, had taken up arms against the king, with support deriving from discontent caused by harvest failures in the two preceding autumns. This revolt lasted only a few weeks, and Llywelyn suffered a traitor's gruesome death.

Meanwhile, an ambitious Marcher lord, Roger Mortimer of Chirk, had become justice of north Wales from 1308 to 1322. In 1322 Mortimer, along with his nephew Roger Mortimer of Wigmore, led a revolt against Edward II. This resulted in Roger's imprisonment along with his nephew. Roger Mortimer of Wigmore escaped prison and fled to France. Here he met and had an affair with Isabella, Queen of England, while in exile, during which time they plotted to overthrow the king. Meanwhile, Hugh Despenser, Edward's favourite, was brought back from exile and effectively ruled England from 1322 to 1326 at the behest of the king.

The troublesome Despensers were captured and executed in 1326 by Roger Mortimer. Edward II was denounced in parliament in 1327 and imprisoned in Berkeley castle on the banks of the Severn in January. He was murdered in September of the same year, thus becoming the first English Prince of Wales to be mourned predominantly by Welsh supporters. Edward's son, Edward III, was only 14 at the time of the king's death, so Roger Mortimer manipulated the situation to effectively rule England from 1327 to 1330. He consolidated power in Wales and took the title Earl of the March in 1328. Roger was hanged, drawn and quartered as a traitor in 1330 for 'having accroached royal powers', and his son was consequently denied any rights to land until 1354, when the Mortimers became the biggest and most powerful landowners of the Marcher lords.

Despite the political drama of Edward II's rule and the revolts during Edward III's reign, this was a period of relative stability in Wales, shored up by the new civil structures and English military authority, which quelled most native anger. The Welsh Church also experienced a golden age in the 50 years following the conquest, while a large quantity of Welsh literature had been amassed in a tradition established before the conquest. Wales, however, would face a new threat – not political this time but natural, uncontrollable and indiscriminate.

When a crew of sailors with 'sickness clinging to their very bones' entered the port of Medina, Sicily, in October 1347, no one could have foretold the devastating consequences of the spread of the disease they had brought with them from the East. It was a sickness that had originated in the Gobi Desert and then spread virulently via China to India and on to the Middle East and the Mediterranean.

In Medina it jumped ship, quite literally, because the plague that had afflicted the sailors was carried in the digestive tract of the fleas of ship rats. So when the rats made landfall, so too did an epidemic cocktail of three plagues – bubonic, pneumonic and septicaemic – which was to devastate the Western world from 1347 to 1351, killing up to half the population of Europe, approximately 25 million people.[2]

The Black Death reached England, in the form of bubonic plague, via the busy seaport of Bristol in the summer of 1348, and by winter of that year, the even more dangerous pneumonic plague which attacked the respiratory system and was spread by infected people rather than fleas had also developed. It ravaged London from September 1348 and had travelled throughout East Anglia by the beginning of 1349. By spring, the English midlands and Wales were riddled with it, and by the summer it had reached Ireland and the north of England. In an attempt to take advantage of the weakened northerners along their border, the Scots raided Durham, but returned with more than they bargained for. By 1350 the plague had spread throughout Scotland.

It was inevitable that Wales would also be struck down by the virulent and venomous spread of *Y Farwolaeth Fawr*, the 'Great Mortality'. An estimated quarter of the Welsh population fell to the plague in just two years, 1349 and 1350. Casualty rates of up to 40 per cent were reported in some places. The population was already weakened by the effects of periods of famine, which had starved Europe between 1315 and 1322, as well as between 1330 and 1331. Children who had grown up sick and malnourished were not strong enough to withstand the onslaught of the plague when it arrived. This was the arrow of death, *saeth y farwolaeth yw fo*, as the poet Gruffydd ab Ieuan ap Llywelyn Fychan put it, and the fatal arrow could strike anyone. A

ABOVE: The burial chamber at Bryn Celli Ddu, Anglesey.

BELOW: Pentre Ifan on Carn Ingli (the Hill of Angels), near Nevern. The portal is large enough to ride a horse through and boasts a breath-taking view to the sea.

ABOVE: The reconstructed Mold Cape, found in Hope, northeast Wales. Its existence suggests a highly skilled and rich cultural centre 'comparable to the contemporary courts of the Pharaohs of Egypt'.

BELOW: The large, early ninth-century cross called the Pillar of Eliseg, near Llangollen, bears an inscription detailing how King Eliseg freed Powys from Mercia.

ABOVE: The deep, trench-like remnants of Offa's Dyke, built to protect Mercia from the Britons of Wales, between 757 and 796 CE.

RIGHT: An impressive tenth-century Celtic cross found in the graveyard of St Brynach's Church, Nevern, Pembrokeshire.

LEFT: The ruins of Strata
Florida, the mighty
twelfth-century Cistercian
monastery patronized by
Lord Rhys until his
death in 1197.

BELOW: Llantwit Major, the
fifth-century monastery
established by Abbot
Illtud. St David is also said
to have studied here under
Illtud, before moving to
the Valley of the Rose.

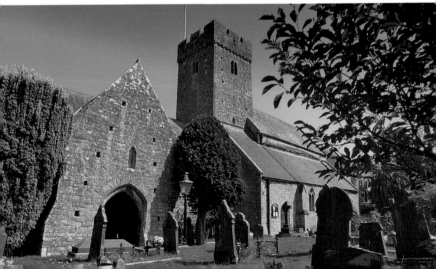

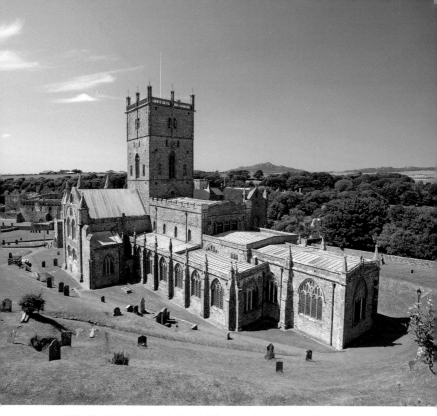

ABOVE: St David's Cathedral, Pembrokeshire. Building began in c. 1181, most likely near to the site St David chose for his original monastery in the Valley of the Rose.

BELOW: 'The very epitome of impregnability': work on Chepstow castle began one year after the Battle of Hastings.

ABOVE: Pembroke castle, one of the most menacing reminders of Norman authority and repression.

LEFT: A monument to Owain Glyndŵr in Corwen, who is still celebrated as a national hero throughout Wales.

ABOVE: The lunar landscape of Parys Mountain, Anglesey, as it looks now after years of copper mining.

BELOW: The former Dinorwic slate quarry at Llanberis, North Wales, was once the second largest slate quarry in the world after Penrhyn quarry. Slate was whisked from here along railways linking the quarry to Port Dinorwic, where ships waited to be loaded with this highly in-demand cargo.

ABOVE: Bute docks, Cardiff, c.1880, packed with ships that once exporting Welsh coal across the globe, including to South America and India.

BELOW: An engraving of Penrhyn Castle, c. 1840. The castle was built in 1837 with the profits amassed by quarry owner Richard Pennant, and included a slate four-poster bed made for the visiting Queen Victoria.

later poet, Dafydd Nanmor, blamed the sinister planet Saturn for its grievous effects.*

In 1300 the population of Wales stood at over 300,000 inhabitants. A century later there were fewer than 200,000. There had been plagues in Wales before this outbreak. One, in 549, claimed the life of many, including Maelgwn Fawr, or Maelgwn Gwynedd, the ruler of Gwynedd at the time. His particular plague-death might have been divine retribution though, for this ruler had been described by Gildas as a man of impressive sinfulness.

Death for the afflicted came within days. By March or April 1349 the poet and gentleman Ieuan Gethin, who held court at Baglan in northern Glamorgan, was registering its arrival, and describing the painful effects of the buboes, those 'spring onion-like' boils that sprouted on the bodies of the afflicted. In one of his poems he offers terrifying detail, telling his contemporaries about the many symptoms, and of the excruciating pain attendant on the disease, which Gethin knew only too well: he lost seven sons to the plague.

We see death coming into our midst like black smoke, a plague which cuts off the young, a rootless phantom which has no mercy for fair countenance. Woe is me of the 'shilling' in the arm-pit; it is seething, terrible, wherever it may come, a head that gives pain

---

* Historian Mark Williams suggests that the poet Dafydd Nanmor, who flourished between 1450 and 1490, had some knowledge of planetary movements and was writing at a time when people questioned whether or not God intervened in the world directly or governed through the cosmic mechanism of heavenly bodies. Dafydd Nanmor's plague poem seems to connect the outbreak of plague with the malign influence of Saturn and may refer to the astrological Saturn conjunction of 1478. For more information, see Further Reading, page 356.

> *and causes a loud cry, a burden carried under the arms, a painful*
> *angry knob, a white lump. It is of the form of an apple, like the*
> *head of an onion, a small boil that spares no one …*[3]

The symptoms he describes were those of the bubonic strain of the plague, where the black pustule at the point of the flea bite was followed by a swelling of the lymph nodes, resulting in the 'shillings' in the armpits as described by Gethin. These shillings would develop into the purple blotches and swollen lymphatic glands that marked the disease's progress, finally leading to complex neurological and psychological disorders, sometimes exhibited as a *danse macabre*, a jerky dance of death. Other poets, such as Gruffudd ap Maredudd and Gruffydd ab Ieuan ap Llywelyn Fychan, were left 'barely alive in a harsh world' after witnessing deaths in the family – in Fychan's case, those of five of his children, while fellow poet Gwilym ap Sefnyn lost ten children.[4] There were other losses in the poets' corner too, as arguably the finest medieval Welsh language poet of them all, Dafydd ap Gwilym, succumbed to it, along with the two main loves of his life, Dyddgu and Morfudd, women to whom many of his poems were addressed.

We know in some detail what happened in Ruthin through the surviving court rolls. These records tell the story of a mass killer come to town: at the end of May there was no evidence of the plague, but by the second week of June, seven deaths were recorded. During the next two weeks, 77 of the town's inhabitants, or one-third of its entire population, encountered the 'rootless phantom'. In Llangollen, 10 people died, 13 in Llannerch and 25 in nearby Dogfeilyn. In the Vale of Clwyd, where mortality had stood at 12 per thousand from 1340 to

1348, that figure had shot up to 173 per thousand in 1349. For weeks during that mortal summer the death rate stayed high. Then there was a brief respite, before the Black Death returned with a vengeance in August. The highlands of Snowdonia and the whole of low-lying Anglesey were afflicted.

In other parts of Wales the plague came as a seaborne disease. It probably made its first landfall in Carmarthen in March 1359, when the two Collectors of Customs of the King's Staple fell victim. Such harbour officials, of course, were often in the front line. The plague spread briskly, dispatching all the tenants of the nearby village of Llanllwch. The Lord of Carmarthen, also the Prince of Wales, saw receipts from mills and fisheries fall dramatically, while fairs, which had been one of the most lucrative sources of revenue, had to be cancelled altogether. In Cardigan many of the town's offices, such as beadle, reeve or serjeant, were vacant and the scale of suffering among the townspeople was heart-rending. Out of a total of 104 rent-paying tenants, 97 had died or fled before midsummer.

Some ascribed the plague to political events. The death of one victim, Evan ap Robert, who died in 1471 'in the flower of his age, being but one and thirty years old', was attributed to plague that 'commonly followeth war and desolation'.[5]

Society itself, shocked and demoralized by the rapidity of the grim reaping, started to fragment, the rule of law breaking down. Two burglars, Madoc Ap Ririd and his brother Kenwric, 'came by night in the Pestilence to the house of Aylmar after the death of the wife of Aylmar and took from the same house one water pitcher and basin, value one shilling, old iron, value fourpence', and again 'came by night to the house of Aylmar in the vill of Rewe in the pestilence, and from that house stole three oxen of John Le Parker and three cows, value six shillings'. In the wake of the plague, looting the dead became a common career option.

The social and economic structure of England and Wales was dramatically affected by the Black Death. On a local level, for example, the whole lordship of Abergavenny suffered, as there were fewer tenants to collects rents from and, as a result, the value of its land dropped to a third of its pre-plague level. Before 1349 rents in the village of Werneryth came to a total of £14 annually: a year later this was less than £2. Similarly, in Trefgoythel rents that had been £4 per annum had declined to just six shillings 'because of the mortality'.

Why should rents matter when so many people were dying? In Wales the Black Death attacked the manorial system. The manor gardens, left without any gardeners, reverted to pasture. The lords of the manors began to let out land at the best rent they could find, and the principle of bondage began to unravel because of the shortage of labour and the new bargaining strength of the surviving *taeogion*, the rent-paying tenants. Soil exhaustion played a part too, but it could be argued that the Black Death also caused the death of serfdom in Wales.

In the lead mines of Holywell in Flintshire, it left so few men alive that the ones who survived refused to work. Mills stopped production 'for lack of grinding, because there was no grain, and this because of the pestilence'.[6] In other areas circumstances demanded that women step into the breach in the labour market, with many of them becoming 'bakers, brewers, harvesters, spinners and weavers,'[7] tipping the social balance further still.

The plague left a traumatized country, its people numbed by suffering and from seeing too much death at close hand. The economic system was hugely weakened, with towns, commercial and industrial ventures all affected. There were, however, pockets of prosperity from early lead mines and the extraction of iron and coal. But little wealth trickled from the lords' pockets to their tenants, and the masters exploited the forests, ran all the fulling mills (for wool cleansing) and took tolls. Indeed, tenants were not even allowed to gather wood for fuel or building, nor were they permitted to hunt in the forest, or put their pigs to pasture there. Forests became symbols of oppression just as much as the castles were.

Resentment led to more radical political upheaval as the fourteenth century came to a close. The English Crown was unstable again, as Edward the Black Prince, Edward III's son and heir, died prematurely in 1346. On Edward III's death in 1377, his ten-year-old grandson Richard II succeeded him. Against this backdrop of change and uncertainty, a new leader emerged from Wales to challenge English rule.

CHAPTER TWELVE

A LAST REVOLT

Owain Glyndŵr was the middle-aged squire of Sycharth and Glyn-dyfrdwy who had been assimilated into, and cooperated with, the English system in Wales for many years. In return he had enjoyed a comfortable life with his family in the Marches – until 1400, when he suddenly turned rebel.

Owain was born around 1354 into a powerful family of the Anglo-Welsh nobility, a continuation of the line of Powys Fadog. He entered the world at a time of relative peace between Wales and the English aristocracy, both of which had been brought low by a combination of the ravages of the Black Death and a succession of famines, resulting as they did in the gradual unravelling of the manorial system.

Owain's father, Gruffydd Fychan II, had been a hereditary prince of Powys Fadog and Lord of Glyndyfrdwy, one of the lines of Welsh lords and princes who traced their royal lineage back way before the Norman conquest, all the way to Madog ap Maredudd, the last prince of Powys. Owain's mother, Elen Ferch Tomas Ap Llywelyn of Deheubarth, also had noble blood in her veins, and descended from Rhys ap Tewdwr. Owain was very well connected, and to every part of Wales.

It is thought that his father died sometime before Owain was 11 years old, and that the young prince was fostered to the household of Sir David Hanmer, of Maelor Saesneg, one of the leading judges of the age. It is possible that Owain followed Hanmer's profession by going to study law at the Inns of Court in London, but did not necessarily become a 'man of law'. But he was well educated, of that there is no doubt.

Owain had been brought up listening to stories about Welsh knights of previous generations, and like every other young man who had the same status, dreamed of becoming a knight. His dream was realized when he became a soldier in the years after 1383. In 1384 Owain enlisted under Sir Gregory Sais in the Marches and found himself fighting in Berwick in Scotland. A year later he enlisted under another patron, the Earl of Arundel, fighting for Richard II in Scotland, and in 1387 he took part in a naval engagement against the French on behalf of the Crown.

Owain married Hanmer's daughter Margaret, with whom he had six sons and several daughters. This marriage brought him the title of Squire of Sycharth and Glyndyfrdwy, and a comfortable home. Some of the features of Glyndŵr's home were Norman, not least the rabbits that shared the deer-grazing. The comforts and culture found at Sycharth during Owain's years as squire and aristocratic soldier for the king were captured in a famous poem by Iolo Goch, written around 1386. In his Continental-style hall, Owain could sip his cup of Shrewsbury beer as his family surrounded him:

Llys barwn, lle syberwyd
Lle daw beirdd aml, lle da byd.

A baron's hall, a place of generosity
Where many poets came and life was good.

A gwraig orau o'r gwragedd …
A'i blant a ddeuant bob ddau,
Nythaid teg o benaethau.

And the best wife of all women …
And the children coming in two by two,
A fair nestful of princes.[1]

So why did this noble rebel? Between 1389 and 1400 feudal ties were irrevocably damaged by events when Richard II came of age and thus threatened the power of his barons. One noble with a claim to the throne, Henry Bolingbroke, had been exiled by Richard I but returned to England in 1399 while the king was distracted by campaigns in Ireland. He seized Richard in Wales and imprisoned him in Flint castle, usurping the king and crowning himself Henry IV in 1399. Shortly thereafter Richard I was murdered.

With this usurpation of Richard I, the inherited authoritative power of the kings of England had been lost, and the right of the English king to rule over Wales had been undermined. Henry IV nevertheless taxed the Welsh and enacted draconian legislation, which he then enforced. It is against this backdrop that we must view the Glyndŵr Rising of 1400.

At the ascent of the new king, Henry IV, Owain found himself in dispute with his neighbour Reginald Grey, Lord of Ruthin, seemingly over land boundaries. An additional reason for the quarrel was that Grey had deliberately withheld a summons from the king, who was seeking support for an invasion of Scotland, thus making it appear that Glyndŵr had committed treason when he failed to respond. This was the stuff of a classic feudal squabble, a hangover from Edward I's conquest of the country. However, it had one key difference. One of the men in this envenomed dispute, namely Glyndŵr, saw history as his precedent. His appeal to the king to arbitrate in the dispute between him and Grey had not merely fallen on deaf ears; his claim was callously dismissed in words that could only inflame: 'What care we for these barefoot rascals?'[2]

Soured by the king's lack of support in his dispute with Grey, Owain reacted by opting for open revolt. Yet this local dispute soon assumed bigger dimensions, turning into a fully fledged national revolt even from day one.

On 16 September 1400 Owain's supporters proclaimed him Prince of Wales at Glyndyfrdwy near Corwen. Some, such as Rhys and Gwilym ap Tudur, sons of Tudur ap Gronw of Penmynydd, had been part of Richard II's personal retinue. After Richard was dethroned, they had lost a patron – just as Owain had done after the death of the Earl of Arundel, who had been executed in 1397. The three were linked by loss and blood and might well have acted in concert to restore Richard to the throne, had it not been for his murder at Ponte-fract castle. The complicated machinations of English politics fed into the rebellion.

The proclamation by 300 supporters was an act that led to outbreaks of fighting in the northeast, as small war bands marched through Ruthin intent on burning. Soon all that was left was the castle and one house. Some blamed *levitas cervicosa*, a giddiness of the mind considered by some observers to be the weakness of the Welsh. Soon the 'giddy' force was attacking other boroughs and little English towns, such as Denbigh, Rhuddlan, Flint, Hawarden, Oswestry, Holt and

Welshpool. This prompted Henry IV to lead a force made up of armed men from ten counties into the area to quell the uprising.

What is interesting about the revolt is the breadth of social classes that flocked to support Glyndŵr's cause. Bondsmen Gwilym and Rhys Tudur were the chief fighters in the revolt on Anglesey. Rhys Ddu, a former sheriff of Cardiganshire and previously an enthusiastic official in Richard II's retinue, attacked the English army who had burnt down the Franciscan monastery of Llan-faes by way of retaliation.

Family after Welsh family rallied to Owain's cause, and it wasn't simply nobles such as Rhys Gethin from the Conwy valley and Gwilym Gwyn ap Rhys Llwyd from Cydweli. Junior officials and priests, such as the brothers of the orders, also pledged their support for Owain. There had already been anti-Welsh protests in Oxford, and in this city of learning, as well as Cambridge, many Welsh students left their colleges during the uprising and returned home to support the new Welsh leader. Labourers too crossed back over the border from England.

It was all enough to send waves of nervousness rippling through Parliament, where reports had been received that 'Owain Glyndŵr and others have made insurrection and have gathered together in the marches of Carmarthenshire. They conspire to invade the realm and destroy the English.'[3]

In 1401 Owain made a new ally in the shape of Henry Dunn of Cydweli. Dunn, like Owain, was a war veteran and provided useful strategic advice as well as strength. That same year Gwilym ap Tudur of Penmynydd seized control of Conwy castle on behalf of Glyndŵr. Owain further consolidated his position by winning the Battle of Hyddgen on the slopes of Pumlumon in the summer of 1401 against an English force far superior in number.

After this defeat the king regrouped in Worcester, but it was autumn before he could mount another invasion. In the meantime, he plundered the south, taking children prisoner and executing supporters of Owain, such as Llywelyn ap Gruffydd Fychan, before evicting the monks of Strata Florida and setting up a war centre.

In response to the uprising, Henry IV enacted the 'Lancastrian penal code' in 1401–2, which banned the Welsh from gaining land or property over the border, or fortifying their houses, or bearing arms, or congregating en masse, or encouraging bards. But it did little to quell the revolt. Indeed, it fanned the flames.

In 1402 the army of Henry IV finally mobilized, moving from three bases on the border. The attempt, however, was thwarted by atrocious weather, leading to a widespread belief that Owain had supernatural powers. In the *Annales Henrici Quarti*, published in 1402, it is said that Glyndŵr 'almost destroyed the king and his armies, by magic as it was thought, for from the time they entered Wales to the time they left, never did a gentle air breathe on them, but throughout whole days and nights, rain mixed with snow and hail afflicted them with cold beyond endurance.'[4]

The success of this 'extraordinary man' on Hyddgen's slopes, and the inability of the rain-drenched royal army to hunt him down, certainly bolstered the insurrectionary spirit throughout Wales. Despite further attempts by the Crown to dampen, if not extinguish, the flames of rebellion, Glyndŵr marched and manoeuvred his men ever more successfully. Owain appealed for help from Irish leaders and from Robert III in Scotland, though some of these pleas seem to have been ignored.

In 1403 came personal success when Owain took his old enemy, Reginald Grey, prisoner. About the same time Owain also won a decisive battle at Bryn Glas, Maeliennydd, where he captured Edmund Mortimer, who subsequently became an ally. Meanwhile, Owain claimed a ransom of 10,000 marks for the release of Grey. The year 1403 was studded with other successes, especially in the south. In July the men of Ystrad Tywi proclaimed their allegiance to Owain as Prince of Wales, and he joined them and their leaders, the outsize Henry Dwnn and the constable of Dryslwyn, Rhys ap Gruffydd. The 8,000 men at his command were supplemented by a force led by Rhys Gethin of the Conwy valley, Rhys Ddu of Ceredigion, and William Gwyn of Cydweli. In a sparsely populated country, this was a mighty gathering of men.

A rabid panic spread through the English ranks as the Welsh fanned out, as suggested in a letter from the constable of Dinefwr castle, Jankyn Havard, who wrote on 7 July to John Fairford, a royal official:

> *I do now write that Owain Glyndŵr, Henry Dwnn, Rhys ap Gruffudd ap Llywellyn, Rhys Gethin, have won the town and castle of Carmarthen, and Wigmore constable of the castle has yielded up the castle of Carmarthen to Owain Glyndŵr: and has burned the town, and slain the men of the town more than 50 men; and they be in purpose to Cydweli; and to besiege as he has ordained at the castle that I keep, and that is a great peril for me, and all that be within; for they have made their vow that they will have us all dead therein.*[5]

The progress of the rebel army was thereafter swift, brutal and effective. Owain captured Newcastle Emlyn, Carreg Cennen and

Llansteffan. Then, at Laugharne and St Clears, Owain was ambushed and lost 700 men in the fight.

Henry IV was facing other challenges at the time. Having usurped the crown from his cousin Richard, he was now being challenged for it by Henry, known as Hotspur, the son of Henry Percy, the Earl of Northumberland. That same July in 1403, as Owain's men scythed through south Wales, Hotspur proclaimed war on the king in Chester. Henry moved swiftly against him, and at the Battle of Shrewsbury, Hotspur was killed, thereby robbing Owain of an important ally.

Meanwhile, all over south Wales the people were rising, attacking Usk, Caerleon, Abergavenny, Newport and Cardiff. Henry IV again entered Wales at the helm of three armies, but to no avail. Owain captured Aberystwyth castle and then Harlech in 1404. Harlech had been under siege for months and would eventually become home to Owain and his family. This was the key year in which he also briefly held the town of Cardiff and, importantly, convened a parliament in Machynlleth, enforcing his status as Prince of Wales. Here he signed a famous treaty with France at a ceremony attended not only by French representatives, but ones from Scotland and Castile too.

This was also a period that saw significant defections to his cause by clerics, not least John Trefor, Bishop of St Asaph, and Gruffudd Young, Archdeacon of Merioneth, who went on to become Owain's chancellor. Some of the documents attributed to Glyndŵr might well have been scribed by the hands of advisers such as these.

Owain had already appealed once previously to Irish and Scottish leaders by letter, so the second time he decided to appeal by emissary and sent a knight, Dafydd ab Ifan Goch. He also dispatched his brother-in-law, John Hanmer, as an ambassador to France, along with Gruffydd Young.

These acts of statesmanship and manoeuvre paid off. In 1405 the revolt took on an international dimension when a French force of 2,500 men arrived at Milford Haven to support him. They were met by Owain and his 10,000 men, but this alliance was not a game changer, even though Owain did manage to lead his new army – comprising possibly five per cent of the entire population – to attack Haverfordwest and Tenby. They then went on to capture Cardigan and Carmarthen, and ultimately marched into England, as far as Woodbury Hill near Worcester.

That year also saw the drawing up of the Tripartite Indenture, an agreement between Owain Glyndŵr, Percy, Earl of Northumberland and Edmund Mortimer in which they agreed how England and Wales might look. England would be cleft in two and Wales made more significant, extending north from Worcester as far as the river Trent and up to the Mersey. Interestingly, one of the boundary markers suggested by Owain were 'the ash trees of Meigon', a location connected with a victory by Cadwallon, and connected intimately with some of Merlin's prophecies.

The Indenture was an example of clever political manoeuvring, complete with clever recourse to myth, both of which served to exploit English divisions at a stroke. Owain was attempting to create an independent Welsh state and he tried to consolidate this by acts of diplomacy.

A second parliament was held at Harlech in August 1405, but the mood of success was blighted by royal gains when a force dispatched from Ireland managed to retake the Isle of Anglesey at the Battle of Rhos-meirch, and then regain the castle at Beaumaris. These defeats prompted capitulation to the king's will by individuals and communities throughout the country, and the French left for home in November.

Despite these considerable setbacks, Owain – 'Owynus dei gratia princeps Wallie' (by the grace of God Prince of Wales) – still wrote a letter to Charles VI of France on 31 March 1406. The so-called Pennal letter (after the parliament held in Pennal) offered to transfer Welsh spiritual allegiance to the pope in Avignon, namely Benedict XIII, rather than the pope in Rome. In the same letter Owain explained how his nation had 'been trodden underfoot by the fury of the barbarous Saxons', and set down terms requiring the establishment of two universities – one in the north and one in the south. He also wanted an independent Church with its headquarters at St David's, priests who could speak Welsh, and furthermore asked that the flow of money from the Welsh Church into England be stopped. The policy had many hallmarks of a political tradition connecting him to the two Llywelyns.

In France, however, a camp calling for peace with England was gaining favour, while in England itself, Owain's ally, the Earl of Northumberland, was killed at the Battle of Bramham Moor in 1408. That same year, Aberystwyth castle, a key holding, was wrested from Owain's grip. The following year, Harlech castle was taken from him, and members of his family were captured. This was a turning point in the revolt. Owain and his son were forced to become fugitives while his houses at Sycharth and Glyndyfrdwy were razed to the ground. In the main, the revolt had failed because of inadequate support by the French, making it very difficult to compete with English military superiority and supplies.

The final battles of the revolt occurred in 1412, including an attack on Shrewsbury and the capture of Dafydd Gam of Brecon, but from then on little is known of the fate of Owain Glyndŵr. Flashes of sporadic violence against the English continued, but now by nimble bands of bandits and outlaws rather than by any semblance of an organized military force.

Henry IV died in 1413 and was succeeded by Henry of Monmouth. Under Henry V, retribution for the uprising was noticeably absent, and many rebels found themselves pardoned and restored to their old roles. Owain's son Maredudd, however, refused a pardon until 1421, leading some historians to suspect that this was the year in which his father actually died.

One theory suggests that Owain ended his life as the family chaplain on his daughter Alis's estate, which she shared with her husband, Sir Henry Scudamore, sheriff of Herefordshire. Here he might have pondered some of the events that had shaped his life, such as the death of his brother Tudur, who had been killed in the Battle of Pwllmelyn, the same battle in which Owain's son Gruffydd was also captured. Gruffydd died in the Tower of London in 1411 and it was here that Owain's wife Margaret also passed away, along with her two daughters after they had been seized at Harlech.

The rebellion was arguably more destructive than constructive for Welsh politics and economy. The Glyndŵr rebellion was typified by acts of serious destruction of property and a significant loss of life, which had a deleterious effect on the country's economy for a long time afterwards. Even today, Glyndŵr's violent uprising resonates in Wales: a decade-long arson campaign directed against holiday homes in the 1980s was conducted by a spectral organization called Meibion Glyndŵr, the Sons of Glyndŵr.

The rebellion had to a large extent ruined the fragile but comfortable coexistence between the English and Welsh. Chroniclers at the time reported that Glyndŵr had 'brought all things to waste' and that the English king had 'proclaimed havoc in Wales'. There had been extensive destruction of towns and villages, and agricultural land had gone to waste. It was at least a generation before most of the areas caught up in the revolt got back to any semblance of normal working life.

Politically too the Welsh were knocked back where they had been making progress. It would be 150 years until they were allowed to become more prominent in society again.

On the other hand, the rebellion inspired Welsh nationalism throughout all the social classes in Wales, from labourers to nobles and from students to clerics. Glyndŵr was not to be forgotten, and became for some a heroic mythical figure. In *Henry IV,* Shakespeare portrays Owain Glyndŵr as a wild, exotic, magical and spiritual man, playing up the romantic 'Celtic' traits.

In the nineteenth century his life and legacy would be re-evaluated as the Welsh 'nation' began to find its voice once more. The discovery of letters and his seal with the four lions rampant of the House of Gwynedd (which had replaced the single lion rampant of Powys) were proof that he had been a national leader of some importance: a learned head of a country with diplomatic ties such as any other head of state might have.

The nationalist movement has always held Owain Glyndŵr in high regard, but he is now a figure of mass culture in Wales, with dedicated statues and monuments, alongside pub and street names commemorating him. Indeed, the historian R. R. Davies refers to

Owain's 'second career' as a talisman. The travel writer Thomas Pennant's warm portrait of a hero in *Tours in Wales* (1778–87) helped the creation of a sort of cult around the strong 'wild heart', a Braveheart for the Welsh.

Owain Glyndŵr had proved an effective talisman and a key touchstone for nascent nationalist energies. In offering a vision of a separate nation and a self-determining future, he was unwittingly anticipating future moves toward a devolved country.

Not for nothing has the last native Prince of Wales been credited as 'the father of Welsh nationalism'.[6]

CHAPTER THIRTEEN

TUDOR WALES

Lo, where he shineth yonder,
A fixed star in heaven,
Whose motion here came under
None of the planets seven.
If that the Moon should tender
The Sun her love, and marry,
They both could not engender
So sweet a star as Henry.[1]

It is one of the most haunting images in British history: a crown has fallen and is caught on a thorn bush on a bloody battlefield. Thomas Stanley picks up the crown and hands it to his stepson, Henry Tudor, who will become Henry VII, the first King of England of Welsh descent. This takes place on Bosworth Field, the birthplace of the great dynasty of the Tudors.

The Tudors were a Welsh family with roots as long and strong as an oak's, extending way back to Ednyfed Fychan, the seneschal (military chief of staff) who served Llywelyn the Great. Ednyfed had three sons: Goronwy, Tudur and Gruffudd, and Ednyfed's descendants had accepted the new order under Edward I – that of handing an entire inheritance to one son rather than dividing it. From the line of

Ednyfed's son Goronwy grew the family of Penmynydd, which had its seat on Anglesey. One of Tudur's sons, Maredudd, was the actual ancestor of the royal Tudor line, and it was his son, Owain ap Maredudd ap Tudur (c.1400–61), who fixed the Anglicized surname, Tudor. Owain had fought for the English king Henry V, and after Henry's death Owain had somehow won the favour of Henry's widow, Queen Catherine, or Catherine of Valois, supposedly marrying her in secret and having six children together. One of the six, Edmund, would become the father of the future Henry VII. This was a family that moved with ease in exalted circles.

If the revolt of Owain Glyndŵr had awoken a dormant sense of nationality, then the Wars of the Roses, the struggle over dynastic claims for the English throne by the two branches (York and Lancaster) of the Plantagenet House fostered it even further. The wars saw support for each side from the Welsh. The Yorkists were backed by the huge Mortimer estates, which extended along the Welsh border, and the Lancastrians were backed by south Wales.

The House of York was further bolstered in Wales as it had history on its side: the Yorkist claimant to the throne, Henry, claimed descent from Gwladus Ddu, the daughter of Llywelyn the Great.

Henry Tudor's uncle, Jasper Tudor, Earl of Pembroke, had taken 'the only imp now left of Henry VI's brood' into exile in Brittany in 1471, from where he harnessed the Welsh tradition of poetic prophecy to marshal support for his young charge. The bards had long sung of a deliverer from Anglo-Saxon or Norman oppression, who might have been Arthur or Owain Glyndŵr. But *might*, conveniently, be Henry Tudor.

Henry Tudor had spent the first 14 years of his life in Wales, having been born in Pembroke castle, where he grew up in the care of a Welsh nurse who might well have taught him to speak Welsh, though there is no direct evidence for this. But even though he was only a quarter Welsh and had spent much of his adult life away from his homeland, it was enough to make the Welsh discern, or possibly yearn for, a special connection with him, and subsequently with his son and grandchildren – the Tudor kings and queens who followed him, from Henry VIII to Elizabeth I.

Henry, the exiled prince with pronounced Welsh roots, was a perfect fit for these bardic descriptions or predictions. There were a good many of these: no fewer than 35 poets penned prophetic poems about this deliverer – not least of which was Dafydd Llwyd at Mathafarn. His poems were eagerly passed from one person to another in a version of Chinese whispers in Welsh verse, spreading a desire for 'the coming of the long golden summer' and with it the 'long foretold triumph of the red dragon over the white'.

Detailed preparations were made to facilitate Henry's claim to the throne, though things did not start auspiciously. His invasion in 1483 was far from successful as 13 of his 15 ships were driven back to harbour by wild gales. Then, in the summer of 1485, Henry landed at Mill Bay on the north side of Milford Haven in Pembrokeshire, where the French had landed years before to aid Owain Glyndŵr. Henry was hoping for support from Rhys ap Thomas of Dinefwr and others, and had sent persuasive messages in advance to curry favour and drum up support. But he did not know yet if they had been heeded.

If truth be told, rallying the Welsh at that time was not easy: there was no court, no capital, no institutions of state and no means of steering the country's destiny. Wales still felt the damaging effects of both the Black Death and a string of failed harvests. Owain Glyndŵr's defeat about 70 years before had left a country debilitated and without a leader.

Henry's troops slogged through Wales at a rate of 14 miles a day. His soldiers tramped from Haverfordwest through Fagwr Lwyd to Cardigan and then northwards, to cross the Dyfi at Machynlleth, picking up support as they went. They were passing through a poor, ravaged land, where the average life expectancy was well below 40.

One might imagine that poetry would have been the last thing on young Henry's mind as he prepared for battle, yet he made a detour to consult with the bard Dafydd Llwyd at his house in Mathafarn. Henry did not get an answer when he posed the question of whether or not he would wear the crown of England – not, that is, until Dafydd's wife advised him to say 'yes', reckoning that Henry would not soon be passing that way again. It was the answer Henry needed. Prophecy was going to create and cement his future.

By 13 August, Henry and his footsore warriors were at the Long Mynd near Welshpool, where Rhys ap Thomas and his 2,000 troops finally answered Henry's prayers and joined him, along with a force drawn from mid-Wales. This in turn was augmented by the Herberts from the southeast of Wales, and chiefs such as William ap Griffith from Penrhyn and Richard ap Howel from Mostyn in the north, who brought cattle with them by way of food supplies. With all this Welsh support now rallying around Henry, he had doubled the size of his army.

How had he got them on his side? On the march to Bosworth, he had sent messages to these chiefs, those 'nobles and commons of this our principality of Wales', which claimed that he was determined that 'when that odious tyrant, Richard, late Duke of Gloucester' had been overthrown, he would restore not only England to its ancient estate, honour and prosperity but 'our said principality, of Wales and the people of the same to their former liberties, delivering them of such miserable servitudes as they have piteously long stood in.'[2] These persuasive words had the desired effect.

Richard watched the battle from a hill overlooking the site. He had not slept and his face looked more 'ghastly and livid than usual'. Probably he was sensing that his time as king was rapidly ebbing away. Henry's troops soon looked as if they were gaining the upper hand, so Richard panicked and charged into battle, where he was unhorsed. One of Henry's lieutenants, either Rhys ap Maredudd or Rhys ap Thomas, allegedly drove a spear through his heart and Richard's forces disintegrated when they realized that the king was dead.

Henry was young, just 28 years of age, when he became king in 1485. The battlefield coronation of this grandson of Owain ap Mare-dudd from Anglesey and cousin of Owain Glyndŵr can be seen as a momentous event. In the words of a Venetian emissary's report to his government, 'The Welsh may now be said to have recovered their former independence, for the most wise and fortunate Henry VII is a Welshman.'[3]

It was no coincidence that Henry unfurled the standard of Cadwal-adr at Bosworth, a flag bearing a red dragon on a field of white and green sarcenet (fine cloth), as this King of Gwynedd was believed to be the last of Henry's predecessors to have ruled over southern Britain. Just as it was for early rulers such as Rhodri Mawr, lineage was impor-tant to the new Tudor king. In fact, Henry VII soon appointed a small team of commissioners to explore further his own genealogy and they took evidence from experts such as the poet Gutun Owen.

Henry Tudor was to confirm the richness of his genealogy when he named his son, born a year after Bosworth, Arthur, allowing for the possibility of another King Arthur to rule Britain, and thus tapping into a rich vein of Brythonic history. Henry would send Arthur to live at Ludlow and make him the Prince of Wales. He was clearly intent on teaching him how to be a king by first managing Wales. Ludlow was also home to the body that administered the legal system, the Council of the Marches. In 1501, Arthur married Catherine of Aragon, but a year later he died of unknown causes.

When Richard III was killed at Bosworth the Welsh saw it as a Welsh victory, and Jasper Tudor, Henry's uncle, as a reward for his propagandist efforts, earned himself the title of Duke of Bedford, not to mention substantial tracts of land along with the title of chief justice of south Wales.

And there were rewards too for Thomas Stanley, who had handed Henry the crown on the field of battle, and for Rhys ap Thomas, who was knighted within days of the Bosworth victory.

Many of Henry's followers were given letters of denizenship, granting them the same rights as Englishmen. There were Welsh sheriffs and Welsh bishops, and the cattle-driving William ap Griffith, the chief who rallied around Henry, became chamberlain of north Wales.

The Welsh were favoured in London too, where they gained many minor posts. It was an unseemly scramble. Henry's security detail, the yeomen of the guard, were mainly Welsh. They had been hand-picked from those who had looked after him in exile and he gave them extra money for their St David's Day feast as further thanks.

The English court poet John Skelton was clearly put out by all these Welsh opportunists in Tudor London. He made fun of their accents and tastes in food in some famously vitriolic lines. He described how St Peter and a better class of people in Heaven were suddenly over-whelmed by an abrupt influx of the Welsh, driving everyone crazy with their incessant talk. So the keeper of the keys arranged for an angel to stand outside Heaven and to shout in loud voice, '*Caws pobi*' – a refer-ence to the basic version of Welsh rarebit, or cheese on toast. The Welsh promptly rushed towards their national delicacy and the gates were slammed shut behind them, much to everyone's relief.[4]

The Welsh might have been thriving at court, but it was not their court; in the end, it was an English court. Historian John Davies has concluded that the Welsh in this period were 'a conservative people, bereft of control over their fate and lacking any centres of wealth'.[5] The wealth lay elsewhere. The contrast with Scotland was certainly marked; Scotland still had its own court and, as a result, the urban development that was largely lacking in Wales. The absence of insti-tutions and the commerce that could foster change would plague Wales for generations to come.

After Prince Arthur's untimely death in 1509 his younger brother Henry inherited the crown, his brother's wife and the title of Prince of Wales, along with the task of governing the Welsh.

During Henry VIII's reign (1509–47), two Parliamentary Acts of 1536 and 1543, collectively known as the 'Acts of Union' or 'The Laws in Wales Acts', were passed with the aim 'for law and justice to be administered in Wales in like form as it is in this realm'. Inaugurated by Thomas Cromwell, chief minister to Henry VIII, they were intended to integrate the legal, political and administrative systems in England and Wales, not to mention making English the official language of the courts and thus of a mainly Welsh-speaking nation.

Cromwell, a forward-looking, ruthless pragmatist had helped the king divorce Catherine so he could marry Anne Boleyn. He wanted to sweep away the past and usher in a new beginning in the form of a unitary British state and he was not alone in his ambitions. It was to Cromwell that some Welsh gentlemen addressed their requests for 'major administrative surgery' as they were beguiled by the prospect of formal marriage between the two countries.[6]

The Acts of Union can be seen to be not just an imposition, but also a punishment that rendered the Welsh second-class citizens and decried their 'sinister usages and customs' for daring to rise up to back Owain Glyndŵr. Far from being a marriage of equals, it had the effect of making the weaker partner even weaker. The preamble to the Act suggests that the difference in laws and language in the two countries, amply demonstrated by the Laws of Hywel, led to discord and discontent. These would no longer be allowed to fester or develop further.

English was now the language of the law, which discriminated against monoglot Welsh speakers. After the passing of the Acts, a criminal could be hanged on the gallows without understanding a single word uttered by one of the chief justices in the Courts of the Great Sessions.

Another consequence of the Acts was the division of Marcher lordships into shires, with seven new counties within Wales, namely Denbigh, Montgomery, Radnor, Brecknock, Pembroke, Glamorgan and Monmouth, being added to the existing six counties within England. It was a legal change that altered the map of Wales.

The second Act of 1543 also paid methodical and meticulous attention to the details of government. Whereas the first Act had been

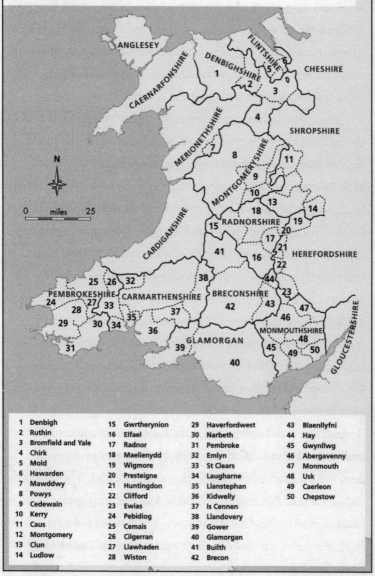

WELSH COUNTIES ESTABLISHED UNDER THE ACT OF UNION, 1536

ANGLESEY

CAERNARFONSHIRE

DENBIGHSHIRE

FLINTSHIRE

CHESHIRE

SHROPSHIRE

MERIONETHSHIRE

MONTGOMERYSHIRE

CARDIGANSHIRE

RADNORSHIRE

HEREFORDSHIRE

PEMBROKESHIRE

CARMARTHENSHIRE

BRECONSHIRE

GLAMORGAN

MONMOUTHSHIRE

GLOUCESTERSHIRE

N

0 miles 25

1 Denbigh	15 Gwrtherynion	29 Haverfordwest	43 Blaenllyfni
2 Ruthin	16 Elfael	30 Narbeth	44 Hay
3 Bromfield and Yale	17 Radnor	31 Pembroke	45 Gwynllwg
4 Chirk	18 Maelienydd	32 Emlyn	46 Abergavenny
5 Mold	19 Wigmore	33 St Clears	47 Monmouth
6 Hawarden	20 Presteigne	34 Laugharne	48 Usk
7 Mawddwy	21 Huntingdon	35 Llanstephan	49 Caerleon
8 Powys	22 Clifford	36 Kidwelly	50 Chepstow
9 Cedewain	23 Ewias	37 Is Cennen	
10 Kerry	24 Pebidiog	38 Llandovery	
11 Caus	25 Cemais	39 Gower	
12 Montgomery	26 Cilgerran	40 Glamorgan	
13 Clun	27 Llawhaden	41 Builth	
14 Ludlow	28 Wiston	42 Brecon	

somewhat nebulous, the second was much more prescriptive and specific. It required that the apparatus of English government be employed in Wales so that a system of sheriffs, justices of the peace, coroners and constables would be introduced. It also created a system of higher courts markedly distinct from those in England, namely the Courts of the Great Sessions, which were to remain in existence until 1830, and which heard both civil and criminal cases.

This seemingly devastating legislative assault on Wales was actually the culmination of a long process of assimilation, of the country drawing ever closer to its eastern neighbour. Welsh gentry wanted to be rid of the pervasive influence of the Marcher lords who controlled large swathes of the map, so the Acts of Union were welcomed by many in Wales. Although time has assessed the Acts as being damaging to the language, at the time, reaction from the normally voluble bards was muted to say the least: 'No protests were organized, no shots were fired in anger, and Welsh poets, who could normally be relied upon to dramatize key events, were uncharacteristically lost for words'.[7]

For those at the top of the Welsh pile, for the larger landowning families, such as the Stanleys and Wynns, whose wealth compared favourably with that of the aristocracy, this was a time when they were particularly successful, both in their home patch and at the 'English' court in London. For them the Acts of Union created huge opportunities, and union was high on the list of priorities for the gentry. As justices of the peace, they dominated local government. As Members of Parliament, profitable doors were opened to them in London. And because the statute abolished division of legacy among heirs, their efforts to build up their estates were facilitated, and grow them they did.

There was to be another big shift in Welsh life, driven by Henry VIII's ambitions and sex life. His marriage to Arthur's widow, Catherine of Aragon, and then his subsequent desire to annul the marriage meant that in 1533–34 Henry broke all ties with Rome and made himself the head of the Church in England. This set in train many acts of vandalism and destruction against monasteries and Church property, with effigies desecrated and shrines destroyed. Monasteries in England and Wales were razed, severing the links between these holy houses and the Welsh culture they were recording.

The Welsh devotion to Mary and to Marian shrines was especially targeted by Henry's chief minister, Thomas Cromwell, particularly at the hugely significant shrine and pilgrimage centre of Penrhys in the Rhondda. When Henry ordered the miraculous 'Image of Penrhys' of the Virgin Mary to be taken to Tyburn to be burned, it had to be removed secretly at night before being destroyed publicly in London.

Henry died a Catholic, but his son, Edward, had been raised a Protestant. Edward ruled briefly from 1547 to 1553, before a premature death at the age of 15. His successor, his eldest sister Mary, had been raised a Catholic, so Catholicism was reinstated between 1553 and 1558.

Queen Mary I's reign did not witness too much discontent in Wales, but rather seemed to indicate a propensity for going back to the Roman fold, which was familiar to its people, and therefore in some ways comforting. One Welsh poet, Siôn Brwynog, summed up this attachment to the 'old faith' thus:

Wele fraint y saint yn neshau – eilwaith
Wele'r hen 'fferenau'

Wele Duw a'i law ddehau
Yn gallu oll ein gwellhau.

Behold once more the privilege of the saints draws near,
Behold the old masses;
Behold God making us whole
With his right hand.[8]

Whilst England and Wales switched from Protestant to Catholic, some priests lost their livelihoods because they were married, something forbidden under Catholic rules, but few people in Wales lost their lives. The paucity of martyrdoms suggests how readily the Welsh returned to observing the mass and witnessing the altars re-established. In fact, throughout the whole of Wales there were only three martyrdoms for heresy under Catholic rule.

At Mary's death, the final Tudor heir, Elizabeth I, became queen, and with her coronation she reimposed the Protestant religion on England and Wales. With all the vacillations of faith back and forth, it is little wonder that worshippers were confused. Old relics had disappeared and then reappeared to disappear again. Pilgrimages were a thing of the past. Shrines had been desecrated. Churches went from being brightly coloured to plain white boxes, stripped of adornment, only for that to all briefly change back again.

Catholicism persisted in Wales, but during Elizabeth's long reign (1558–1603), she was keen to stamp out alternatives to the Protestant faith, forcing both the Catholic faith and the faithful into hiding, whether to priest-holes hidden in houses or abroad. Priests were given 40 days to leave the country or face charges of high treason.

Interestingly, the first book printed in Wales, and that on an illegal press in a cave near Llandudno, was the Catholic *Y Drych Cristionogawl* in 1585. Its foreword depicted a godless Wales in need of spiritual edification:

> ... *And now I hear that there are many places in Wales, yea, whole shires knowing nothing of virtue, except that they retain the name of Christ in their memory, knowing hardly anything more of what Christ is than animals do. And in those places where some of them are Christians, only a few poor common people follow Christ. The gentry and the wealthy think nothing of any faith in the world and are neither hot nor cold.*[9]

For one Wrexham man, this Elizabethan period showed him the path to sainthood. Richard Gwyn was a well-educated family man who refused to give up the Catholic faith, which outraged local officials. In May 1581, six men forced Gwyn to attend the Anglican service in the church in Wrexham. They carried him around the font on their shoulders and placed him in heavy shackles in front of the pulpit. Then he 'so stirred his legs that with the voice of his irons the preacher's voice could not be heard'.[10]

Such seeming disrespect had to be punished, and he was put in the stocks and taunted by a local Anglican minister. Gwyn's riposte was to suggest 'That there is a difference – whereas Peter received the keys to the Kingdom of Heaven, the keys you received were clearly those of the beer cellar.' These were fighting words.

Gwyn was subsequently convicted of attempting to convert others to the Catholic faith, and of treason, and as a consequence was condemned to death by being hanged, drawn and quartered in October 1584.

This bloody process meant that Gwyn was literally butchered alive – hanged until he was at the very point of death, at which stage his genitals were cut off and thrown into a fire. His chest cage and belly were then ripped open and the intestines and innards unlooped before onlookers. Throughout this ordeal the victim was still alive and eventually died in the most excruciating agony.

Richard Gwyn's last words were, '*Iesu, trugarha wrthyf*' (Jesus, have mercy upon me). Gwyn was canonized by Pope Paul VI in 1970.

Religious exiles were active across the Catholic Continent, in strongholds such as Paris, Douai, Milan and, of course, Rome. In fact, the first Welsh grammar was published in Milan. But despite Catholic activity abroad, the Counter-Reformation did not take a strong hold, and the remaining pockets of Catholicism in England, in places such as the Jesuit college in Cwm in Herefordshire, came to be viewed as something foreign. In fact, by the end of Elizabeth's reign there were only a little over 800 open Catholic objectors compared with 212,000 regular churchgoers.

While the few Catholics in England were marginalized, there were others in Wales who were really prospering. The leading Welsh families enjoyed refined living in the fine houses of the Elizabethan Age. The Wynn family homes of Plas Mawr and Gwydir castle were elaborately decorated and benefited from high-quality European craftsmanship. Gwydir castle, near Llanrwst in the Conwy valley, was built by one of Henry Tudor's great supporters, Maredudd ap Ieuan ap Robert. After Henry VIII's dissolution of the monasteries between 1536 and 1540, building material from nearby Maenan Abbey was used to expand and decorate the place, complete with a fine front porch and gardens in the very latest style.

A central character in this refined and privileged world was Katheryn of Berain, who, with her six children, and scores of very well-connected descendants and relations, became known as the 'Mother of Wales'. Said to be a cousin of Queen Elizabeth, this Denbighshire daughter of a bastard son of Henry VII made four profitable marriages with men from the leading Welsh families, including Maurice Wynn. Some have subsequently suggested that she helped her husbands to their graves. A fine Dutch portrait of her from 1560 hangs in the National Museum. In it she appears intelligent, attractive and purposive, though not necessarily bent on murder.

Katheryn's first marriage was to John Salusbury, son and heir to Sir John Salusbury of Lleweni. The femme fatale's next short-lived husband was Sir Richard Clough, and it is said that the third candidate for her bed, Maurice Wynn of Gwydir, had proposed to her even as he led her from church after her first husband's funeral, but she refused as she had already accepted Sir Richard on the way to the church. She had promised, however, 'that in case she performed the same sad duty to this husband, he might depend on being the third'.[11] Clough died in 1570, and three years later she kept her word to Wynn. After his death she took her final husband, Edward Thelwall, who lived happily ever after.

But it wasn't just Katheryn of Berain who made a mark. During the second half of the sixteenth century, London seemed to be awash with the Welsh. In a frenzy of socializing, networking and influencing, they were sufficient in number to make up the biggest 'ethnic' group. They managed to blend in well, although they had a reputation for being quick to quarrel and boastful of their ancient pedigrees. The Welsh were tradesmen, drovers and cattlemen, and prominent in the law. The Inns of Court especially were where the Welsh formed a network in which they could put their taste for dispute to good use. A Welshman, it was said, was 'precious in his owne conceit, and upon Saint Davies day without comparison'.[12]

However, this boom time for the landowning class did little for general economic development in Wales. There was no trickle-down effect – in fact, if anything, the gap between the social classes widened. The rise of the gentry did not lead to a complex system of trades, skills and wealth creation, such as that in prosperous, growing towns in England at the end of the sixteenth century. Poverty afflicted the majority of people, and crippling poverty at that.

There were, of course, signs of enlightened humanism in Elizabeth's day. One of the finest expressions was William Morgan's Bible of 1588, which remains a glorious literary, as well as a singular religious, achievement.

This Welsh Bible came into being due to some shrewd lobbying by three north Walian Protestants, namely Bishop Richard Davies, Humphrey Llwyd and William Salesbury, who suggested that one could best reform the Welsh by doing so in their own language. In 1563 this resulted in Parliament ordering the translation of the Bible and Book of Common Prayer into Welsh from English, 'the which tongue is not understood by the greatest number of Her Majesty's most loving and obedient subjects inhabiting the country of Wales who are therefore destituted of God's holy word'.

The translation of the New Testament by William Salesbury in 1567 did not meet with full approval because of the scholastic and rather impenetrable language. So William Morgan, a Cambridge graduate and vicar of Llanrhaeadr-ym-Mochnant in Denbighshire undertook the task of translating the whole Bible. During the process of translation he also standardized the language where he 'found the Welsh vernacular a congeries of dialects and spellings, some of them deserving only of death, and he left it a language that has held its place with increasing estimation during a period of three hundred years'.[13]

Morgan dedicated his monumental work to Elizabeth I, who had commissioned it, saying 'Faith indeed comes by hearing and hearing by the word of God: a word that until now has only barely sounded in the ears of our fellow-countrymen, as it is hidden in a foreign tongue.'[14]

The Welsh Bible was intended to be placed in every parish church in Wales, so a thousand copies were printed. This not only helped to save the Welsh language, but also brought the Church closer to the people of Wales.

By the end of Elizabeth's reign in 1603, and the beginning of the Stuart period under James I, the Welsh gentry and the Welsh people were much more strongly aligned with the monarchy. Some places, such as south Pembrokeshire, were as wealthy as places in England, with towns such as Tenby thriving on sales of high-end goods. The coastal ports here had trade links with countries such as Portugal and Morocco, which chose Wales because of its lower tariffs and more efficient service. But away from the towns, commercial development was slow.

This period also saw the stirrings of popular learning in the grammar schools set up in market towns, such as Bangor, Carmarthen and Cowbridge, and the rise of Puritanism.

Puritanism, a movement for Church reform that wanted to eliminate every last vestige of Catholicism, was much slower to take off in

Wales than in England. Wales was still a poor and underdeveloped country that lacked a strong middle class. Puritanism appealed to literate middling sorts, so outside Pembrokeshire and the borders, there were few supporters. What was perceived as the plight of Wales led to the London Welsh paying to translate Puritan tracts and texts by authors such as William Perkins and Arthur Dent. Some effort was also made to provide the common reader with the Scriptures. In 1630 the first octavo Welsh Bible, known as *y Beibl bach* (the small Bible), was published. Significantly, some Puritans, drawing their inspiration from the death of John Penry, a Puritan martyr in 1593, resolved to set up separatist congregations. The first of these was established by Independents at Llanfaches in Monmouthshire in 1639.

Initially, although Welsh Puritans were relatively few in number, they were ferociously committed and determined to be influential. A few are recorded as taking up the new Dissenting strain of Protestantism, including the Pritchard family of Llancaiach Fawr and the Williamses of Whitchurch. One of the Williamses' sons would marry into the family of Thomas Cromwell, and his son Oliver would take his mother's family name. It would be a bitter irony for Oliver Cromwell, the son of a Welshman, that when civil war broke out, Wales was overwhelmingly on the side of the king. For when the civil war came, it would be particularly harsh in Wales. And Oliver Cromwell was convinced that Wales needed a fresh start.

CHAPTER FOURTEEN

CIVIL WAR

Poor Taffy, up to her knees in blood.[1]

What was so often called the English Civil War is a misnomer, because the consequences of this profound political event in seventeenth-century Europe tore through not only England but also Scotland, Ireland and Wales. The four countries were hugely unsettled by religious and political unrest, all of which were part of the wider struggle for supremacy between Catholics and Protestants across the Continent.

The civil war showed Wales to be markedly conservative and royalist – this may be surprising, given the reputation Wales had gained for violent rebellion in medieval times. But the Acts of Union, respect for the Crown and the growth of Protestantism had made the Welsh a more obedient and benign people.

What's also interesting about the civil war is how Oliver Cromwell viewed and dealt with the Welsh during and afterwards. It might have been that his Welsh heritage (represented in his personal seal, which included the heraldry of the princes of Powys, Glamorgan, Ardudwy and Gwent) influenced his religious and political policies in Wales. He seemed to feel particular concern for the country that he called 'that dark corner of the Kingdom' and he viewed the Welsh as a 'seduced, ignorant people' lacking in Puritan zeal.

It can be argued that at the beginning of the Protestant Reformation the people of Wales were nominally Catholic, but this was to change. In 1533, Henry VIII severed links with Rome, a political manoeuvre that enabled him to divorce his first wife Catherine of Aragon, and marry Anne Boleyn. But his break with Rome also, unintentionally, started a process of religious change. The Protestant faith subsequently spread throughout Britain as the national religion under Edward IV, Elizabeth I and James I, and would eventually lead to widespread Anglicanism in Wales.

James's successor, Charles I (r.1625–49) favoured a High Anglican form of worship, while his wife was Catholic. This was the inspiration behind his plans to reform the Church of England to a High Church blueprint, drawn up by a former Bishop of St David's. This made many of his subjects suspicious of him, fearing a hidden religious agenda. Meanwhile, tensions between the king and Parliament over the cost of waging war overseas against Spain and France resulted in his dissolving Parliament three times between 1625 and 1629, eventually dissolving it entirely in 1629. There was a growing divide between king and country.

Beyond England's borders, there were varying alignments in loyalty. In Scotland, Charles's attempt to introduce a new hymn book caused tensions, and rumours that the king was recruiting an army in Ireland to help him fight in Scotland, where there was also an uprising, made some people in Wales wary of an Irish invasion.

The Welsh gentry, who had been very loyal to the Tudors, had transferred their allegiance to the House of Stuart – not least because James I was a descendant of Henry VII, whom they had viewed as a Welsh king. In the hopes of continued rewards, they stayed steadfastly royalist; this, in turn, implied the support of their tenants as well.

The Acts of Union during Henry VIII's reign had bound England and Wales closer together in law, and the Bible translated during Elizabeth's reign had helped spread a common religion throughout England and Wales, bringing some unity between the two countries.

Yet relations between the Welsh and the authoritarian Charles I had had their strains, especially as his go-it-alone loftiness and personal rule coincided with bad harvests and unemployment at a time when there was little extra cash to raise so-called Ship Money to support the navy. Indeed, some Welsh counties failed to contribute a single penny.

The issue of money, or lack of it, may explain the reluctance of the Welsh to support Parliament's cause. There was no Welsh mercantile class, so Charles I's commercial and financial policies, which were the cause of furore among politicians and in the world of English commerce, stoked very few fires of outrage in Wales. Prior to the outbreak of civil war, only five Welsh MPs opposed Charles, and only two areas in Wales backed the Parliamentary forces: Pembrokeshire and Denbighshire.

South Pembrokeshire was a predominantly merchant community under the influence of the Earl of Essex, who held lands there. Philip Herbert, fourth Earl of Pembroke and keeper of Cardiff castle, was central to the debates about kingship and was a committed Parliamentarian.

In the northeast, Wrexham had well-established connections with Puritans in Cheshire. The influential Thomas Myddelton of Wrexham was the MP for Denbighshire. He would later defeat Royalist forces at Montgomery in 1644, although in 1648 he was expelled from Parliament by Oliver Cromwell for not being sufficiently antagonistic to the Royalist cause. Incidentally, Myddelton also happened to be the son of a lord mayor of London who had helped bankroll the Welsh Bible of 1630.

These two parts of Wales were the only areas that supported Parliament during the First Civil War. Throughout the rest of Wales, Royalism was encouraged by key figures, such as the Catholic Earl of Worcester, Charles's biggest financial supporter, based at Raglan castle, until the castle fell under Parliamentary control in 1647. But just as in England, patterns of loyalty during the civil war were constantly shifting, and taking sides was often nothing more than personal choice.

When the Long Parliament met in November 1640, for instance, Welsh MPs spoke out virulently against the king and his bishops. Yet by 1642 their strident criticism had dampened and both opinion and backing swung in the king's favour. As a result, Charles I found that Wales was a fertile ground for recruiting soldiers. Wales was strategically important for the king too because of its land routes, north and south, to Ireland. During the course of the war, control of these early highways yo-yoed back and forth between the two sides.

The First Civil War broke out in August 1642 with the inconclusive Battle of Edgehill, the culmination of over 15 years of autocratic rule. The map of England was roughly divided between the Royalist north and west and the Parliamentarian south and east. The First Civil War stuttered towards a truce after the Siege of Oxford in 1645, where Charles escaped with his life, eventually surrendering to the Scots. He escaped from them too and found sanctuary on the Isle of Wight, from where he stoked discontentment among some Scots and encouraged them to invade. In Pembrokeshire Parliamentarian soldiers switched sides and offered their services to the king. The governor of Pembroke castle, John Poyer, led the antipathy towards Parliament, which thereby lost one of its strongholds and gained an enemy. This fomented the Second Civil War, a short-lived affair, which lasted for a year and came to an end with the rout of Royalists by the Parliamentarian general.

Some of the bitterest and biggest battles between Parliament and king were fought in Wales, caused in great measure by the discontent that arose from the ending of the first war, and the disbanding of Parliament's army. This occurred in Pembrokeshire in February 1648, leaving many former soldiers without pay, and angry about arrears of pay. Now backing the restoration of the king, the disaffected soldiers under the control of Poyer, his brother-in-law Rowland Laugharne and fellow veteran soldier Rice Powell marched across south Wales. They started by attacking Carmarthen, then seizing Swansea and Neath, before pressing eastwards, where they fought in the Battle of St Fagans, near Cardiff, in May 1648, in which they faced a section of the Parliamentarian New Model Army. This was one of the final battles of the Second Civil War and is commemorated in local pub names such as Tŷ Pwll Coch (The Red House) in Ely.

These events were sufficient a touchstone for Cromwell himself to take control of the Welsh campaign and march five regiments across south Wales in 1648 to subdue the rebellious inhabitants. They started at Chepstow castle, which they swiftly captured.

Turbulent months followed the execution of Charles I in January 1649. Two Welsh Parliamentarians, John Jones, MP for Meirionnydd, and Thomas Wogan, MP for the Cardigan Boroughs, were among those who had signed the king's death warrant. Despite the upheaval following the king's execution, Cromwell maintained his extraordinary commitment to reforming Welsh religion whilst he consolidated his political position as leader of England and Wales: The Commission for the Propagation of the Gospel in Wales was formed in 1650 and was tasked with rooting out what Cromwell saw as superstitious practices in the Welsh Church.

The result of the commission was that only licensed ministers were allowed to preach, and a total of 287 ministers were deemed unfit to do so. When, in 1653, the Rump Parliament (so named after the purge of original members sympathetic to Charles) refused to extend the commission's three-year tenure, Cromwell dissolved Parliament.

During this period, there was much popular resentment against the hounding of the Welsh church and its Anglican representatives by some of the more militant Puritan ministers. Vavasor Powell was a restlessly energetic preacher, often travelling 161 kilometres (100 miles) in a week and preaching three times a day. Born in Powys, he converted to Puritanism in 1638. By 1642 Powell had moved to London, where he became the vicar of Dartford, but after he resigned in 1646, he was given the approval of the Committee for Plundered Ministers to preach in Wales.

Powell was a Parliamentarian, but his doctrines, and the vehemence with which he clung to them, brought him into opposition to Cromwell. Powell, the so-called 'archbishop of the new saints', was incensed by Cromwell's self-elevation, which would result in his becoming lord protector. On 18 December 1653, Powell denounced Cromwell and was arrested. On his release on 24 December, Powell fled to Wales to organize opposition to Cromwell, but supported the Protectorate during a Royalist rising in 1655. His opposition continued in the 1655 protest broadside called 'A Word for God... against Wickedness in High Places', which was presented in November 1655. Signed by 322 people, it alienated many Welsh Puritans as well as the government authorities. From 1660 until his death in 1670, aged 53, Powell spent his life either preaching his beliefs or in prison. His story is richly revealing of a time when the Catholic-Protestant conflict turned the world upside down and left Wales reeling.

The social hierarchy of Britain had been swept aside by civil war and the land had been left without a king. Puritanism had been pressed upon the conservative inhabitants of Wales by a new political figurehead, who had not been ordained by God. These were dramatic changes indeed. The following century would see Wales evolve again, this time emerging as an economic and religious world leader. Characters such as Vavasor Powell were sowing the seeds of Nonconformity, which would become a prevalent religion in Wales. Meanwhile, the harnessing of Wales's natural resources in the Industrial Revolution would permanently change the country's landscape and place Wales prominently on the world stage. It would be quite a turnaround.

PART FOUR

INDUSTRIAL WALES

CHAPTER FIFTEEN

A FLURRY OF
THOUGHT

Despite the conservatism of the eighteenth century, as the Hanoverian dynasty settled on to the throne of England, there was a steady growth in Wales of intellectual and populist ideas. In this Age of Enlightenment there were pulses of a new, intellectual energy as a handful of thinkers and scholars made connections with the wider world.

It was during this time of radical thought that Wales went through a religious awakening that would play a crucial role in shaping the country's identity.

In Germany in the 1730s, and across the Atlantic in Massachusetts in the 1740s, the Moravians had conducted the first large-scale Protestant missionary movement. Methodism had its roots in eighteenth-century Anglicanism. Its founder was a Church of England minister, John Wesley (1703–91), who, along with his brother Charles, sought to challenge the religious assumptions of the day. During a period of time in Oxford, he and others met regularly to study the Bible, to pray and to receive communion. They became known as 'The Holy Club' or 'Methodists' because of the methodical way in which they carried out their Christian faith. John Wesley later used the term Methodist himself to mean the methodical pursuit of biblical holiness.

The rise of the similarly missionary Methodism in Wales should be viewed as an independent Welsh movement led by two very influential leaders: Howell Harris and Daniel Rowland. Initially, the leaders in Wales and England cooperated, but before long fracture lines appeared as the Welsh embraced Calvinism, which derived from the thinking of the sixteenth-century Protestant Reformer John Calvin. Calvin argued that God was sovereign in the salvation of humanity and that living the Christian life was essential for the Church, especially in the context of humanity's depravity.

Calvinistic Methodism took root slowly in Wales and initially focused around Llangeitho, Trefeca and Bala. An evangelical movement, it had a strong sense of moral self-discipline that seemed to chime with the experiences of the Welsh, who liked to work hard and pray hard.

Howell Harris, born in Trefeca, south of Talgarth in Powys, had been educated at the Nonconformist Academy at Llanigon, where he was baptized on Palm Sunday in 1735. Fired by the spirit, he preached zealously around his native village, gathering his converts into *seiadau*, or societies that were designed 'to keep the believer from back-sliding'. By the middle of the eighteenth century there were 428 of these clinics for the soul, and each one was organized under a superintendent who oversaw a regular pattern of worship, with monthly and quarterly meetings, and a great many in between.

Howell Harris made connections outside Wales too. Together with George Whitefield, the leader of the Calvinist wing of English Methodism, he travelled to London, where he had meetings with the

Wesley brothers. He then set about organizing his movement, intent on disseminating his mainly Calvinistic theology, which emphasized the sovereignty of God and His grace in Christ, and on the election of the saints.

One of the pivotal meetings in Howell Harris's life was with Daniel Rowland, who had been born in Nancwnlle in the Ceredigion countryside and became a priest in 1735. Rowland converted to Methodism in 1735, the same year as Harris, who had vowed to lead a new life having heard a sermon by Pryce Davies, the vicar of Talgarth, about partaking of the Lord's Supper.

There was more than a whiff of brimstone about the Methodists' preaching, warning as they did about the eternal torture and torment that was the lot of those who did not embrace Christ and his teachings. Thousands travelled to Llangeitho, dubbed the Jerusalem of Wales, to hear Rowland dramatically depict the boundless pain that awaited the unconverted. He was loquacious, articulate and erudite in a way that was accessible to the rural populace. Each sermon was a dramatic monologue. Transfixed by the preacher's words and manner, those in the congregation who saw the light, or heard the call, literally jumped in the air, as if electrified by the truth. On one famous occasion, these so-called 'jumpers' caused a chapel balcony to collapse.

Harris too made a meal of the Judgement Day that awaited recalcitrant sinners, even though his slightly scandalous relationship with one Madam Griffith of Cefnamwlch made him the subject of more day-to-day judgements. Just as with later revivals in Wales, such as that of 1904–5, there was an erotic undercurrent to the fervid actions of preacher and congregation, as if faith was triggered as much by hormones as by God.

Harris crossed and recrossed Wales tirelessly. A key meeting for him came when he met the man destined to be the third leader of the Methodist revival, William Williams Pantycelyn, who would also become one of Wales's finest hymn writers and the foremost literary figure of the eighteenth century. Williams's soaring, often anthemic songs of the spirit were to become the soundtrack to Methodist Sundays. Not for nothing would he be called *Y Pêr Ganiedydd*, 'the sweet singer'. His songs were conduits for both Old Testament and New Testament thinking, and through their catchy tunes and words could guide his increasing flock to safe pasturage. 'Guide Me O Thou Great Jehovah', he would implore.

William Williams had originally planned to become a doctor and had embarked on a course of studies at the dissenting academy at Llanigon. On hearing Howell Harris preach in a nearby Talgarth churchyard, however, he saw the divine light. Although he became a deacon in 1740, his work with the *seiadau*, or fellowship meetings, meant that he was denied any opportunity of becoming a priest.

Williams penned an enormous number of hymns, no fewer than 800 of them, all shot through with raw and uncomplicated emotion, and adorned with powerful biblical imagery. But his writing wasn't confined to hymns; he also published almost 90 other works, including long poems such as *Golwg ar Deyrnas Crist*, which was a survey of Christ's kingdom, and *Bywyd a Marwolaeth Theomemphus*, an account of the journey of a soul from a reprobate condition to final redemption. Williams also found time to pen a vast history of world religions, the *Pantheologia, neu Hanes Holl Grefyddau'r Byd*, a guide to marriage, *Ductor Nuptiarum*, and *Templum Experientiae Apertum*, which collected his thoughts about his ministry.

Because of Rowland, Harris and Williams, a distinctive type of Protestantism emerged in Wales. It claimed to be 'of the people ' – a genuinely popular movement that captured hearts and minds.

Religion and education became inextricably linked when Harris met Griffith Jones, rector of Llanddowror in Carmarthenshire, in 1736. Jones played a vital role in the Welsh education system, ensuring democratic access to literacy just as surely as his contemporaries spread the good word. It is perhaps no coincidence that the hubs of Methodist activity corresponded with the areas that had greatest preponderance of schools set up by Jones.

Up until the 1730s, there had not been enough literacy in Welsh to support book-based Protestantism. Griffith Jones set up a system of schools to teach people to read, and it proved to be phenomenally successful. Even though he was himself a gifted and eloquent preacher, Jones thought that literacy would give people a different kind of access to the Bible, a personal empowerment. And he was right in his assumptions because the growth of literacy dovetailed with the dynamic expansion of Methodism.

In 1737 Jones devised a system of travelling schools, which aimed to do nothing more ambitious than allow the rural population to be able read the Bible and the catechism in Welsh. Jones harnessed the enthusiasm of men and women, who would set up instant schools in farm and church buildings.

His efforts also helped the Welsh language too, and it is more than slightly ironic that this work was funded in the main by English gentlefolk. To ensure the flow of patronage, Griffith Jones detailed his work and its myriad successes, and defended the rationale of teaching through the medium of Welsh in an annual report, *Welch Piety*.

Less than 40 years after instigating the scheme, it was possible to tally that over 200,000 had attended the circulating schools, a number that equated pretty much with half the population at the time. This vast number of young and adult scholars had been educated in 3,225 schools in 1,600 locations. News of Jones's scheme travelled as far as Russia, and Empress Catherine the Great sent inspectors in 1764 to analyse his grassroots crusade with a view to replicating it in Russia. After his death, the work was carried on by his confidante and patron Madam Bridget Bevan. Charity schools and newly licensed printing presses built on the emergence of a book-reading public.

By the 1740s, the rise in literacy and Methodism had released a new energy in Welsh society. By the mid-nineteenth century, mass religious zeal would reach its peak, mirroring the dizzy rise of industrialized Wales.

Philosophy, politics and literature also experienced a surge of new energy. There was revolution in the air, both in mainland Europe and in America, as intellectuals discussion themselves hoarse with talk of equality, fraternity and democracy.

The county of Glamorgan, thrumming to the soundtrack of new foundries and heavy metal industry, produced two major international philosophers: Dr Richard Price, born in Llangeinor, and David Williams, a native of Caerphilly. Both Price and Williams were outward-looking thinkers, with a sense of far horizons.

Price was a moral philosopher, preacher and pamphleteer. The son of a Dissenting minister, Price received his education at an assortment of Dissenting academies before moving to London, where he held a pastorate at the famous Hackney Academy. He won a name for himself as a prolific Unitarian thinker – rejecting the idea of God as Trinity – and a supporter of the Americans during the American War of Independence (1775–83). His pamphlet *Observations on the Nature of Civil Liberty* sold 60,000 copies after it first appeared in 1776, and it was reprinted a dozen times in that very same year, a year, of course, that witnessed the Declaration of Independence. Price argued that each community had the inherent right to govern itself, that MPs were just the trustees of their electors' wishes, and that to run counter to this was tantamount to treason – opinions that found a ready audience in the new America. He was given many honours, including the Freedom of the City of London and an LLD (Doctor of Laws) in the sole company of George Washington from Yale. When Price died in 1791, the new French National Assembly felt duty bound to enter a period of official mourning for him.

David Williams's writings about religious freedom and education resonated in France, where his advice was sought on matters of democracy, and he was made a citizen of the New French Republic. Of particular note were his *Letters on Political Liberty*, which came out in 1782 and argued a similar role for MPs as set out by Price – sophisticated political thinking that predated the demands of the Chartists.

This was a time when newspapers were the vehicles of political education, but it was also a period that saw a burgeoning in book production. In the 1760s there were some 230 books in Welsh; 30 years later there were nearly 500 such tomes. Bodies such as the Cowbridge Book Society busily distributed the latest volumes, while a bookseller in Merthyr took weekly consignments to London. Native printing presses, coupled with the publishing efforts of the London

Welsh, energized poets and balladeers, historians and political pamphleteers.

Wales also helped light up the intellectual life of London and other English cities, and key Welsh figures delved back into the past to establish the tradition, the ancient dignity and identity of the Welsh.

Edward Lhuyd, keeper of Oxford's Ashmolean Museum, did pioneering work on science, Celtic history and languages. Indeed, this illegitimate son of an Oswestry squire combined scientific observation, wide travel and a logical approach in the *Archaeologica Britannica* of 1707, which was to become the basis of all later studies of Celtic languages. Meanwhile, under the influence of the Morris brothers of Anglesey and their circle of scholars, the Honourable Society of Cymmrodorion was set up in London in 1751. It published ancient texts that linked the Welsh to the ancient Britons, and investigated prehistoric links.

There was a touch of Celtomania in the air of the London salons and societies where Edward Williams, a remarkably many-sided stonemason who was better known by his bardic name Iolo Morganwg (Edward of Glamorgan), was busy conjuring up a new past for his own country, or at least giving it new meaning and resonance, between 1773 and 1774. Iolo Morganwg was steadfast in his belief that the Welsh were the most important people in the British Isles, and that they could trace an unbroken line back to the Druids. Seldom has Wales seen a writer who was so prolific over so long a period. Even as an old man, he could be found giving lectures in Merthyr about the history of metallurgy.

Iolo Morganwg took enormous delight in reading and acquiring the works of local poets and lexicographers, such as Thomas Richards and John Walters, and especially in imitating their work. He was an avid copyist and collector of manuscripts.

He seemed to be addicted to words, but from a relatively early age he had found another addiction, namely laudanum, a tincture of opium that he used to relieve chronic asthma. There are echoes here of the life of another Romantic, Samuel Taylor Coleridge, who became so addicted to laudanum that he had to move in with the doctor treating him for his addiction, or with those other poetic addicts George Crabbe and Thomas de Quincey. Despite, or arguably with the help of, opiates, Iolo Morganwg found energy to embrace an encyclopedic range of enthusiasms: folk music, geology, gardening, architecture, botany and theology. Even reading about his interests is somewhat exhausting, and he himself had to concede, 'I have always had too many irons in the fire.'[1]

The eighteenth-century revival in literature and antiquarianism proved to be a personal touchstone for Iolo Morganwg, and he started to compose his own verse in Welsh and English. At some stage it occurred to him that he could add to the already impressive legacy of the past. Thus *Barddoniaeth Dafydd ap Gwilym*, or 'The Poetry of Dafydd ap Gwilym', published by the Gwyneddigion in 1789, the year of the French Revolution featured 'newly discovered' poems, written by Morganwg himself, which appeared in an appendix to the poems written by Owain Myfyr and William Owen Pughe. Iolo Morganwg also published an anthology of his English poems, *Poems, Lyrics and Pastoral*, in 1794, and was one of the editors of the highly influential three-volume *The Myvyrian Archaiology of Wales* (1801–7).

Iolo Morganwg was also deeply committed to the cause of radical religious and political dissent. He liked to be called 'Bard of Liberty', and his circle of friends and acquaintances widened to include Thomas Paine, author of the *Rights of Man*; Thomas Hardy, founder of the London Corresponding Society; David Williams, the philosopher and political activist; Horne Tooke, the philologist and politician; and John Thelwall, the political orator and elocutionist. Iolo befriended many leading Unitarians in London, including Joseph Priestley, Andrew Kippis and Theophilus Lindsey, all of whom were deeply impressed by his agile mind and humanitarian principles. Iolo Morganwg was complicated and charismatic and some, such as the historian Geraint H. Jenkins, go so far as to describe Iolo Morganwg as 'arguably the most gifted, complex and intriguing figure in the annals of Welsh culture'.[2]

But there was a shadow looming on the horizon, a cloud to dampen the enthusiasm and dismantle the self-belief of a God-fearing and Welsh-speaking people.

After this Age of Enlightenment, of religious and political populist thought, of the enduring hymns of William Williams Pantycelyn, not to mention the work of the indefatigable Iolo Morganwg to glorify Welsh culture, the work of another William Williams, during the nineteenth century, might come as a surprise. While men such as Richard Price, David Williams, Edward Lhuyd and Iolo Morganwg conducted a liberal trade in ideas with the world, they were exceptions. Radicals weren't numerous and belonged in the main to the 'left wing' of Nonconformity.

William Williams, a successful businessman, Welsh speaker and avowedly radical MP, stood up in the House of Commons in March 1846 and made a speech. The burden of it was that the government had done nothing to help the Welsh learn English, and Williams asked for a commission to address this lack of provision.

William Williams came from a rural background in Llanpump-
saint, Cardiganshire, as poor as Iolo Morganwg's in the Vale of
Glamorgan. Williams worked his way up from draper's assistant in
London to become a wholesaler in linens, and ascribed much of his
success to learning English.

He saw the Welsh as educationally and linguistically disadvan-
taged in comparison with, say, the Irish and the Scots, and saw the
English language as a passport to success, a means to law and order
and 'the only road to knowledge ... the road to improvement and civilization' which would spread 'the arts and comforts of civilized life
among the poor Welshmen, which while it improves the face of their
beautiful country, will make them a more happy, a less servile – a
superior people'.[3]

In response, Williams was given a three-man team of English
Anglican barristers, appointed to 'enquire into the state of education ... in Wales, especially into the means afforded to the labouring
classes of acquiring a knowledge of the English language'.[4] Their
credentials didn't exactly dovetail with the job: they knew no
Welsh, understood precious little about Nonconformity, or indeed
about education.

The inspectors each covered and reported on different parts of
Wales. Ralph Robert Wheeler Lingen covered Glamorgan, Pembrokeshire and Carmarthenshire, where he found that 30,000 children were
taught in day schools and 80,000 attended Sunday schools. Jellinger
Symons chronicled the situation in Brecknockshire, Cardiganshire,
Radnorshire and Monmouthshire, while Henry Johnson looked at
north Wales, which basically included everywhere else not included in
the preceding two reports. The three inspectors and their assistants

threw themselves into the task with enormous energy, amassing gargantuan volumes of evidence so that their resulting report, bound into three volumes, contained no fewer than 1,252 pages. It became known as the Blue Books.

Much of their evidence was based on confused answers to complicated questions that were inadequately translated to the children they met, but there was little doubt that education was in a parlous state. On their wedding day almost half the bridegrooms in Wales couldn't spell their own names. In the day schools, by and large, Welsh-speaking children were taught in English by teachers who couldn't speak Welsh. Some schools, it was revealed, contained no more than a third of the children between five and ten years of age who should have been in class.

The Welsh language, it was concluded, was the main cause of these profound failings. Jellinger Symons's devastating critique is oft-quoted and no less lacerating for that:

> *The Welsh language is a vast drawback to Wales, and a manifold barrier to the moral progress and commercial prosperity of its people. It is not easy to over-estimate its evil effects. It is the language of the Cymri, and anterior to that of the ancient Britons. It dissevers the people from intercourse which would help advance their civilization, and bars the access of improving knowledge to their minds. As proof of this, there is no Welsh literature worthy of the name.*[5]

Nonconformity was labelled as the other root cause of Wales's ills. When Symons visited the mid-Wales town of Tregaron, he concluded that:

Welsh Methodism sprung [sic] from this immediate neighbour-
hood, though its spread has been so extensive of late years that
neither this place nor Llangeitho can be said to present any pecu-
liar characteristics or results of Methodist instruction. I think the
extreme filthiness of the habits of the poor, though observable
everywhere, are as striking in this place, if not more so, than else-
where, inasmuch as in a town it might be expected that a little
more of the outward observances of cleanliness and decency
would be met with.[6]

The reports also portrayed the Welsh, especially women, as a deeply immoral people. The newspaper, the *Morning Chronicle*, commenting on the Blue Books, went so far as to call for the extinction of the Welsh.

The reports concluded with a recommendation that the government's intervention to stem any further decline should include establishing a comprehensive network of English-medium elementary schools.

The effect of the publication of the reports went beyond the initial sting of the criticism. It plunged people into a deep morass of shame. But it also set off a series of counter-attacks from the likes of Thomas Phillips, the mayor of Newport in 1839, and most notably in a lampooning play by R. J. Derfel called *Brad y Llyfrau Gleision* (The Treachery of the Blue Books), which captured the public's outraged mood and acted as a ready conduit for collective rage.

The Anglican clergy, hoping to undermine the Nonconformist movement, were seen in general to have encouraged the reports, but there were some members of the Church, such as the Dean of Bangor, J. H. Cotton, who were sufficiently outraged by the Blue Books that they attacked them, adding their voices to the strident clamour of the backlash. And of course the Nonconformists reacted strongly. The Congregationalist minister and journalist M. P. Henry Richard made loquacious speeches, while the journalist Ieuan Gwynedd penned passionate and lucid essays.

But in these days of empire, many in Wales nudged ever closer to the way the commissioners thought, believing that in order to be a country of progress, the people should learn English and embrace English ways.

One of the other by-products of the education reports was a growth in a protective kind of nationalism, one that spawned new institutions to defend the nation from criticism. New institutions were created to counter the Blue Books, from the Cambrian Archaeological Association, established in 1846, to the new Baptist and Independent Unions formed alongside the Methodists. Together they added to the already authoritative tone of Welsh Dissent, eloquently expressed in a new song, 'Hen Wlad Fy Nhadau', destined to become the national anthem.

Of the three verses, only one is usually sung.

Mae hen wlad fy nhadau yn annwyl i mi.
Gwlad beirdd a chantorion, enwogion o fri,
Ei gwrol ryfelwyr, gwladgarwyr tra mad,
Dros ryddid collasant ei gwaed.

The old land of my fathers is dear to me,
Land of poets and singers, famous and renowned;
Her brave warriors, patriots so fine,
For freedom they shed their blood.

As a people, the Welsh had been stung by the treachery of the Blue Books, but there was further ignominy ahead. The Welsh *Not* (note), a piece of wood hung as a plaque around the neck of a child who had the temerity to utter any Welsh words in class, was the physical expression of a widespread attempt to stigmatize Welsh as a backward language.

Many people all over Wales wanted to answer the criticism in the Blue Books by simply improving the overall standard of education and they campaigned long and hard to establish state-run secondary schools throughout the country. In 1889 their diligence and agitation paid off. A new law was passed in Westminster called the Welsh Intermediate Education Act, which facilitated the creation of such schools, but with one crucial and damaging proviso, namely that all the teaching should be conducted in the English language.

And so after the Age of Enlightenment, during which Wales provided globally celebrated political and religious figureheads, composers who celebrated the native language, and scholars who treasured Welsh history and literature and added to its rich store, the Welsh language was set to be knocked off its perch. The work of Griffith Jones in promoting Welsh-language education was now frowned upon by so-called progressives among the Welsh middle class. The Welsh were expected to embrace the English language even at the expense of their own native tongue.

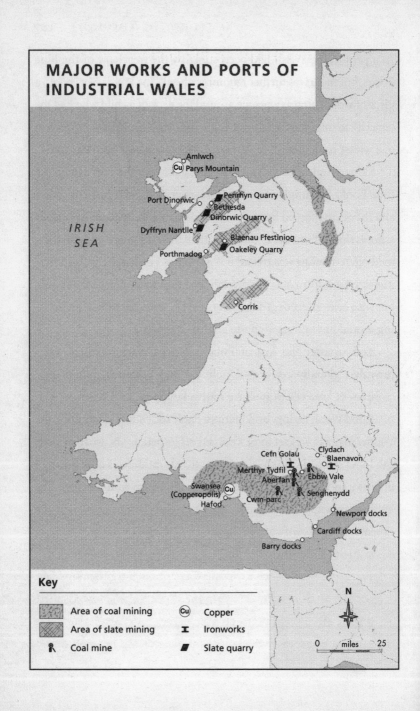

MAJOR WORKS AND PORTS OF INDUSTRIAL WALES

Amlwch
Cu Parys Mountain

Port Dinorwic
Penrhyn Quarry
Bethesda
Dinorwic Quarry
Dyffryn Nantlle
Blaenau Ffestiniog
Oakeley Quarry
Porthmadog

IRISH SEA

Corris

Cefn Golau
Clydach
Blaenavon
Merthyr Tydfil
Ebbw Vale
Aberfan
Swansea (Copperopolis) Cu
Senghenydd
Hafod
Cwm-parc
Newport docks
Cardiff docks
Barry docks

Key

Area of coal mining
Area of slate mining
Coal mine
Cu Copper
Ironworks
Slate quarry

N

0   miles   25

CHAPTER SIXTEEN

THE RISE OF INDUSTRY

The foundries, mines and manufactories of the Industrial Revolution would move Wales from the periphery of events to centre stage, creating incredible wealth – even if it was unfairly distributed – not to mention plentiful job opportunities for the thousands and thousands of people drawn to the pits and ironworks, and the new towns that accreted around them. Coal, slate, copper and iron, along with a slew of other metals, had been mined and refined in Wales over the centuries, but now new technologies for their extraction and manufacture sped up the juggernaut processes of industrialization.

A 1791 engraving by Thomas Rothwell, showing the Forest Copper Works in Morriston, depicts no fewer than 25 stacks pumping dense smoke into the air, turning the sky inkily dark. By the next century there would be some 20 copperworks in the lower Swansea valley, with other metals worked nearby.

Just as copper had dramatically changed Bronze Age Wales, in modern times (along with coal), the metal quickly ushered in a golden age for places such as Swansea. It grew at a tremendous rate and made a lot of money for a handful of people. The town gained the nickname 'Copperopolis', and the name stuck, just as surely as the landscape was to be disfigured for generations by spoil, smog and slag.

Many of the copper mines of Wales often sprang up alongside coal-mining areas. Neath had a smelter, able to process 520 tons of ore a week, and worked under the Mines Royal Society as early as 1584. The area consolidated its reputation for copper-working from the early 1700s, when pioneers such as John Lane from Bristol set up a smelter at Landore. Indeed, working metals such as copper, zinc and nickel was a major industry along a swathe of coast between Cydweli and Port Talbot, and at the centre of it all was 'Copperopolis'. At its apogee this stretch of the south Wales coast was the hub of copper production for the whole of Britain, boasting as much as 90 per cent of its total production in the eighteenth and nineteenth centuries.

From 1845, the British Navy plumped for copper-bottomed ships (hence the term 'copper-bottomed' for anything that is secure or reliable), the Royal Mint favoured copper for manufacturing coinage, and housewives opted for copper saucepans – all of which created a soaring demand. Soon copper ore had been discovered in many countries, and it was subsequently imported from harbours such as Burra and Adelaide in South Australia, Valparaiso in Chile, and from Santiago de Cuba in eastern Cuba, where slaves toiled underground to extract the raw material. Companies such as the East India Company made sure they were involved in this lucrative copper trade.

The deregulation of metal mining by the Crown towards the end of the seventeenth century triggered the reopening and reworking of disused mines in mid and north Wales. The scale of such enterprises was sometimes staggering: the workings on Parys Mountain and in Mona mines on Anglesey made it unequivocally the biggest production centre for copper in the world by the latter stages of the eighteenth century, when its enormous seams were worked very hard and comprehensively.

Parys Mountain was originally named Mynydd Trysglwyn, but it was renamed in 1406 after Robert Parys the younger, a royal fine collector working for Henry IV, whose job it was to extract money from over 2,000 islanders who had had the temerity to support Owain Glyndŵr's revolt. The king gave Parys the land without realizing it had subterranean treasure, thereby giving away one of the most precious parcels of land in his realm.

After copper was discovered on Parys Mountain, the nearby port of Amlwch became Wales's fifth biggest parish when an influx of people arrived to work the mines. By the census year of 1801, it had 5,000 inhabitants compared with Cardiff's relatively meagre 1,809. It also became the biggest copper-exporting harbour in the world. The mining here used up 15,000 tons of gunpowder in 1815 alone, blasting away the landscape and replacing it with a moonscape. The creation of this 'stupendous gulch, its sides aglow with orange and yellow tints', as historian John Davies puts it, also led to the crowning of Anglesey attorney Thomas Williams of Llanidan, the owner of the copper workings of Parys Mountain, as 'the Copper King'.[1]

Williams built warehouses, offices, roasting kilns and smelters, turning a local industry into a global enterprise. He exported ore to Swansea and to the coal-rich Greenfield valley in Flintshire. By 1780 the yawning chasms formed the largest mine in the world, producing 3,000 tons of ore each year and employing 1,500 men and women, while Williams was the one-man dominant force in world copper from about 1788 until his death in 1802.

Not that everybody saw him in the same regal light. Those who toiled at the Parys mines were not treated at all fairly. They were not paid for their first month of work, and their small subsistence was quickly swallowed up when they had to buy their own chisels, powders, fuses, hammers and candles at exorbitant prices from the company stores. The workforce were paid half the amount received by Cornish workers and by the late eighteenth century they were not paid in real money at all, as the owners were minting their own copper tokens instead of coins of the realm. These weren't deemed illegal until 1817.

Thus in the north and south these were pioneering and transformative years when the country's first integrated global industry came into being, ushering in a period when Wales could be fairly described as the first industrialized nation in the world.*

Some of the magnates of the Cornish mines, such as the Vivians, poured money into new ventures in places such as Neath and Swansea – money they had made by harnessing steam to reach ore supplies deep underground. Not only did these entrepreneurs create work, but they also brought a degree of civic pride and urban sophistication. Workers' housing was properly planned rather than jerry-built. The Victorian Gothic-style Singleton Abbey, now part of Swansea University, was built as a mansion for John Henry Vivian. Today's city still has the Glynn Vivian art gallery, built to house the extensive collections of John's fourth son, Richard Glynn Vivian.

---

* The United Nations determines the status of 'industrial nations' by comparing the numbers of people who work in industry (such as mining, processing, manufacturing and transportation) with those who work in agriculture. When the numbers in industry outweigh those in agriculture, a nation can be defined as industrialized. The 1851 census suggests that this happened in Wales before anywhere else. For more information, see Further Reading, page 351.

But gradually other countries discovered their own coal resources, enabling smelters to be built nearer the sources of ore in South America and Australia. So a slow, steady decline began in Wale's copper industry. Even then, the last of the copperworks in Swansea, the Hafod works – established by John Vivian in 1810 and finally owned by Yorkshire Imperial Metals – closed its doors as recently as 1981. In its heyday this had been quite simply the largest copperworks in the world.

The impact on Swansea was very clearly seen in the town's demographic profile in 1801. It had the biggest population centre in Wales, and the wealth generated even made it fashionable: an observer in 1786 said, 'Swansea, in point of spirit, fashion, and politeness has become the Brighton of Wales'. [2]

Despite such favourable reviews, Swansea was at the mercy of the poisonous fumes, a veritable fog of sulphuric acid mixed with arsenic, that were the by-products of the copper plants. The 'Brighton of Wales' had to request an Act of Parliament that moved copper production to the lower Swansea valley, away from the town centre, but even then the problem was not eradicated. Breathing problems were experienced as far away as Neath, and generally weakened people's constitutions so that they were more vulnerable to other diseases, such as tuberculosis.

The copper masters were also spin doctors, arguing that the smoke wasn't injurious to health, but rather that it was good for the constitution. A report to the Board of Health by a local doctor, Thomas Williams in 1854, claimed that the presence of copper smoke was in fact extremely beneficial, since its antiseptic properties acted as a protective cordon to keep disease at bay. [3]

The copper industry showed Welsh inventiveness and connectedness to a wider world. It showcased an ability to sustain innovation through technical skills and engineering. But the copper industry didn't create the same large communities that iron-working did, or that coal would most certainly do: non-ferrous smelting kept fewer than 4,000 people in work even in its heyday. Most of the investment came from English entrepreneurs, particularly from Bristol – figures such as Vivian and Watt, and characters such as Chauncey Townsend, who set up the Middle Bank Works.

The Vivian family, who had their roots in Cornwall, kept strict control on every stage of the process, from the extraction through the smelting to the final marketing of the product. The Welsh were mainly relegated to the position of workers, and hard-pressed workers at that, harnessed to other people's interests. Soon the copper of Anglesey was exhausted, just as foreign countries managed to become geared up for manufacturing copper themselves. By the 1880s copper was in decline.

Luckily, there was another metal waiting in the wings. Some copperworks became zincworks, and in areas such as the upper Swansea valley, nickel was also produced. The history of zinc manufacture was also considerable, with the plant established by the Imperial Smelting Company in 1876 working for over a century. As well as zinc, Alfred Mond and his three sons created the largest nickel plant in the world in Clydach. This went into production in 1902, working ore that was imported across the Atlantic from Canada, and is one of the few metal plants in the Swansea valley still working today.

Metal smelting had taken off in Bersham as early as the 1720s, and fortunes were made by providing artillery for Britain's eighteenth-century wars. A small coalfield sprang up around Wrexham, while the digging of a network of canals was key to reaching the ports of the Mersey. Thomas Telford was a major figure in developing the transport infrastructure of north Wales. The Pontcysyllte Aqueduct, designed by him and finished in 1805, remains a thrilling construction in the landscape.

The perfect combination of natural resources in the southern coalfield made the ironworks of Merthyr one of the largest manufacturing concerns in the world. Indeed, during the eighteenth century, a time of multifarious wars, the British Empire, not to mention belligerent overseas customers, craved iron. The entrepreneurs of Merthyr, such as the Crawshays of Cyfarthfa and the Guests of Dowlais, geared themselves up to deal with the demand. By the mid-nineteenth century there were no fewer than 26 ironworks smelting over a third of Britain's pig iron.

Dowlais employed 5,000 people in 1850. Capital investment in the Welsh iron trade allowed it to stay ahead of its competitors, so it was able to feed the hungry maw of a new consumer: the railways of Britain and the world, which welcomed the fact that Welsh works were able to supply the heavy bar iron necessary for laying tracks. Indeed Wales supplied most of the world's burgeoning railways.

In 1802 Admiral Nelson paid a personal visit to Cyfarthfa ironworks, drawing huge crowds amidst the smoke and fire. The naval hero was struck by the gigantic water wheel, known as 'Helios', which powered the works and was considered by some to be the eighth wonder of the world. By 1811 the Cyfarthfa ironworks were the wealthiest in the world, with seven furnaces producing 18,000 tons of iron, and all part of a network of iron mines, collieries, limestone quarries and kilns. They were so renowned that one day two crates arrived from Italy containing Italian iron ore sent by Napoleon, who enquired whether it might be possible to smelt it in Wales. Unfortunately, this was just before his defeat at the Battle of Waterloo in 1815, so the iron was never processed at Cyfarthfa.

While the southeast of Wales produced bar iron and rail tracks, the northeast, at places such as John Wilkinson's Bersham Ironworks, manufactured cylinders for beam engines. The nearby Bersham and Brymbo works produced cannons to be used in the French wars.

Moving metal was hard work, so the ironmasters created canals to replace the travails of heavily-laden pack animals. Some of these involved sophisticated hydrology: the Glamorgan Canal had a series of no fewer than 16 locks as it passed through Abercynon. Canals formed a necessary network. The Glamorgan Canal was complemented by the Monmouthshire Canal, and each in turn was complemented by horse-drawn tram roads and branch canals.

Merthyr grew swiftly, sucking in migrants from all over Wales, Ireland, England and Scotland. It was a place of tough tasks and notoriously dangerous work. At the height of its prosperity it became notorious for its hideously deformed beggars and its crippled and blind musicians. A Merthyr surgeon in 1809 even used the risks of health and safety to advertise his practice, emphasizing that 'the situation is in the immediate neighbourhood of an ironworks and subsequently has the advantage of a very extensive practice'.[4]

Injury was a part of iron-making, and the working life of the average puddler, or iron-worker, was usually over by the time he was 40, with men often going blind after years of looking at the white light of the furnaces. There were also many other hazards to contend with, such as rivulets of molten iron, burning coals and boilers of scalding water. The thunderous machinery took a grim toll of lost and crushed limbs almost casually.

Workers were forced to live cheek-by-jowl in exceedingly cramped conditions. Skilled workers could expect to have a house with four rooms, while unskilled workers might have a house with only two. Sub-letting meant that living space was even more cramped, with maybe a dozen people sharing four rooms in a tiny cottage. Houses were in such short supply that unscrupulous speculators threw up new buildings in next to no time, and in these miserable hovels poverty and squalor were natural bedfellows.

The buildings themselves were often nothing more than wooden or stone huts built on top of piles of slag or human waste. These were some of the first slums in Wales, and in 1841 around 1,500 people were living amid crime, filth and perpetual misery in Merthyr. Gangs formed in the slums, whose gang leaders were known as 'Emperors'. Young thieves, pimps or bullies were known as 'rodnies', while prostitutes were known as 'nymphs'. It was no place for strangers. It even had a 'Forbidden City'.

With so many people crammed into insanitary conditions – human waste was slopped onto the streets on a daily basis – it was little wonder that a panoply of diseases affected the populace, from typhoid to dysentery. But there was one disease among all others that struck fear into the heart of these teeming, squalid communities: cholera.

Merthyr suffered various outbreaks in the early nineteenth century, and other communities suffered too. At Cefn Golau, outside Tredegar, 235 victims of cholera outbreaks were buried. Cholera had been around in Wales for some time, but this ruthless, indiscriminate killer was able to capitalize on the lack of hygiene and clean water, moving quickly through the slums. Whole families might be fit and healthy in the morning, but struck dead by the end of the day.

In 1849, some 1,800 lives were lost to cholera in Merthyr, the victims suffering vomiting, diarrhoea and cramps before dying after several hours of excruciating pain. The *Merthyr Express* in October 1849 gave an update: 'The Cholera is still raging very bad here: there were 30 funerals here on Monday, 16 in the churchyard at the same time … The Parish hearse is going about all day… no less than 36 parish orders for coffins were given at Merthyr last week.'

A small watercolour called *Rolling Mills* by Thomas Hornor, dating from about 1817, shows the skies above Merthyr lit up by shafts of orange light emanating from the metal-smelting furnaces. There is a sufficiently infernal glow to make the iron-workers in the yard seem slightly luminous, or suggest that the owners of the mills, the Craw-shays – who owned the Cyfarthfa works – had managed to turn night into day. Or it might be that the smoke, rising in billowing clouds, is thick enough to blot out the sun. In any case, it is a striking image, especially in light of the fact that Hornor found a ready market for his images of industrial scenes among the gentry of Glamorgan, selling no fewer than 400 watercolours, which kept him in gainful employ-ment for four years.

Cyfarthfa castle, built in 1825 by the ironworks owner William Crawshay II, is a testament to the wealth generated by the iron indus-try in Merthyr. Now a school and museum, it was so ostentatious at the time of building that William's father almost wrote him out of his will, seeing his son as being too extravagant. It was an architectural confection with mock battlements, 15 towers and 72 rooms, includ-ing a lavish ballroom. When William's son Robert Crawshay married Rose Mary Yates, a holiday was declared and a thousand guests invited, including the workers, who enjoyed 10,000 quarts of beer, 16 main dishes, seven sweets and six different desserts, with the dancing continuing until dawn.

Cyfarthfa was the home of invention: John Hughes, the son of a Cyfarthfa engineer, devised a naval fitting for heavy guns that was so successful he was able to establish his own ironworks in Donetzk in the Ukraine, renamed Hughesovka in Hughes's honour. Merthyr historian, Gwyn A. Williams, suggested that when Anna Karenina laid her head down on the railway tracks at the end of Tolstoy's novel that she would have been doing so on iron that had come from Wales!

Men ran all of these enterprises and it would be several generations before women were able to join them, but some women did play a direct part in the metal trades. Lady Charlotte Guest managed the Dowlais Ironworks after the death of her husband John in 1852, while the Llangrannog-born poet and editor Sarah Jane Rees, also known as Cranogwen, worked on her father's boats around the copper ports near Swansea, and travelled to Brittany and Holland. There was also Swansea-born Amy Dillwyn, the granddaughter of the industrialist, botanist and first president of the Royal Institution of South Wales, Lewis Weston Dillwyn. Amy became a very successful novelist, writing about political subjects such as the anti-tollgate Rebecca Riots, which she depicted in her 1880 novel *The Rebecca Rioter*. Dillwyn, who spent most of her life in Swansea, was an early campaigner for votes for women and ran the Dillwyn Spelter Works after the death of her father.

While copper was at one time supremely dominant among north Wales exports, one of the products most commonly associated with the area was slate, hewn from the Great Slate Belt of central Caernarfonshire and north Merioneth. It was a localized industry driven by water-power and the adventitious arrival of the railways to transport such a heavy material from the quarries to the sea, and, in turn, open up what were previously remote mountain areas. Narrow-gauge railways were constructed from Penrhyn to the sea at Port Penrhyn, from Dinorwic to Port Dinorwic, or Y Felinheli, and down from Blaenau Ffestiniog to Porthmadog, where a fleet of local slate ships had a reputation for speed on the high seas. The port of Porthmadog itself was created specifically to serve the needs of the slate industry. The slate taken from these ports was then transported by rail and cart all over Britain, especially to the north of England and beyond. 'Beyond' included Germany, an important market after fire destroyed the city of Hamburg in 1842. From a relatively modest 2,000 tons in 1782, slate production rose to over 130,000 tons in 1862, bolstered by the repeal of slate duty in 1831.

Slate was mainly used as a roofing material, although it also had myriad other uses, such as fencing, writing surfaces, pencils, laboratory work surfaces, blackboards, billiard tables and gravestones.

There were slate quarries throughout northwest Wales. Samuel Horner, a Lancashire businessman who would later become a Liberal MP, managed to turn the barren slopes of Blaenau Ffestiniog into a thriving township after he moved there from Liverpool in 1821. Money flowed into slate, with investors such as Nathan Rothschild venturing capital, and in Dyffryn Nantlle a well-known Nonconformist, John Jones Tal-y-sarn, actively pursued numerous slate ventures.

However, the largest was the Penrhyn quarry, started by Liverpool merchant prince Richard Pennant in the early 1780s. It was the largest handmade hole on the surface of the Earth at the end of the 1800s, and for all of the nineteenth century it led the world in the production of slate. Such a quarry replaced what had been, until then, the province of small family businesses. Pennant had made much of his fortune as a consequence of the slave trade and the wealth generated by West Indian sugar plantations.

The owners of the quarries could chalk up huge profits on their slates. In 1859 the net annual income at Penrhyn was a staggering £100,000 (£4.5 million in present-day values), while the estate itself was the third largest in the whole of Wales. Penrhyn castle was built on slate money in 1837 and came complete with a gargantuan slate four-poster bed made especially for the visit of Queen Victoria and 'rooms like crematoria'[5] set within an estate that would encompass no fewer than 72,000 acres by the 1790s. In the grounds of the castle a statue of Richard Pennant was erected with a motto proclaiming that 'he improved the condition of the peasantry, exciting them to habits of industry by employment'.

The Pennant family, bloated with profit, were able to graduate from wealthy business folk to mock aristocracy when Edward Gordon Douglas Pennant was ennobled in 1866, becoming Baron Penrhyn of Llandygái. Thus it was a Lord Penrhyn who built roads, schools, houses and churches, although magnanimity was traded for animosity when his cold attitude to the slate-workers led to the longest dispute in the industrial history of Britain, a bitter lock-out that lasted for three years between 1900 and 1903 and attracted national attention.

As production in the northwest increased, so too did the work-force, which tripled from 1,000 men in 1820 to 3,000 towards the end of the century, and this despite the increased use of technology. In the area as a whole the workforce had grown to 15,000 men by its heyday towards the end of the nineteenth century. Slate, like copper and iron, caused towns to boom. The parish of Ffestiniog saw its population quadruple in 30 years up to 1881. In Llanddeiniolen, between 1831 and 1841, there was an increase of 61 per cent, a rise mirrored in other parts of Caernarfonshire, which outstripped other parts of north Wales when it came to growth.

The way of life of the north Wales quarrymen was tough. Organized into work gangs or *criws*, which varied in size from two to 20, they worked long hours hewing away at huge blocks of slate with chisels and wedges to break them free from the surrounding rock face.

The workforce extracting and fashioning the slate was mainly Welsh-speaking, making it 'the most Welsh of Welsh industries' according to A. H. Dodd.[6] The men who worked there held cultural competitions known as *eisteddfodau* and discussed a wide range of books and pamphlets during their breaks.

One of the by-products of the slate industry was a slew of Welsh-language writers: indeed, the slate communities produced the majority of writers of significance of the twentieth century, including R. Williams Parry, Kate Roberts, Sir T. H. Parry-Williams, W. J. Gruffydd and Caradog Prichard, whose *Un Nos Ola Leuad* (*One Moonlit Night*) is arguably the finest modern prose work in Welsh.

An amalgam of materials drawn from the Earth helped turn Wales into the world's first industrial nation. While towns rapidly grew from the metal, slate and coal industries, by 1851 only a third of the Welsh population was working on the land, and agriculture had declined. Swathes of Wales began to fill with what seemed like instant communities. As rural folk decamped into new urban centres, it also marked the genesis of working-class Wales, with its own values and concerns.

Hard work toughened the people of Wales, and the vagaries of industry steeled them to disappointment, while also forcing them to be adaptable and transfer skills as industries boomed and declined.

CHAPTER SEVENTEEN

THE REIGN
OF KING COAL

Coal would totally transform parts of south and northeast Wales, just as much as slate would reconfigure the landscape of the northwest. Coal, the blackened, time-hardened and weight-compressed remains of fossilized plants, had been mined in Wales as far back as Roman times, when it was used for drying grain and lighting funeral pyres. There had been small coal mines, often just one simple tunnel or 'adit', in medieval times too, when this fossil fuel had been extracted in both Glamorgan and Flintshire. By the fifteenth century, rudimentary mines were fairly widespread in the country, with coal being used mainly for domestic purposes.

From as early as the sixteenth century, the black 'diamonds' were being exported from places such as Flintshire, Swansea and Pembrokeshire and sent to Ireland, France and the west of England. Coal was increasingly accepted as a house fuel, and became a staple of life in towns.

In the seventeenth century, the first proper pits were sunk in the middle of Glamorgan and Monmouthshire, presaging the growth of these areas as nothing short of titanic production centres later on. These mines were deeper than those of Tudor times, 360 feet as opposed to 100 feet, and the danger to workers increased with the extra depth. Roofs, always in danger of caving in, were held up by un-carved coal, using the so-called 'pillar-and-stall' method. Men, women and children scaled down rickety ladders in the pitch dark, and at the bottom they had only candlelight to see the coal, which would be hewn and moved by barrow and sledge. Seeping water led to serious problems of drainage until the advent of mechanical pumps in the early eighteenth century. There was gas too, which could kill without a whisper.

Denbighshire, Glamorgan and Flintshire saw new mines opening in the seventeenth century, and between 1638 and 1639 the Flintshire mines alone exported over 10,000 tons of the black stuff to Ireland. The shipments left from Chester, which was in those days one of the principal ports in the region.

The local gentry benefited, of course; the Myddelton family of Chirk owned coal mines at Brymbo and Rhos. In south Wales seams were busily being worked at production centres in Carmarthenshire and Pembrokeshire, and the Gower Peninsula, now an Area of Out-standing Natural Beauty, was riddled by a warren of small mines, as was the hinterland around Neath. Neath gentry, such as Bussy Mansel and William Phillips, were beneficiaries of overseas' demand, selling to Normandy, Brittany and the Channel Islands.

The first boom in the coal trade came in the eighteenth century, when the coalfields started extracting gargantuan quantities from deep under the Earth. Demand was fuelled in part by the needs of the burgeoning iron smelters around Merthyr and, further east, in Blae-navon. Technology drove many of the changes, such as Abraham Darby's success in smelting iron with coke at Coalbrookdale in 1709,

which was bolstered by demands for extra iron in times of war –
namely the Seven Years War, the American War of Independence, and
the French wars. By the late eighteenth century, coal had also replaced
timber as a fuel source for the iron manufactories, so the coalfields
had to expand. This required huge injections of capital, supplied by
entrepreneurs such as ironmasters Richard and William Crawshay,
Anthony Bacon and John Guest.

By 1828 the south Wales coalfields were producing 3 million tons
annually. Twelve years later this had risen to 4.5 million tons, with
half that amount being consumed by the rapacious appetites of the
various ironworks. In the south, new pits were opened seemingly by
the week to mine the anthracite coal in places such as the Gwendraeth
valley, and the softer steam coal found in the crimped and crenellated
southeastern valleys, such as Pontypool. In northeast Wales production was ratcheted up in areas such as Rhosllannerchrugog, Wrexham,
Gresford and Bersham.

The demand for housing for the colliers and their families led to
exponential growth in sprawling terraced houses, which hugged the
valley sides like strings of limpets. Pit-head wheels punctuated the
skyline, and slag heaps grew to create artificial hills.

Fleets of ships at sea became crucially important in the success
story. By the 1840s, coal, and in particular Welsh coal, became the fuel
of choice for the British Empire, the result of a little-known series of
laboratory experiments. Scientists based at the Admiralty in London
carried them out, keen to discover which variety of British coal was
best suited to fuelling the steam-driven ships of Queen Victoria's navy
– the largest and most formidable fighting force of the age. They
weighed, burned, crushed and measured coal samples from all over

the country, and it was Welsh coal that consistently came up trumps, resulting in the placing of huge bulk orders.

Soon, Aberdare's mines – bolstered by others in the southern valleys and connected to new port facilities at Cardiff – were supplying much of the British Navy's fuel. Before too long, the ships of other navies, from Russia to Japan, were also crossing the high seas and plying the oceans courtesy of supplies of Welsh coal.

John Crichton-Stuart, the second Marquess of Bute, was already one of Britain's richest landowners and a descendant of Scottish and English kings. He was as keen as can be to exploit the coal measures, and, to this end, took a huge gamble in creating and paying for a masonry dock in Cardiff in 1839. This would benefit from the Taff Vale Railway, the first major line in Wales, which opened in 1841 and connected Merthyr and the coal seams with the sea.

In 1848, John Crichton-Stuart died. The trustees looking after his wealth (until his son came of age) located a 1.22 metre (4 foot) seam of high-grade steam coal at Treherbert, near the head of the Rhondda Fawr, the larger of the two Rhondda river valleys. The Bute-Merthyr Pit opened in 1855, the first of a string of profitable Bute mines. The pit at Cwmsaerbren Farm was located in what were then rather remote reaches of the Rhondda: indeed the valleys of the Rhondda Fawr and Rhondda Fach rivers had only 1,000 inhabitants between them.

The Crichton-Stuart family was keen to get quick returns on land and mineral rights in their possession, so miners were swiftly housed in Treherbert, a town that was soon to become an important access point for the Taff Vale Railway, just as Ferndale was to the Rhondda Fach. The Rhondda was poised to outstrip the Cynon valley, as its deep shafts reached ever deeper into the darkness, down as far as 1.46 kilometres (4,800 feet) by the 1870s.

The coal travelled to the coast, fuelling Cardiff's growth. Cardiff had been a busy centre for exporting coal from the 1830s onwards, when Lucy Thomas sent coal from Abercanaid, a small village north of Cardiff, to London.

Lucy's mine-owner husband had died soon after opening a new mine in 1828, but along with her son, William, Lucy decided to keep the pit open, and eventually opened a series of others, including the eponymous Lucy Drift. Meanwhile, in London people had been beginning to express concern about the amount of smoke coming off Newcastle coal. In 1830, two coal merchants arranged to meet Lucy Thomas and offered to buy all she could supply for four shillings a ton. By the time it arrived in London, its price had increased to 14 shillings.

Moving coal, be it by road, canal or sea, was a lucrative affair. The docks at Cardiff, or rather the Bute West Dock, first created by the John Crichton-Stuart in 1839, grew to monumental importance. From here coal was sent to all four compass points, to South America and India and a host of far-flung destinations. The city grew to match the scale of imports and exports. The repeal of duty on coal carried by British ships in 1842 made this export even more attractive. But Cardiff was not without its rivals: Swansea, the port of departure for smokeless anthracite from the Amman and Gwendraeth valleys, grew to rival Cardiff for a while.

The growth of the coalfield, from the 1850s onwards, didn't simply put money in the pockets of already wealthy families such as the Crichton-Stuarts. It also gave the Welsh people as a whole a much-needed shot in the arm, for it had repercussions far beyond the export of coal. The mills of the Teifi valley were inundated with orders for warm, woollen clothes for the colliers. Tourism of a sort grew in the west as miners and their families visited the coastal resorts. It was even argued that in rural Wales the rate of marriage fluctuated in line with the price of coal.[1]

There was a cultural blossoming to accompany the wealth genera-tion. In the popular imagination Wales became, and still remains, the 'Land of Song', and the growth of the valleys' townships, and the deepening of their sense of community, was aided by *eisteddfodau*, cele-brations of the twin Welsh heritages of poetry and music, which flourished through the second half of the nineteenth century and during the first decades of the twentieth century. Even some of the smaller *eisteddfodau* were attended by substantial crowds, who enjoyed the opportunity to express their devotion to Wales and all things Welsh.

From the 1860s onwards they increasingly chose to do so by singing one particular parlour song, 'Hen Wlad Fy Nhadau', or 'Land of My Fathers'. Composed by the Pontypridd father and son team of Evan and James James, it had echoes of folk songs in the melody, coupled with heroic sentiment in the lyrics.

And central on the map of the Land of Song was the choir. Enthu-siastic hymn singing, not to mention monastic choirs, had been part of Welsh life for centuries, long before the first choral societies started to spring up in the early years of the coal boom, but the explosion of choral singing is remarkable nevertheless. In places such as the Rhondda, a surge of population also meant a prominence for the culture the incomers brought with them, which was often Non-conformist, with an emphasis on the chapel – itself a dominant form of entertainment, with something going on all the time, not just on Sundays.

Over the course of some 30 years, inspirational conductors such as Griffith Rhys Jones, better known as Caradog, whipped novice singers into single musical entities, able to tackle even the most ornate and complicated works, and garner fame throughout the UK. He led the South Wales Choral Union, which beat allcomers at the Crystal Palace two years running, a crucial moment in the creation of a choral nation, and helped to lay to rest the image of Wales as the backward country of the Blue Books.

Caradog may even have coined the phrase 'Land of Song', and it appealed to the Welsh. A competitive spirit in the late nineteenth century led rival choirs to tackle works of increasing difficulty, with test pieces of ambition and complexity, such as Handel's *Messiah*, being performed all over the valleys with the regularity of a railway clock. And because temperance was in the air – attempting to curb the excesses of drink – such choral competitions couldn't happen in pubs, which weren't big enough anyway, so they were always held in chapels.

There were up to 150 chapels in the Rhondda valleys by the end of the nineteenth century, with room for congregations up to 2,000 strong, so religious music went down well. Handel and Mendelssohn were prominent among the favourite composers of religious works, and the tonic sol-fa movement (a way of representing music in which every tone was given a name – do, re, mi, fa, sol, la, ti or do, according to its relationship with other tones in the key) made music more accessible, and the individual editions of the music itself that much cheaper.

In the nineteenth century a new form of singing, a Welsh *style* of singing, emerged that was dramatic, emotionally intense and literally articulate. New forms of transport facilitated moving large choirs around, and not just in Wales, as some of the choirs travelled abroad, especially to emigrant communities in America. They were also a palatable way of exploring and expressing local rivalries.

The crowds attending musical events often far outstripped those for sport: in 1893, when Wales won the rugby Triple Crown for the first time, they beat England in front of a crowd of 15,000; the same year there were 20,000 people enjoying the chief choral competitions at the National Eisteddfod, held that year in Pontypridd. It wasn't entirely unknown for choir competitions to disintegrate into mass brawls in which hitting the wrong note was the least of one's worries. A bout of fisticuffs occurred between the Treorchy Male Voice Choir and the Rhondda Glee Men in 1890.

Full employment gave everyone something to sing about. When the age of coal began, Welsh morale was at rock bottom, yet by the end of the nineteenth century the Welsh were seen as an upright and honest people. And the south Wales coal boom was one of the principal causes of change, driven by tough and courageous coal magnates such as David Davies.

Born in 1818, in Llandinam, Montgomeryshire, Davies was quite the opposite of his great rival the Marquess of Bute. The son of an impoverished tenant farmer, he did not have any of the social advantages of his competitor. A self-made man, he accumulated his early wealth by building railway lines in mid-Wales, before diverting his attention to the south of the country.

Davies started his search for coal near Treorchy in the 1860s, but exploratory pits, sunk over a period of 15 months, reaped nothing of any significance. It was sufficiently draining an enterprise to use up all of Davies's cash, leaving him with a dilemma. He called his men together to give them the money he owed them, but also to tell them that he could not afford to pay them to continue digging. In fact, he told them he had only a half-crown left in the world. A voice in the crowd said they would have that too, and Davies happily obliged, tossing the coin towards them. The men liked his style, so they agreed to work for a further week for no pay whatsoever. Fortuitously, on the seventh day of exploring, Davies struck it lucky, hitting a six-foot-wide seam of high-quality steam coal. This soon became the Cwm-parc pit near Treorchy, an important component of the success of Davies's Ocean Coal Company.

Using the Taff Vale Railway, Davies moved large quantities of coal to Cardiff. By 1859, Cardiff had a new East Dock to complement the older West Dock, but the two docks between them couldn't cope with the stupendous volume of trade, and consequently trucks laden with coal lay idle in the sidings. Many owners pilloried Cardiff because of the wealth it created for the Butes, so David Davies decided to build another dock, this time in Barry. He submitted a Parliamentary Bill in 1883, occasioning a veritable battle in Parliament, which passed it a year later. The new dock would eventually have millions of tons of coal passing through it, transforming a small fishing village into a busy town. Two years after it opened, Barry was exporting no less than four million tons of coal a year.

Davies had hoped his rival dock would 'cause grass to grow in the streets of Cardiff'.[2] However, instead of stealing trade from Cardiff, the growth of additional docks underlined the importance of the whole south Wales seaboard, and nowhere was this more visible than in Cardiff's Coal Exchange, with its clocks that indicated high and low tide (the points at which trading started and ended on any given day).

At its busiest, hundreds of men filled the capacious hall of Cardiff's Coal Exchange, shouting out prices and cementing deals. Prices were chalked up on blackboards and at the end of another day's frenetic trading, champagne, claret and hock were quaffed in great quantities. Myth has it that the first ever million-pound cheque was signed here.

Things were changing underground too. The new longwall method of extraction, in which a whole section of a coal seam was removed in one fell swoop, was safer than the old pillar-and-stall method. Safety lamps, or 'Davy' lamps – after their inventor, Humphry Davy – helped at least anticipate the danger of methane leaks, which led to deadly explosions in the mines. But despite these advances in techniques and safety measures, there was still a terrifying catalogue of death and injury underground. In just four years, between 1851 and 1855, a total of 738 people died in accidents in south Wales, such as the terrible Albion colliery disaster of 1894, which claimed the lives of 290 miners. One in five of those who died in Welsh accidents in this period were boys under the age of 15.

Legislation to inspect mines and cap the working day of under-16s to ten hours was hard to enforce, but accidents were less frequent by 1875. Miners didn't earn much and job security was non-existent. A dispute in 1898 arose between miners and owners over the linking of their pay to the price of coal. The law sided with the mine owners, who could lay off the colliers without any notice, and in return the colliers protested in a way that was to become so familiar in the 1980s – they went on strike. The strike fizzled out after six months, but feelings ran sufficiently high to warrant establishing a trade union the same year – the South Wales Miners' Federation, which came to be familiarly known as 'The Fed'. It would play a central role in the life of Wales for half a century, providing leadership for the coalfield communities through good times and bad.

Its leading light in the early years was the Rhondda MP, William Abraham, nicknamed 'Mabon'. This Welsh-speaking advocate of a 'softly, softly' approach to industrial relations drew scorn from younger and more hot-headed men, such as Noah Ablett.

The writing of the Syndicalist* pamphlet *The Miners' Next Step* in 1912 threw up a revealing comparison between the two men. On one hand, there was 'Mabon', the first Federation President who was elected 'Lib-Lab' MP for the Rhondda in 1885. He was deeply rooted in a Welsh-speaking world and a broker of political compromises. On the other hand, the Ruskin-educated miner and former check-weigher Noah Ablett had no time for the conciliatory attitude of older leaders, and thought the future lay with a more confrontational and confident workforce, and organized Labour politics. Ablett paved the way for the next generation of Labour leaders, such as Aneurin Bevan.

Such men achieved a great deal in different ways. Mabon, using consensus, helped agree a sliding scale of wages in 1875. From 1892 to 1898, in order to limit production and maintain wages, the workers did not work Mondays. As a result, the day became known as 'Mabon's Monday'. Ablett, in *The Miners' Next Step*, argued for industrial action and effective strikes to deliver a seven-hour day and a daily minimum wage of eight shillings.

---

* Syndicalism was a movement that argued for transferring the ownership and control of the means of production and distribution to workers' unions.

The whole picture of employment in Wales was skewed by this one industry. It was so dominant by 1920 that 271,516 miners were employed in the south, or almost a third of all the men employed in the country. From the 1890s the coalfield was sucking in English-speakers from the West Country and the Midlands. By 1914 Rhondda had 53 large mines, each employing over a thousand people. And with the rise in employment, the population of Wales around the coal hotspots exploded as well, along with shops, public houses and chapels for the workers and their families. Coal also created opportunities away from the coalfields. Despite the negative effects of the First World War and of subsequent post-war German reparation payments in coal, there were still 120 shipping companies in Cardiff in 1920 compared with two today.

Coalfield sport, especially rugby, drew passionate crowds and created tough and skilful players. Theatres were built alongside the chapels, and also workmen's institutes with their comprehensive libraries. There is no doubt that coal communities in both the south and the north of the country were vibrant.

Industrial Wales was also experiencing another more economi- cally motivated invasion: Irish, Italian and English settlers came to Wales in search of work. By 1914, Wales almost matched the USA as a magnet for immigrants, who eventually made up one-sixth of the country's population. In some areas, the newcomers learned Welsh, in others it was the Welsh who turned to the English language. Half the population of Wales spoke Welsh in 1901 and by 1911, the number of speakers peaked at over 977,000. Thereafter the numbers plummeted, as people left to seek work elsewhere and two world wars reduced the male population available to work.

While money stayed mainly in private hands, some of it spilled over into civic society. The Bute family bankrolled the great buildings of Cardiff's civic centre, while yet another John Crichton-Stuart, third Marquess of Bute, commissioned a brilliant architect called William Burges to modify Cardiff castle in 1865. This marquess was very different from his father, as he was scholarly and pious with a lifelong interest in the Middle Ages. With coal money and Burges's vision, he also rebuilt Castell Coch in Tongwynlais in the 1870s, a fairytale castle on the outskirts of Cardiff, which still commands the view from the depths of extensive beech woods.

While the coal boom helped Wales to thrive economically, social pressures were building. Welsh coal was still in demand but seams were getting much harder to work, and pit owners' profits were being squeezed as a result. To maintain profits, they ignored their miners' demands for better pay and conditions. In 1910–11 an extraordinary wave of class-based violence swept through the South Wales Coalfield. This was the dawning of the consumer age, and people could see the items required to live the good life in the many shops along the high street, but couldn't afford any of them.

Tonypandy, in the Rhondda Fawr, was the first place to erupt, with rioting breaking out in November 1910, at the height of an acrimonious strike. Hundreds of people were injured and one man died. Sadly, there was a racist component to these attacks, as Jewish shopkeepers and Chinese immigrants were subject to harassment. The police and the army were sent into restore order, and an uneasy calm descended on the entire region, but it wouldn't last.

During the very hot summer of 1911, further disturbances took place in widely separated parts of the coalfield. Riots broke out in Llanelli, where two men were shot dead, and in Cardiff, Tredegar,

Bargoed and Brynmawr. All involved extensive damage to property, but there were many injuries too.

As the Edwardian age succeeded the long reign of Queen Victoria, Wales was dressed in the finery of a new prosperity. Both the National Museum of Wales and the Library of Wales were created in 1907, the latter after a heated competition between Aberystwyth and Cardiff to site it. The University of Wales, formed in 1893, was a key cultural institution, and other bodies followed, such as the Royal Commission on the Ancient and Historical Monuments of Wales in 1908. Cardiff became a city in 1905, 50 years before it became a capital, and this burgeoning place now boasted an impressive complex of grand buildings in Cathays Park.

It's hard to imagine the sheer scale of the Welsh coal industry on the eve of the First World War. In 1913, some 26 million tons of coal were shipped from Barry – enough to fill the Millennium Stadium 19 times. This was the golden age of Welsh maritime history, with ships taking coal out and grain in, trading as far as South America and the Black Sea. Coal's reign was long lived, and it left a kingly inheritance of buildings and spirited communities. But it would also cause enormous pain in the latter half of the century as the coalfield communities were undermined by the mass closure of pits.

The industrial age in Wales is marked by an inventiveness and entrepreneurship that clearly highlighted the country on the globe, but it was also a time of class iniquity and tension, which would simmer and erupt into violent riots and strikes that would pepper the eighteenth and nineteenth centuries. This was the period in which unions emerged, parliamentary speakers argued for better working conditions for the men in the pits and the smelting works, and working-class Wales started to develop a sense of worth and a political voice.

CHAPTER EIGHTEEN

MAKING TRACKS

There were parts of the Welsh landscape that had escaped the ravages of the Industrial Revolution: scenery that had not been razed, blasted or blackened, and picturesque scenery at that.

The Napoleonic Wars of 1803–15 had closed down the educational rite of passage that was the 'Grand Tour' of Europe, by which prosperous young men, in the main, travelled the Continent in some style for their edification and education. As a consequence of Continental wars, tourism took off in Britain and Wales underwent an image-change. Once seen as bleak and inhospitable, it now became impressive and mystical.

A country that had been dismissed by Ned Ward as 'the fag-end of Creation, the very rubbish of Noah's flood' in his 1700 travelogue, *A Trip to North Wales*, had become a sublime destination by the end of the same century, attracting painters such as J. M. W. Turner, who visited Wales five times in eight years, as well as tribes of scribes, including Thomas De Quincey.

De Quincy had, as a young man, spent four months in the Welsh mountains, where he encountered a 'happier life'. It was hard to find something better to 'imagine than this vagrancy, if the weather were but tolerable, through endless successions of changing beauty and towards evening in a pretty rustic home'.[1]

Other writers tramped the hills and traipsed the vales. Walter Savage Landor, Thomas Love Peacock, William Wordsworth, Samuel Taylor Coleridge and Robert Southey all came here in search of mouldy ruins, Gothic overhangs and remarkable cataracts of water – experiences that they often transmuted into words, such as Wordsworth's sonnets 'To the Torrent at Devil's Bridge in North Wales' and 'Composed Among the Ruins of a Castle in North Wales'.

The poet Percy Bysshe Shelley was one of those most affected by the country, although the time he spent at his cousin's summer home in the Elan valley was marred by mental torment. Even then, some of his letters register a dizzy delight in the place:

Rocks piled on each other to an immense height, and clouds intersecting them; in other places, waterfalls midst the umbrage of a thousand shadowy trees form the principal features of scenery. I am not wholly uninfluenced by its magic in my lonely walks.[2]

One of the torch-bearers for early tourism and the determined quest for the picturesque was William Gilpin, whose *Observations on the River Wye* evoked the beauty of these scenes which arose 'chiefly from two circumstances: the lofty banks of the river and its mazy course.' His *Observations* had considerable impact and led to a tourism equivalent to the Gold Rush, as people rushed to claim the various treasures for themselves – the sublime vistas, the ample panoramas and the transcendent views. The Wye Tours had started before Gilpin, back in 1745 in fact, when Dr John Egerton, started taking friends on river trips from the rectory at Ross-on-Wye.

Gilpin's *Observations* were not published until 1782, even though those in the know had been aware of them for a decade. By the early part of the nineteenth century there were eight craft plying the Wye in the summer months, cruising slowly past picturesque ruined castles such as Wilton, Goodrich and Chepstow. By 1850 no fewer than 20 writers had published guides to the river's attractions, including poets such as Thomas Gray who published his own gushing guide to the riverbanks' 'succession of nameless beauties.'

The Wye Tour became famous and very well established. Visitors glided in comfort from Ross-on-Wye to Chepstow in boats equipped with drawing tables and protective awnings. The riparian reaches of the Wye remained an attraction well into the nineteenth century, but even as it lost a little of its sheen and social cachet, the coming of the railways added a new boost to the numbers of river gawpers.

Through the eyes of Wordsworth and other Romantic visitors, Wales possessed an awe-inspiring landscape and its inhabitants mystical qualities: bumpkins speaking a strange tongue were soon transformed into bards and seers. Wordsworth, as a young Cambridge graduate, went on two walking tours of Wales in 1791 and 1793, both in the company of a fellow graduate, the Welshman Robert Jones from Llangynhafal in Denbighshire. The landscape moved Wordsworth deeply, and 'The Prelude' was inspired by his walk to the top of Snowdon with his sister Dorothy Wordsworth. One of her letters captures their friendship and the sublime and mountainous landscape they both enjoyed:

I often hear from my brother William who is now in Wales where
I think he seems so happy that it is probable he will remain there

all summer or a great part of it ... His friend Jones is a charm-
ing young man ... then there are mountains, rivers, woods and
rocks, whose charms without any other inducement would be
sufficient to tempt William to continue amongst them as long as
possible ... his pleasures are chiefly of the imagination, he is
never so happy as when in a beautiful country.[3]

On other visits, such as the one in the summer of 1793, Wordsworth travelled up the Wye before heading on to north Wales and the Vale of Clwyd and, as a consequence, wrote the beautiful meditation 'Lines Composed a Few Miles Above Tintern Abbey', which has come to be considered as 'the consecrated formulary of Wordsworthian faith'.[4]

But there was another kind of transport developing besides these transports of delight. Alongside all the radical activity and industrial development, there emerged an early form of mass tourism, as transport links, especially railways, changed the world. Some of the early tramways, such as the Mumbles Railway on the edge of Swansea Bay, started life in 1804 as a mineral line. It was adapted for passenger use by 1807 and became the first horse-drawn passenger railway.

Tramways complemented and connected with the canals, and these carried huge quantities of coal and iron in south Wales, with no fewer than 240 kilometres (150 miles) of canals linking with a system of 560 kilometres (348 miles) of tramways. In the north of the country, tramways served the slate industry, taking materials from the quarries that pockmarked the mountains to the coast and to ports such as Port Penrhyn, Porthmadog and Port Dinorwic. In the north-east too harbours were linked to the coal-production centres and limestone quarries of Denbighshire via tramways.

But it was on the tramway connecting the Penydarren Ironworks with the Glamorganshire Canal that the most important transport development took place, namely the testing in 1804 by Richard Trevithick of a steam locomotive, and thus the first experiment in railway locomotion.

Samuel Homfray, owner of Penydarren Ironworks in Merthyr, made a bet. He wagered Richard Crawshay 1,000 guineas that he could construct a steam engine to haul ten tons of iron from Merthyr to Abercynon nine miles away. Homfray had enlisted the assistance of a Cornish engineer, Richard Trevithick, who built a high-pressure tram engine that ran on rails – the first steam-powered rail locomotive.

On 14 February 1804 people came from far and wide to witness the great experiment. Five trams were loaded with iron and 70 men. With shouts of encouragement, the engine started its journey. Unfortunately, disaster soon struck. The chimney of the locomotive collided with a low bridge and both were damaged. But Trevithick repaired the engine, cleared the debris and made good the chimney. Soon he was off at a hair-raising five miles an hour. Nine hours later, he, his engine and his precious cargo reached Abercynon still intact. Trevithick and the ironmaster's experiment had proved that railways were the future.

But it would be some decades before they became a reality: by 1839 the wager between two men had led to a domino effect of discovery and development, which led to the opening of the first Welsh railway specifically for locomotion, between the harbour in Llanelli and Pontarddulais.

Naturally, some of the early railways pioneered in different ways. The Taff Vale Railway connecting the port of Cardiff with Merthyr

Tydfil became the most profitable railway company in Britain. Mineral railways proliferated everywhere, running along many south Wales valleys, such as the Neath, the Rhymney and the Ebbw.

Passenger networks followed in rapid order, with a line running from Chester to Holyhead, carried at one point by Robert Stephenson's elegant Britannia Bridge. In the south of the country Isambard Kingdom Brunel's line ran from Gloucester across south Wales, originally terminating at Swansea. This was then extended as far as Carmarthen and eventually to Neyland, where Brunel had a vision of creating a major port to connect with Ireland.

The railway age had most certainly arrived. In a period of about 30 years approximately 2,300 kilometres (1,430 miles) of track were laid across Wales, which equated to an investment of £20 million.

The pace of railway building slowed down by the 1880s, but there were still two major developments to come, namely the digging of the Severn Tunnel, which was opened in 1885, when it ranked as the longest undersea tunnel in the world.

In 1888 the Barry Railway came into being, a component of David Davies Llandinam's vision of creating an integrated rail and dock system to rival the connectivity between the Bute Dock Company in Cardiff and the Taff Vale Railway.

The mass tourism that rail brought was evident. While the Butes built a port in Cardiff, the Mostyns of Llandudno built a resort. The town was laid out as it now stands in 1849. The Mostyn family leased out plots for development, but this was not a hands-off approach, for they strongly influenced the building design and uses of the land. Meanwhile, Aberystwyth on the Ceredigion coast became known as the 'Biarritz of Wales'.

RIGHT AND BELOW: 'Biarritz of Wales':
The colourful posters created for the Great
Western Railway to promote the Welsh
coastal resort of Aberystwyth.

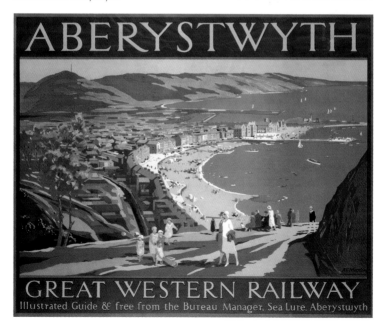

LEFT: David Lloyd George, photographed in 1913, while he was still Chancellor of the Exchequer.

BELOW AND OPPOSITE TOP: Unemployed miners scavenge for coal during the bleak Depression years, in Merthyr Tydfil.

BELOW: Bute Street in Cardiff, after sustaining extensive bomb damage during the Second World War.

ABOVE: Taking a break at the Powell Duffryn Colliery, June 1931. The miners sit underground, near the coalface, with safety lamps at their feet.

LEFT: Miners drilling and shovelling coal at the Powell Duffryn Colliery, near Merthyr Tydfil. The mine opened in 1862 and closed in 1940.

BELOW: An aerial photograph taken of Aberfan on 21 October 1966 shortly after the disaster. Two million tonnes of slag submerged the mining village and claimed 144 lives.

ABOVE: Llyn Celyn reservoir, which was officially opened on 28 October 1965. The project cost £20 million to construct and consumed the homes of 48 Welsh villagers and one church.

BELOW: On 8 September 1966, the first crowds crossed the newly opened Severn Bridge.

ABOVE: Miners from Celynen North Colliery march against proposed mine closures, 18 August 1984, along with family and local supporters.

BELOW: 'Your class needs you': Militant posters during the 1984 miners' strikes in South Wales.

ABOVE: More than 60,000 Welsh rugby fans watching the 2011 Rugby World Cup Semi-finals on a giant screen in the Millennium Stadium.

BELOW: The cathedral of Welsh rugby: the Millennium Stadium during the Rugby Union Heineken Cup Final, 2008.

LEFT: The Debating Chamber of the National Assembly for Wales, opened in 2006.

BELOW: The reception area at the National Assembly for Wales, with its beautiful curved ceiling, designed by Richard Rogers.

Barmouth, which had suffered a decline in its exports after years of busily shipping out slate, lead, manganese and zinc, was thrown a veritable lifeline by the railway, which reached across the Mawddach estuary via an extraordinary wooden viaduct in 1867. Tall Victorian guest houses mushroomed on its streets, and Queen Victoria's daughter, Beatrice, opened a large church in the town in 1889. Barmouth had much to admire scenically, and little wonder that the very first property to be acquired by the National Trust came courtesy of three Victorian philanthropists who wanted to create 'open-air sitting rooms for city dwellers to have a place to breathe'. The open-air sitting room they chose was Dinas Olau, 'The Fortress of Light', which is a hump of rock that dominates the skyline above the town, and is spanned by the Panorama Walk with its commanding and uplifting views of the estuary and the mountains beyond. It became a renowned place to stay and walk. The town attracted visitors such as the naturalist and evolutionary theorist Charles Darwin, and the writer on art and architecture, John Ruskin.

Tenby, on the southeast coast of Pembrokeshire, was similarly transformed by the landlord, politician and wealthy Bengal merchant William Paxton, and his dream of creating a saltwater therapy spa, capitalizing on the town's views over Carmarthen Bay and as far as the Gower Peninsula. Paxton – a controversial figure who during one famous election had tried to gather popular support for his political ambitions by supplying 200,000 bottles of beer and 11,000 bottles of liquor to his supporters – built public baths and instituted a network of stately promenades and terraces. By the time the railway connected with the town in 1866, everything was in place to make it a grand tourist centre.

Meanwhile, landlocked Llandrindod in mid-Wales attracted a great deal of attention from the much-trumpeted benefits of its smelly and sulphurous water, and the rebuilding of the town's Pump Room, which ushered in an era of successful tourism, especially when the railway arrived in 1865. Towns such as these saw themselves appear on newly minted tourist maps, where the range of scenery that had attracted writers such as Dickens and Thackeray combined with the advantages of mass transportation to open up the whole country as a centre for rest and relaxation.

New seaside resorts came into being too, as the nineteenth century gave way to the twentieth. The former iron and coal terminus of Porthcawl grew to become a seaside resort, funded by investment by Maesteg ironmasters the Brogdens, just as the town's docks declined. Its popularity grew, not least as a side-benefit of the growth of the South Wales Coalfield. Legions of guest houses and caravan sites, such as sprawling Trecco Bay, benefited from the institution of the miners' fortnight in August, when miners and their families flocked to the coast to enjoy the sands and the sea air.

From Gothic overhangs to the elegance of Victorian piers, from cleansing spas to elegant stately hotels, this was the evolving apparatus of a tourism industry that would eventually become one of the most important in the land.

CHAPTER NINETEEN

REVOLT
AND UNREST

While the grandeur of the landscape delighted some, others were still busy changing it forever. As the hard labour of lower classes continued, in increasingly worse conditions, for the profit of a rich minority, the workers began to ponder the fairness of the divide between themselves and those with power.

Jacobin thought, which had fuelled the revolution in France, was a fervent movement for political and economic change that underlined equality and the rights of man. This movement had been gathering momentum in the towns and the dissenting academies of Wales, and had even impacted on the pace of book production. Pamphlets, broadsides and lengthy tracts all poured off the presses. Indeed, the first political book in Welsh was a translated pamphlet about the war between Britain and her colonies.

Coupled with this interest in political dissent, the Methodist fervour of the eighteenth century continued to grow, and during the first half of the nineteenth century the Nonconformist chapels exerted a substantial influence on the population of Wales. Nonconformism was an appealing spiritual and social movement, which empowered local congregations. As its influence grew, Wales was seen as a 'land of

Revivals', where the bulk of worshippers devoted a large part of their leisure time to worship. By the time of the Religious Census of 1851, four-fifths of the worshippers in Wales attended Nonconformist chapels. Many of those who worshipped, and many more who did not, were involved in a long struggle against the Establishment.

As people took matters into their own hands there was the very real sense that there was strength in numbers. Welsh food riots peaked in the 1790s after another cycle of grain shortages, followed by famine prices, led to an outbreak of rioting throughout the country, from Conwy to Bridgend. People were incensed not just by the perceived unfairness, but also by new moves to force recruitment into the military. Rural counties, such as Merioneth and Montgomeryshire, were plunged into turmoil, and in Haverfordwest, a stronghold of Jacobin sympathy, events took an insurrectionist turn in 1795 as price riots brought angry crowds onto the streets.

There were widespread and deep grumblings of discontent in many parts of rural Wales. William Jones of Dolhywel in Llangadfan, Montgomeryshire, lived up to his local reputation as a 'rural Voltaire' by complaining bitterly to the Wynns of Wynnstay about the behaviour of landlords and stewards: 'these rapacious cormorants, not satisfied with open racking, frequently join the fox tail to the bear's claw and make of us base circumventions to fleece us more effectively … and if we happen to complain of our hardships, we are immediately told in a true Aegyptian phrase "that we are idle".'[1]

Even moving through the countryside cost money, collected at toll-gates. In the southwest of Wales small farmers, deeply aggrieved at the monies extracted from them to use roads to roll their wagons, rose up against the toll-gates and their operators in a major social disturbance in the 1840s. The protestors themselves came from an area already gripped by abject poverty.

Poor harvests in the period after 1815, followed by atrocious wet weather, meant that farmers had to buy corn at famine prices for their own use, having produced next to nothing themselves. When live-stock prices, which had remained reasonably high, took a tumble in 1842 and 1843, it made rural living, and making a living, well-nigh impossible. Butter and pig prices fell. Corn prices also plummeted because of one atypically productive harvest.

Away to the east, a slump in the iron trade sent seismic shivers to the west as demand for goods, such as butter and cheese, disappeared. While all these challenges were dished out to them, the rural folk also had to scrape up the money for a barrage of demands in the form of tithes, rents, poor rates, county rates and turnpike tolls. They saw themselves as victims of tyranny and oppression, exacerbated by English toll-renters' exaction of money from those who pushed carts filled with lime along smaller roads and tracks in an effort to avoid paying tolls on the main roads.

It was natural that the targets of attacks would be the tollgates and their keepers. They were attacked at night, by men dressed as women, who aimed to intimidate those who lived in the toll-houses, and to physically destroy the gates themselves with axes.

The leader of each of these protests was called 'Rebecca'; this subterfuge, along with a tight countryside solidarity, meant that no principal leader was ever identified, although a pugilist called Twm Carnabwth is credited with organizing the first attack. The protest name came from the Book of Genesis: 'And they blessed Rebekah and said unto her, thou art our sister, be thou the mother of thousands of millions, and let thy seed possess the gates of those which hate them.'

Right from the beginning, part of the fear associated with Rebecca's 'men' was inspired by the way they were dressed. Not only did they plump for women's garb, but they also blackened their faces or wore masks and made an uncommon noise as they struck, often to carry out a mock trial before setting about the business of wreaking havoc.

Rebeccaism derived from the local custom of the *ceffyl pren* (wooden horse), a means of punishing someone who had affronted the standards of the local community by, say, infidelity, in which the offender was paraded through the village tied to a wooden frame in a ritual humiliation. Menfolk doling out the justice would often have blackened faces. This had counterparts in England's 'rough music' and in the noisy masked festivals of Europe, such as the *charivaris*, *cencerrada*, *katzenmusic* and *scampanate*.[2]

Rebecca's first attack was made at Efail-wen on the border of Carmarthenshire and Pembrokeshire on 13 May 1839. Men armed with axes and sledgehammers destroyed the gate, and this phase of destructive activity lasted for 13 days, culminating with the total destruction of the tollgate at Water Street in Carmarthen. Protest peaked again in the winter of 1842, and by the autumn of the following year Rebecca rioters were active in half a dozen counties. Tollgates weren't the only focus for the people's fury and pent-up anger, as workhouses and weirs – where fishing was tightly controlled – were also targets for acts of destruction.

Thus were the people pitched against the toll collectors, the gentry, the magistrates, the bailiffs, the Anglican clergy and the masters of the poor houses. All were seen as tight-fisted and heedless of the suffering of a mainly poor, rural populace. Unsurprisingly, Rebecca also warned landlords to reduce the rents they charged, which were higher in Wales than in England. The fact that tithes now had to be paid for in cash, rather than in the form of goods, piled misery on top of outrage. One night this grievance against tithe collectors prompted rioters to seriously injure a tithe agent, John Edwards of Gelliwernen House, near Llan-non in Carmarthenshire. Sometimes the focus of complaint was more specific:

> In ye parish (Llanfihangel-ar-Arth) a gentleman farmer a Mr
> Bowen of Wernmackwyth ... had a visit from 'Rebecca and her
> daughters' who brought with them a child which they told him
> was an illegitimate of his own and on pain of having his prem-
> ises fired, made him promise to take care of it in future.[3]

The re-erection and reopening of tollgates fuelled anger, and overall there were over 500 attacks on gates and other targets. In Carmarthen town 2,000 protestors against the Poor Law marched under banners proclaiming, 'We are all lovers of Justice'. These cross-dressers had support across society.

Urban life had its troubles too. Working conditions in industrial Wales were appalling. In the 1840s it was common for four-year-old children to work underground, while some of their older siblings opened and closed ventilation doors in complete darkness. Such children grew up deformed or retarded, if they grew up at all. Cholera was rife and sanitation non-existent, and therefore life expectancy was low: even by the middle of the nineteenth century, almost half the deaths in Aberdare were children under the age of five. In the north of the country, slate quarrymen living collectively in barracks worked 50 hours a week in punishing conditions, which led to a high incidence of chest and stomach disease.

Workers also had to contend with the effects of world events and turn-downs. The boom of the 1790s – fuelled by the demands of war – was the precursor of a bust. Peace overseas led to a slump in demand for iron, and workers' wages took a plunge. Protests ensued against these cuts, although in the absence of trade unions, the protests suffered from disorganization and mainly petered out. Later developments, such as the moderate progressivism of the Poor Law Amendment Act of 1834, seemed completely inadequate to the Welsh radicals who often found themselves in conflict with the forces of the British state.

Social disaffection manifested in a new, spectral terrorist organization in the form of the 'Scotch Cattle', a secret society that took its name from the verb to scotch – that is 'put an end to' – the workers' subservience. This society wanted to control the production of iron and later of coal, and did so by fomenting strikes and fostering intimidation. This mix of coercion and direct action held sway for over a decade between the early 1820s and the mid-1830s.

Led by a leader called 'Lolly', 'Ned' or 'The Bull', the Scotch Cattle dispensed frontier justice. The group operated along the Glamorganshire–Monmouthshire border, with its members sworn to secrecy on pain of death. Anyone threatening the solidarity of a strike would be intimidated by the 'Cattle' coming down from the hills, lowing and banging metal implements together. They sought out the employers' agents who cut the workers' wages to the bone, and

destroyed machinery, tools, pit-props and engines, paying particularly destructive attention to coal wagons, barges and tram roads.

They would also intimidate Irish and English immigrants by visiting in the night, holding mock trials, then smashing windows and
manhandling their victims before spiriting themselves away. Lucky
victims escaped with only a red cross painted on the front door, itself
a disquieting symbol.

To prevent an early return to work by colliers in Clydach, Breconshire, the following message, in a free mixture of Welsh and English,
was posted as a warning to three local colliers:

> *How many times we gave you notice to you about going in to*
> *work before you settle all together to go on better terms than were*
> *before and better than what you ask at present?*
>
> *Notice to you David Thomas John, and David Davies, and*
> *Andrew Cross, that the Bull and his friends are all alive, and the*
> *vale of Llamarch is wide, and woe shall be to you, since death*
> *you shall doubtless have all at once, you may depend on this. It*
> *may be that the night you do not expect, we shall come again.*
> *We are not afraid were you to go all at once to work.*[4]

The death of a woman in one of the Cattle raids led to three men
being sentenced for her murder, and one of them, Edward Morgan,
was hanged, a punishment that marked the end of the Scotch Cattle.

In the 1830s and 1840s, Wales was both industrious and volatile,
and nowhere was this more visible than Merthyr, the tumultuous iron
town that had grown at a ferocious rate. Because workers were housed
in increasingly cramped and insanitary conditions, the whole place

was ripe for epidemics – and a place where discontent could easily mutate into militancy. The Poor Law Amendment Act of 1834 created a system by which parishes created workhouses for the poor. In effect, they were little more than local prisons, with deliberately worse conditions on the inside acting as a deterrent for the poor on the outside. It was also proposed that the poor be means-tested, which, since they did not have the means to pay, was doomed to fail.

In 1831 and 1832 there were strenuous attempts to reform parliamentary representation, and the bulk of Merthyr's population was firmly behind such reforms. The fuse for the workers' rebellion in Merthyr was lit in May 1831 when the owner of the Cyfarthfa Ironworks sacked some of his employees and reduced the wages of the workforce.

A mass meeting of some 10,000 people was convened at the Waun Fair on Twyn y Waun, overlooking the town, and afterwards the crowd – who demanded cheaper bread and better wages – moved into the town's streets. Bedlam ensued as the unpopular Court of Requests, which collected small debts, was attacked, and shops and houses vandalized.

The central, iconic act of the rising was the raising of a red flag made from a sheet soaked in the blood of a calf. It symbolized the workers' solidarity, with pronounced echoes of the French Revolution. For a total of six days the protesters, numbering as many as 10,000 people, roamed freely throughout the town, even as the owners of the ironworks, the magistrates, and assorted other businessmen were pinned down in the Castle Hotel.

On 3 June soldiers arrived in the town, 68 of them in total, and in the resulting mêlée at least 24 members of the public were shot and killed, and 16 soldiers wounded. Sheer weight of numbers was on the protestors' side and they eventually disarmed the soldiers who had been sent from Brecon, but military reinforcements from the Argyll and Sutherland Highlanders were swiftly dispatched, with express orders to take the town and restore order. Four days later the people's authority, chaotic as it was, had been wrested away from them by the military.

One of the protestors, Richard Lewis, or Dic Penderyn, was to become a local hero and working-class legend and martyr. His execution by hanging in Cardiff for wounding a soldier – even though he was completely innocent – was commemorated in popular songs, including 'Who is Dic Penderyn?'

So who's this Dic Penderyn then?
He was Mrs Lewis's son, wasn't he?
He was just one of the ordinary men–
A man like you and me.

The real ringleader, Lewis Lewis, or Lewsyn yr Heliwr, was also due to be executed, but he was punished instead by being transported to Australia.

Another force for equality and egalitarianism was Chartism, which emerged in the late 1830s, fuelled by the radical energies of people such as William Lovett and Ernest Jones. The *People's Charter*, which gave the movement its name, was published in the late spring of 1838. This charter, which demanded political rights for all men, was based on an idea that had been promulgated for some 40 years, but the charter listed six specific points for reform: a vote for every man over 21 years of age; a ballot; no property qualification for Members of Parliament; the payment of MPs, so ensuring a level playing field where a tradesman or working man could serve a constituency just as easily as a man of means; equal constituencies, securing the same amount of representation for the same number of electors; and annual parliaments, which were seen as the most effectual check to bribery and intimidation.

Chartism was a campaign for democratic rights that had witnessed the establishment of such bodies as a Working Men's Association in Carmarthen in 1837. Mid-Wales weaving towns, such as Newtown, proved to be fertile ground for such ideas. Having unsuccessfully petitioned Parliament, people took to the streets in places such as Llanidloes and Newtown to express the depth of their feeling. In Newtown, a society was established in 1838 by tradesmen and craftsmen, who argued against the monopoly of the aristocracy over land and wealth, and railed against the fact that wealth created by the workers did not in any way filter back to them. The answer was to seize political power for themselves.

By the summer of 1839, as many as 25,000 men and women had joined democratic associations. The Working Men's Association in Carmarthen had been followed by three more in mid-Wales weaving towns. Other political societies and radical associations came into being, many expounding the Chartist cause, with the first Chartist convention taking place that same year. Mass protest was in the air.

On the evening of Sunday, 3 November 1839, a 19-year-old cabinetmaker called George Shell from Pontypool sat down to write a letter to his parents in which he described how 'I shall this night be engaged in a struggle for freedom and should it please God to spare my life I shall see you soon.'[5] He was one of many preparing for an astonishing day of mass protest.

There had been months of planning, with many secret meetings. Money had been collected and homemade firearms stashed away, not to mention stolen fire arms, which had been hidden in caves ready for the right moment.

That moment was Parliament's rejection of the Chartist Petition, which had tried to ensure that people other than property owners had the right to vote. In response, 5,000 coal- and iron-workers, not to mention cabinet-makers (including George Shell), from the industrial valleys of Monmouthshire funnelled into the town centre of Newport on the morning of 4 November 1839, and marched on the Westgate Hotel.

On reaching the Westgate, they were faced down by the mayor, Thomas Phillips, backed by a detachment of the 45th Foot Regiment augmented by special constables. It is thought that the Chartists fired the first shot, instigating street fighting that lasted for half an hour, during which 28 men were killed and 50 wounded on the Chartist side, and the mayor and two soldiers seriously wounded.

When troops examined the dead, they found that nearly all were well supplied with ammunition, cartridges and flasks of powder. *The Times* marvelled at the sophistication of it all: 'This was no momentary outbreak but a long planned insurrection, deeply organized, managed with a secrecy truly astonishing.'

Several bodies of shot marchers were buried in unmarked graves, including that of young George Shell, the cabinet-maker. Three of the ringleaders were arrested, tried, found guilty of high treason and sentenced to death, although this sentence was later commuted to transportation to Australia. One of the Chartist leaders, former town councillor and mayor John Frost, had been particularly incensed by the Morgan family of Tredegar House's toll of £3,000 for goods that crossed their land at Tredegar Park, locally and ironically known as the Golden Mile. Frost spent 14 years in Van Diemen's Land (present-day Tasmania) before being pardoned. The other two Chartist leaders, Nant-y-glo publican Zephaniah Williams and a Pontypool watch-maker William Jones, probably believed, like Frost, that their show of strength alone would be enough to cow the opposition. They had drilled and armed their men, but they were not military tacticians, and their efforts were hampered by nothing more fearsome than bucketing rain, giving a farcical edge to the ultimately tragic proceedings.

This was not the end of Chartism in Wales, for angry embers still glowed in places such as Merthyr Tydfil, where men joined the General Strike of 1842, called to secure Chartist demands, but there was to be no comparable display of rage again. Indeed, some of the remaining Chartists were to be drawn into a Liberal frame of mind, encouraged by the proselytizing of parliamentary candidates such as Henry Richard. Class hostility would later recede.

There was industrial unrest in north Wales also: the Wareham Riots of 1830 at Rhosllannerchrugog reflected the pressure for higher wages in the Flintshire coalfield, not to mention hostility to the system that obliged coal miners to buy goods from the company stores or 'Tommy shops'. The strikes in Flintshire were the first large-scale riots in Welsh history, and led to the formation of the first trade union in Wales, in 1830 at Bagillt. A Home Office report of the time said that union activists from Flintshire had been seen in Merthyr with cash collected shortly before the 'disturbances' of 1831.

Strikes and riots would continue to punctuate Welsh history in the decades to come. In 1874, Baron Penrhyn of Llandygái faced a substantial strike for much the same reasons as the coal strikes of the early 1830s – poor wages and poor conditions. The strike enabled the establishment of a union-controlled quarry committee and the removal of managers who had run the quarry for 50 years. Associated strikes broke out in Dinorwig quarry and lasted throughout the bleak winter of 1885-6.

In 1896–7, another strike occurred in Penrhyn. For 11 months, 2,800 men were locked out of the quarry as they argued over their rights to organize and be represented as workers. Lord Penrhyn refused to budge, and the workers and their families suffered hugely. There was a failed strike at the Llechwedd slate quarry too. Here, as at the Oakeley workings near Porthmadog, the slate was produced in enormous underground chambers.

In 1900, industrial relations at Penrhyn ruptured again and a riot against the employment of individual contractors led to the conviction and dismissal of six workers, causing the whole of the workforce to down tools. Many of them did not return to work for three long years. The British press now started paying close and daily attention to 'The Great Strike', which persisted until November 1903. There was widespread support for the striking workers. When London's Bethnal Green raised £300 to support the strikers and their families, £25 of it was raised in farthings.

There were passionate parliamentary interventions on the subject of the strike by the Liberal MP David Lloyd George, who was a doughty enemy of Lord Penrhyn, and in 1901 the quarry reopened, but without sufficient workers. The majority stayed home, while others had moved to the south in search of work in the coalfields.

Society began to dislocate in the slate-quarrying areas: violence flared up in places such as Bethesda, and soldiers had to be called in to protect *cynffonwyr* or blacklegs, men who felt obliged to return to work. Baron Penrhyn even erected houses in places such as Tregarth to accommodate the blacklegs and their families, but a street such as Ffordd Tanrhiw was soon baptized Stryd y Gynffon (Traitors' Row).

The strike polarized the community, setting neighbour against neighbour and engendering angry scenes, not least when local papers printed the names and addresses of those who had returned to work. Those who had chosen to stay on strike put cards in the windows of their homes proclaiming '*Nid oes bradwr yn y tŷ hwn*' (no traitors live here). There was now open warfare in the area, family set against family, village against village, and the pain took generations to heal.

Because of the violence, the Trade Union Congress withdrew its support. By the time the strike ended, the workforce was massively depleted, but meanwhile the building industry was entering a slump, and demand for slate dropped as a natural consequence.

In just 100 years, the Industrial Revolution had utterly changed Wales. A rural economy was now predominantly an industrial one. The countryside haemorrhaged, its people leaving in droves for new towns, which could absorb them and offer work. As the number of people left in the rural hinterlands declined, so too did their grievances.

A new class of people – the working class – had emerged from a grimy, poverty-ridden mire to fight with spirit and dignity for improved rights and conditions. From the middle of the nineteenth century a volatile society full of radicalism and a keen sense of politics had been born in the new industrial Wales.

PART FIVE

THE MAKING OF MODERN WALES

CHAPTER TWENTY

A LIBERAL WALES

The year 1906 was a remarkable one for the Liberal Party in Wales. Following a dramatic electoral landslide in its favour, the Conservatives were routed and the Labour Party gained only one seat. The Liberals would hold sway over Wales for no less than two generations, remaining in power until 1922, when Labour took the reins.

The Liberal Party, which formed in 1859, had been successfully growing its support in Wales during the second half of the nineteenth century and had good relations with the Nonconformist community. In 1865 it had won its first-ever parliamentary majority, and the following year saw the return of 23 former members, but it was the aftershock of the election that really bolstered Liberal Party support. Tory landlords evicted tenants who had voted Liberal and this set voting patterns among the agricultural communities for generations to come, fuelled by a new popular martyrology.

The reaction to an alleged 200 notices to quit in just the county of Cardiganshire alone constituted 'an important episode in the growth of political consciousness. They afforded to radicals and nonconformists of all shades a cause for common action.'[1]

Then, in 1880, the Liberals had further success, winning nine new seats in the general election. One of the real poster boys of Liberalism was William Ewart Gladstone, Squire of Hawarden, who

was married to a Welsh native. His image was to be found prominently displayed in the homes of agricultural labourers and miners
alike, not only because he lived in Flintshire, but also because he
repeatedly showed in Parliament that he was willing to listen to
Welsh public opinion.

Gladstone was key to the party's success. With him as their
eloquent spokesman, the Liberals were able to draw up a charter of
national demands, which included disestablishing the Church,
reforms in education, land reforms, the creation of Welsh national
institutions, and advances in legislation concerning temperance
(reduced use of alcohol). Meanwhile prominent politicians, such as
T. E. Ellis (leader of Cymru Fydd – Young Wales) and Liberal MP
David Lloyd George, established Liberal federations in north and
south Wales, and soon their efforts were being rewarded.

Their popularity was not just on a national scale: in the first
county council elections in 1889 they controlled virtually every one of
the Welsh councils, which were based mainly on the historic counties, although some new boroughs, such as Merthyr, now came into
being, reflecting their surge in population.

One of the first pieces of legislation in modern times specifically
to address a Welsh issue, namely the Welsh Intermediate Education
Act, was passed in 1889. This gave counties and boroughs the right
to establish intermediate or secondary schools. These were quickly
established, and by 1905 there was a network of 95 throughout the
land, in which 8,000 pupils could be educated, and girls outnumbered boys. Laudably, these schools also increased social mobility,
with low fees and ready scholarships available, and this put Wales

ahead of England when it came to matters of state-sponsored secondary education.

There were advances in land reform too, as Gladstone appointed a Commission for Land in Wales, and in 1893 the University of Wales received its charter. These were both pivotal acts in the creation of civic institutions to mirror political advances. After the damning Blue Books of 1847, the future was looking much brighter for Wales.

As one century yielded to another, Liberal Wales was consolidating its success, bedding down ever deeper. Grass-roots support came from shopkeepers and middle-class professionals; media backing came in the form of dozens of local newspapers and periodicals; and there were plenty of links with buoyant industries. The causes of free trade, freedom of the individual, and social equality were enthusiastically embraced and promoted, especially by the Nonconformist chapels.

However, in 1902, these gains appeared to be threatened by the Education Act, an Act put through under the Conservative government, which sought to change the system of school administration, part of which involved channelling funds into Church of England schools. This move was deeply unpopular in Nonconformist Wales and the implications of the Act – that there would be 300 school districts where the only elementary schools would be Church of England caused great dissent. The Act was fiercely opposed by Liberal MP Lloyd George, who was able to rally support throughout the Liberal Party to oppose giving aid to Church schools. His persistence helped to wreck the Act completely. The irony of the children of Nonconformist parents having to attend Church or 'National' schools was not lost on the Welsh: prime minister-to-be Lloyd George had himself been taught in a Church school.

The astounding Liberal victory in Wales in 1906 also ushered in the end of the influence of gentry families on the political life of Wales. Gentry estates had supplied Parliament with Welsh members since time immemorial. As they captured seats, Welsh Liberals replaced the Tory 'toffs' of the gentrified past with lawyers, industrialists and entrepreneurs.

One of the brightest stars in the Liberal firmament, David Lloyd George, would become, in the words of historian Kenneth O. Morgan, 'the greatest Welshman of the day and the outstanding Liberal of the century'.[2] The first politician of genuinely humble origins to become prime minister of the United Kingdom, he was born in Manchester to Welsh-speaking parents and raised in Caernarfonshire. He always viewed Wales as his home, even though he was to acquire a taste for cosmopolitan life, enjoying time in the Alps and on the French Riviera.

A successful solicitor in northwest Wales, Lloyd George won the seat of Caernarfon Boroughs in 1890 at the age of 27, and held the seat until the end of the Second World War. In his early career he was noteworthy for his opposition to the South African or Boer War of 1899–1902 as he believed that 'waging war upon two small Boer republics, run by Calvinist farmers rather like the Welsh, was a political and moral wrong'.[3]

Lloyd George became president of the Board of Trade in 1905 and three years later was made chancellor of the exchequer under Herbert Asquith. During this time he swiftly built two pillars of the welfare system, namely old age pensions and national insurance, thereby creating the bedrock of the welfare state.

Shored up by the success of these reforms, Lloyd George went even further with his 'People's Budget' of 1909, which he described as

a 'war budget' – a war against poverty – in which new taxes were introduced against the wealthy, and new social welfare programmes were
introduced.

These actions also led to constitutional change: the war budget
was rejected by the House of Lords, an action that led to the Parliament Act of 1911, which removed the House of Lord's power to veto.
A pinnacle of Liberal achievement was to follow with the granting of
disestablishment, or the withdrawal of state control from a Church, in
this case the Church in Wales withdrawing from the state Church of
England. In 1920, the Church in Wales became a totally separate
entity, with its own archbishop to represent Anglicanism and its
chapels in Wales.

Lloyd George, who could sound very much like a preacher fired up
with *hwyl* (sudden inspiration), knew the value of Nonconformity in
his political aims and ambitions. In a speech he made as president of
the Baptists' Union, he focused on the Wales he represented, a country veritably shored up by faith, with its chapels nothing less than the
colleges of the common people:

> *Nonconformity was the first power to do that for Wales … It
> taught them perseverance, it taught them organization and the
> importance of permanent work – work that had no flash about
> it, work that brought no immediate fruit, but work that meant
> patience and long waiting.*
>
> *It was Nonconformity that taught Wales her politics … And
> what had been added unto the people of Wales? First the democ-
> racy of Wales had won their self-respect, they had also won their
> independence. They stood like men … the Welsh nation was*

going forward, ever forward; not following the flesh pots in the
land of bondage, but turning its back on these to steadfastly
follow the cloud by day and the pillar of fire by night … forward,
ever forward, fighting the sons of Amalek. Many of us have
ascended the summit of Pisgah and there from afar have gained
a glimpse of the Promised Land. How many of us will reach it? I
know not but in my opinion we are rapidly approaching it, and
the people of Wales can sing 'Bryniau Canaan ddont i'r golwg.[14]

As war broke out in 1914, Lloyd George remained chancellor of the exchequer before becoming minister for munitions in 1915 and secretary of state for war in July 1916. By this time, Lloyd George had become critical of Prime Minister Asquith. A letter from Bryn Roberts, the Liberal MP for north Caernarfonshire, to Asquith warning him of Lloyd George's nationalist tactics, and Asquith's subsequent complaints to Lloyd George about his disloyal behaviour, served to sour the relationship between the two men.

In December that year, with the support of the Conservative and Labour leaders, Lloyd George became Prime Minister. His reputation would now depend not on how he handled industrial relations, but how he managed the task of being a wartime premier.

The First World War had broken out as a consequence of the assassination of the Archduke Franz Ferdinand of Austria-Hungary on 4 August 1914. A crumbling Austro-Hungarian Empire decided to punish Serbia, the country it blamed for the murder. An aggressive Germany decided to back up its neighbour to the hilt. The death of this one man thus became an act that resonated throughout a deeply divided Europe.

As Britain allied itself with France and Russia to fight Germany and Austria-Hungary, no one could have imagined the titanic scale of the carnage that would ensue during the so-called 'war to end all wars'. Certainly no one could even have begun to imagine what would occur, particularly at Ypres and the Somme. The Battle of the Somme, which lasted from July to November 1916, was a human tragedy that claimed the lives of 450,000 British soldiers, no fewer than 19,000 of whom died during the first day's fighting.

At first people at home had no inkling of the scale of the slaughter, and had been led to believe that the war would soon be over. The frustrations of the working class meant that an outbreak of war fever was unlikely, and elements of both the Welsh Nonconformists and the Liberals railed against militarism (Wales had more conscientious objectors than anywhere else in Britain, a fact that infuriated Lloyd George).

Yet the Welsh embraced the war as a means of defending their cherished values. Despite objections from some quarters, the drive to sign men up was mainly enthusiastically endorsed in all sections of society: by scholars such as Sir John Morris Jones in Bangor, by Liberal MPs such as W. Llewelyn Williams in Carmarthen, and south Wales miners' leader William Abraham, not to mention Nonconformist ministers such as John Williams of Brynsiencyn. Indeed, in October 1914, 20 Nonconformist ministers became signatories to *A War Manifesto*. Politicians, union leaders, church ministers, civic leaders, academics and the press overwhelmingly joined the campaign for recruits. The press encouraged communities to compete with one another in gaining recruits, and in August 1915 the recruiting offices in Cardiff and Swansea simply could not cope with the numbers coming forward.

Between 1914 and 1918, 272,924 Welsh men were recruited to fight. Recruits came overwhelmingly from Glamorgan and Monmouthshire, as did half of all those killed. The press were critical of rural counties where able young men were allegedly more reluctant to come forward, yet the final death toll suggests that in some rural counties a larger percentage of men joined the forces than from the industrialized south, and proportionally suffered twice as many killed in the war.

In Briton Ferry in Glamorgan, south Wales, virtually every man of eligible age joined the forces. The Tylorstown Silver Band joined en bloc, and in the Rhondda, miners' agent David Watts Morgan promoted the formation of a 'pals' brigade'. The Pals battalions and brigades were specially constituted units of the British Army, comprising men who had enlisted in local recruiting drives, with the promise that they would be able to serve alongside their friends, neighbours and work colleagues rather than being arbitrarily allocated to regular Army regiments. Friends could therefore live, serve and die together.

So why did Wales respond to the outbreak of the First World War with such enthusiasm? Lloyd George and others reminded Welsh people of their military tradition; resistance to the Normans, defiance at Harlech and against the bowmen of Crécy, but the decisive factor was the Welsh identification with the plight of Belgium. This was a small country like Wales, now apparently defenceless in the face of aggression from its powerful, bullying neighbour. In a speech at the Queen's Hall in London on 19 September 1914, he argued for the founding of a Welsh Army:

Ah! The world owes so much to the little five-foot-five nations. The greatest art in the world was the work of little nations; the most enduring literature of England came when she was a nation the size of Belgium fighting for their freedom. The heroic deeds that thrill humanity through generations were the deeds of little nations fighting for their freedom. Yes, and the salvation of mankind came through a small nation ... Wales must continue doing her duty. I should like to see the race that faced the Normans for hundreds of years in a struggle for freedom, the race that helped to win Crécy, the race that fought for a generation under Glendower against the greatest captain in Europe – I should like to see that race give a good taste of its quality in this struggle in Europe; and they are going to do it.

Only one division of this 'Welsh army', the 38th, was actually created, and it went to France in December 1915 and saw action during the First Battle of the Somme in July 1916. By December 1914 no fewer than 40,000 south Wales miners had enlisted, and four battalions of the Welsh Division were drawn from the Rhondda alone.

Despite this substantial figure, miners were generally expected to stay at home as their work was deemed essential to the war effort, and they were exempted from military service. But they too would be affected by the war. As it progressed, colliery managers came under increasing pressure to maximize production, and working conditions suffered. In response, the men went on strike in 1915, fired by the belief that they were being exploited by the owners, who capitalized on the false view that the miners were unwilling to support the work effort.

Cabinet ministers were incensed by the strike and its effect on the war effort. The leadership of the Fed (the miners' union) offered to

attend talks in London, but the men were solidly against such a conciliatory move. As one of them put it, 'You have gone to that city of
Philistines too often. Let them come to us, here in south Wales.'

Lloyd George went to the miners. He largely accepted most of
their demands, assuring them that the colliery owners would abide
by the agreement they had just reached. It was a promise that proved
difficult to deliver in reality, but it was enough at the time to smooth
over the tension.

Meanwhile, the Russian Revolution, which began in 1917, was
widely seen as a call to arms by disgruntled workers all over Europe,
and it received a sympathetic reception in the South Wales Coalfield. In
Merthyr Tydfil, for example, the editor of the local newspaper recorded
that there wasn't another place on Earth where the revolution had been
greeted with greater joy. In another mining valley local people sang
'Workers of the Vale of Amman/ Echo Russia's mighty thrust …'

In July 1917, while the war was still progressing, 200 delegates
from all over the South Wales Coalfield attended a special conference
in the centre of Swansea with the express aim of deciding whether or
not to set up Russian-style 'soviets' (workers' councils) in Wales. The
meeting was eventually broken up by a mixture of soldiers and arma-
ments' workers, which showed how feelings were running high on
both sides, and the whiff of revolution was set to linger in the air a
good while yet.

Women got behind the war effort by joining the Red Cross and St
John Ambulance, knitting garments for the troops, welcoming Belgian
refugees, making bandages or campaigning for peace, but peace didn't
come. Little wonder that there was a backlash against the Church and
attendances declined. Membership had peaked in 1907 when the

churches of Wales had a total of 750,000 communicants, not to mention a host of occasional 'hearers'; but deep cynicism caused by the clergy-recruiters for the First World War led to numbers falling away.

During the war, women, out of necessity, also started to do jobs formerly carried out by men, and this change irrevocably transformed the role of women in British society. They drove trams, dug graves, worked in shipyards and munitions factories, and become clerks, secretaries, post office workers and chimney sweeps. The Women's Land Army tilled the soil and lent a hand to farmers who had lost their labour force to the battlefields. And there were women who were more directly involved in the war effort in bodies such as the Women's Royal Air Force, the Women's Royal Naval Service, and the Women's Army Auxiliary Corps, which organized support services in offices and canteens.

In the world of munitions manufacture, women entered the work-place very fully and ably, and in the National Shell Factories in Llanelli, Swansea and Newport they mass-produced shells for a greedy artillery overseas. Women also risked their lives and endangered their health as they made explosives such as TNT and gun-cotton in places such as Pembrey and Queensferry, and explosions on the production line weren't unknown.

Welsh women were active in both pro- and anti-suffrage campaigns. They achieved parity with men in 1928, when they were allowed to vote at 21. The following year Megan Lloyd George, daughter of David, became the first woman to be elected in Wales. Despite these changes, employment in domestic service remained the largest single employment opportunity for women till 1939, although there was a massive decline in the numbers. From 1931 government domestic training courses had been set up in Cardiff and eight valley towns to train Welsh women as cheap migrant workers for the homes and hotels of affluent England.

After the war, Welsh women also took up more places in Welsh universities and constituted a higher percentage than their counterparts in Scotland and England. Yet their status more generally in society was ambiguous. Bangor University had not a single female professor before the Second World War. There was also massive social pressure exerted on women to return to the home. It was made virtually impossible for them to claim unemployment benefit, and professions insisted that women resign upon marriage.

The war also precipitated the departure of David Lloyd George. Not everyone was pleased by his wartime leadership and, in particular, his lack of judgement in not removing Field Marshal Sir Douglas Haig, who had lost two million men under his command. In the 1930s, the economist J. M. Keynes ascribed many of the failings of the Treaty of Versailles – the peace treaty between Germany and the Allies – to the manoeuvrings of a prime minister 'from the hag-ridden magic and enchanted woods of Celtic antiquity'.[5] Lloyd George's Welshness was often seen as weakness, a view that persisted until his death in 1945.

Lloyd George had also had trouble in his own camp. The general election of December 1918 was dubbed the 'coupon' election – a reference to the electoral arrangements between Coalition Liberals and the Conservatives. In this agreement 150 Liberals were to be offered the support of Lloyd George and the leader of the Conservative Party at the next general election, but it created sharp lines of division among the Liberals, those with backing and those without, with the latter likely to lose their seats as a consequence.

Black and Tan* violence in Ireland also reflected badly on Lloyd George too, as he had been a highly visible supporter of Irish Home Rule. Such factors ushered in a period when Labour was able to take advantage of splits within the Liberal camp to break the Liberals' hegemony and make gains in by-elections in constituencies in industrial south Wales.

By 1922 the Liberals found themselves representing little more than the rump of rural Wales, and in October of that year Lloyd George had to step down as prime minister. This ushered in a new era for the Labour Party in Wales.

---

* Black and Tans were all armed forces recruited to fight against Sinn Fein (Irish Republicans) in 1920. Their nickname came from the colours of their uniform.

CHAPTER TWENTY-ONE

DEPRESSION WALES

In the 1920s the tightly woven tapestry of Welsh industry quickly unravelled as work opportunities and money dried up. The Depression blighted many parts of the world – including, famously, America, where the popular song 'Buddy Can You Spare a Dime?' became a street-corner mantra. It precipitated a profound slump in Wales – a country that was so very dependent on a handful of products: steel, coal and tin. Here was an economy entirely dependent on extraction and production; if the market shrank, the only way for Wales's economy to go was down, bringing subsidiaries such as commerce and transport with it as well.

Unemployment figures sky-rocketed as the slump truly set in. This was vividly apparent in the mid-1920s, when unemployment among coal miners shot up from 2 per cent in April 1924 to 12.5 per cent by January 1925, before climbing to 28.5 per cent by August of that same year. The South Wales Coalfield, more dependent upon exports than the other British coalfields, was the worst hit.

The reasons for the decline in the British coal industry were multiple. British production methods were inefficient, and the exchange rate of sterling was high. Meanwhile, there was an increase in coal production from elsewhere: South American markets had been captured by the USA, which developed strip mills to service the steel industry, and this was coupled with a loss of European markets because Germany was paying reparations in coal after the First World War. This meant that Germany was supplying free coal to its former enemies at the same time that French, Belgian, Polish and American coal production was stepping up. As a consequence, British coal prices fell through the floor.

To stem their losses, in the spring of 1926, the mine owners of Great Britain tried to impose a brutal cut in the wages of their already struggling workers. The move triggered one of the most harrowing, but also inspiring, episodes in the history of the South Wales Coalfield: the prolonged lockout that followed in the wake of the General Strike.

The strike was a Britain-wide phenomenon. Launched by the trade unions as a response to the mine owners' proposals, it involved dockers, steelworkers and railwaymen, as well as the miners, and was seen as an attempt to bring down the Conservative government led by Stanley Baldwin. Patchily supported by the British public, the strike collapsed after just nine days in most of Britain. In Wales, however, the struggle went on. Welsh miners refused to accept the terms offered elsewhere and were consequently locked out of their pits by the owners. They managed to hold out for seven long months, during which time life in the valleys was turned upside down. Dread spread through communities, as people realized that the work might never return.

Because of the global conditions, a total of 241 coal mines in Wales were shut down between 1921 and 1936, and the workforce of 270,000 was halved as a consequence of these closures. In the northeast too the closure of the steelworks at Brymbo, not to mention the closure of local collieries, ushered in a period of economic trial and tribulation.

It was not the same throughout the coalfield, however. Soft, bitu-minous coal wasn't needed, leading to pit closures and a sharp decline in the business of attendant ports such as Cardiff – where empty ships clogged the harbour – but anthracite, mined on the western rim of the South Wales Coalfield, was still very much in demand, moving toward a peak in production in 1934.

For most, though, this was a period of intense hardship, and low incomes resulted in poor health and sub-standard housing. As the 1920s drew to a close, one in five workers in Wales wasn't working. It was little short of a social cataclysm. People had to scrabble around slag heaps looking for fragments of coal to heat their homes. Malnu-trition took its toll.

An alternative to suffering was Popular Assistance, known as the 'dole', but to qualify for that one had to suffer the ignominies and humiliation of the means test, which was widely and passionately resented. Under this system, poor people already on welfare – includ-ing dole money for the unemployed – saw their money cut if one member of the household was lucky enough to get a job. The means test led to massive protests, including the demonstrations of 3 February 1935, when 300,000 people took to the streets in Wales. They offered conclusive proof that miners and their families weren't prepared to lie down.

At the height of the strike, in that 'Angry Summer' of 1926, jazz bands still struck up defiantly. But the defeat of the strikers was a blow to people already weakened by financial insecurity. In some areas in southeast Wales the local authorities did their best to alleviate suffer-ing, spending tens of thousands of pounds in helping people to cope with hardship. The South Wales Miners' Federation, as well as chari-table bodies, did their bit too by funding soup kitchens.

The Depression halted and reversed the industrial growth that had been in full flow for 150 years. It caused massive emigration – what the Rhondda-born writer Gwyn Thomas called 'a Black Death on wheels'. Wales lost at least 430,000 people between 1921 and 1940, some of whom ventured as far afield as Australia, South Africa and America. The country's population was not to regain its 1925 level until 1973.

The effect of this migration was most acutely felt in Monmouth-shire and Glamorgan. In the latter, over 50,000 people left the Rhondda alone, and as these were mainly young men, this had a dramatic and withering effect on the society they left behind. Men went to the car-making centres of Oxford and Coventry, and to indus-trial cities, such as Birmingham and Liverpool, and to seek work in other urban centres, such as London and Reading. There were also dispersals because of very particular local issues, such as the closure of the naval dockyard in Pembroke Dock in 1926, which prompted a quarter of the borough's population to move away and left half of those who remained blighted by unemployment.

While unemployment was at its most extreme in coal mining, the Depression also affected steel, tinplate, slate and transport work-ers. Agriculture, an area in which many workers were women, also faced worrying decline. There were disquieting social inequalities too. In Carmarthenshire, which had the largest agricultural labour force in Wales, women lost their jobs five times faster than male labourers. In these times of hardship many fully employed small-holders and farm labourers earned less than those on unemployment benefit. Tenant farmers who had just bought land couldn't cope with high interest rates and soaring costs, while rural industries, such as the woollen mills, went out of business, with half of the 50 mills that were operating in the Teifi valley shut by the period just after the war.

This being the age of photography, images proliferated of gaunt men with eyes like wells of hopelessness, of urchin children, and of women beaten down by circumstance. But, as historian Deian Hopkin has noted, there was one fact above all others that summed up the deprivations of the age: between 1920 and 1938 spending on clothes and shoes fell by almost 40 per cent.[1] Men couldn't afford to buy shirts and women just had to make do. The Pontypridd-born writer Alun Richards recalled the shame of it all:

> I think it must have been about 1936 that I first became aware of the humiliating poverty with which so many people were afflicted. Rickets and other malformities due to malnutrition and requiring leg irons, I accepted, because I had always seen them amongst my classmates, but when the boy who sat next to me in school was forced to attend in his sister's shoes, I felt his humiliation deeply.[2]

Yet even in this age of deprivation, some middle-class people continued to prosper. More radios and cars were bought in Cardiff than in Slough or Luton. The suggestion of unremitting and somehow egalitarian suffering was untrue. Middle-class houses were erected on crescents in the Uplands, Swansea, in Cyncoed in Cardiff and Garden Village in Wrexham. In Cardiff, one in six households had a phone, while in the Rhondda it was one in fifty and in Abercarn one in a hundred. It all depended on where you lived.

For those in areas worst hit, enforced idleness created fatalism and despondency, with the newly established football pools offering a dreamer's way out of a predicament. In place of gainful employment, killing time became the principal occupation for legions of laid-off workers.

Sociologist Hilda Jennings portrayed the soul-sapping tedium of life without work:

> Visits to the Exchange at most take up part of two half-days in the week. For the rest, some men stand aimlessly on the Market Square or at the street corners, content apparently with a passive, animal existence, or with the hour-long observation of passers-by, varied by the occasional whiff at a cigarette. Others work on allotment or garden, tend fowls or pigs, or do carpentry in their backyard or kitchen. Others again 'stroll down the valley' or sit on the banks when the sun is warm. On wet days the Miners' Institute offers papers and a shelter, although shop doors and street corners satisfy many. At night, there are the pictures, and the long queues outside the 'Picture House' probably account for more of the pocket-money of the unemployed than do the public-house.[3]

The opening decades of the twentieth century witnessed the rise of a new art form and mode of popular entertainment: film and the cinema. It followed that cinemas proliferated everywhere. Even small towns in Wales had a Plaza, Palace, Hippodrome or Empire, and often more than one. By the interwar period, cinemas had started to appear with the same rapidity that the chapels – the Gerazims, Pisgahs and Rehoboths – had opened their doors when religion was the principal form of entertainment. Indeed, dwindling chapel attendances were blamed on the popularity of celluloid stars such as Clark Gable and Bette Davis.

Chapelgoers naturally bristled at the new mode of entertainment, and novelist Pennar Davies was not alone in sounding notes of caution about its heavenly attractions: 'Babylon, less garish then than now, was setting up its raj, one of its most seductive instruments being the Saturday matinée in the Palace cinema. This, and the rarer and even more intoxicating "legitimate" drama in the Empire, provided a powerful counter-attraction to the Sunday School.'[4]

As far back as the 1880s, the pioneering showman William Haggar had been taking his horse-drawn, and later traction-engine-tugged, travelling theatre around the country. In 1898 he showed his first bioscope film at Aberafan, although a six-month strike in the coalfield at the time meant that it wasn't a big attraction.

Early machines for showing moving pictures were a big draw. As the nineteenth century drew to a close, an industrial exhibition was held in Cathays Park – a direct consequence of the coal money that had made Cardiff, in terms of tonnage, the second largest port in the world after New York. Two of the attractions were penny-in-the-slot Kinetoscope cabinets, developed by Thomas Edison, which allowed viewers to see short films, such as one round of a prize fight or strongman Eugene Sandow lifting weights.

At the beginning of the twentieth century Haggar began to make his own films: taking his cue from melodramas such as *The Maid of Cefn Ydfa*, he and his family would act out similar scenarios. Haggar's films often mocked authority, just as the Keystone Cops did in America, with clumsy and inept policemen a dependable source of ready laughs. Some of these anti-authoritarian films, such as *A Desperate Poaching Affray*, were serious contributions to the development of cinema. This example included one of the first-ever chase sequences and was distributed and shown throughout America.

There were 162 halls and other venues screening films in Wales in 1910, and by 1920 the number had soared to 252. Places such as Blaengarw Working Men's Hall were showing films early in the century, and similar venues sprang up elsewhere. When the new miners' institute, serving the miners of Nine Mile Point colliery near Cwmfelinfach, opened in 1913 they hoped that the top floor cine-matograph would bring them revenue equivalent to half the cost of building the entire place. Miners elsewhere followed suit, with work-men's halls, from Ogmore Vale to Maerdy, opening up new screens for an eager public: the one in Ferndale held almost 2,000 people, and was the go-to destination for the Rhondda valley.

Between 1912 and 1927 some 26 films on Welsh subjects were made, although these would struggle to compete with the allure of films coming out of America, which were by their very nature more exotic. *The Proud Valley*, the 1940 vehicle for black singer and activist Paul Robeson, was built on a special relationship between him and Wales, which began when he sang in places such as Aberdare and Mountain Ash to raise money for the Spanish Civil War. *The Proud Valley* was based on a story written by a communist writer called Herbert Marshall, and told the story of a black stoker who arrived in a valley community, where he joined the choir, worked hard, proved himself a hero, and ulti-mately sacrificed his life to save others underground.

Shot by Pen Tennyson, the Eton- and Oxford-educated great-grandson of the poet Alfred Lord Tennyson, the film was made for

£40,000. Despite his silver-spoon upbringing, the director initially wanted to call the film 'One in Five', a reference to the injury rate in the pits at the time. The original script was tinkered with and watered down by other hands so that the finished product 'shunned reality like a disease', according to the *New Statesman*.

Audiences in places such as Ferndale especially enjoyed watching the biggest male star in Britain of his day, namely the Welshman Ivor Davies (better known as songwriter and singer Ivor Novello), in some of the early films of Alfred Hitchcock. During the 1930s, Welsh actor Emlyn Williams also emerged as a popular star. This decade also saw the first Welsh-language film, *Y Chwarelwr* (The Quarryman), made in Blaenau Ffestiniog by Sir Ifan ab Owen Edwards. By this decade there were more cinemas per capita in south Wales than anywhere else in Britain. Clark Gable was by now as familiar a face as the man next door.

The picture palaces pegged their prices in order to ensure that the cheap seats were always full of customers. Audiences lapped up the hilarious antics of Charlie Chaplin and Buster Keaton in picture houses anywhere from Resolven Miners' Welfare Hall to Risca. In the dark of the cinema one could forget the harsh realities outside.

And the realities were indeed harsh: Wales was much worse off than other parts of Britain. Between 1928 and 1939 the rate of unemployment in Wales never dipped below 20 per cent and at its worst it was as high as 39 per cent. Not only was this rate worse than elsewhere, but men also remained out of work for longer. This resulted in social phthisis – a wasting away of hope and aspiration. Towns and villages such as Merthyr, Dowlais, Pontlottyn, Rhymney, Blaina, Brynmawr and Nant-y-glo, which had been created by labour opportunities, swiftly dissipated into ghost towns, sapped of civic spirit and completely demoralized by the lack of work.

Dowlais, in particular, was affected by the closure of the ironworks in 1931, ten years after the works at Cyfarthfa. The closure marked the end of what, at times, had been the principal world centre of iron production. But no longer. In such places the new mottoes, such as 'New Leisure' or 'Time to Spare', coined by politicians to put a positive spin on the situation, had a hollow ring.

By 1932, when unemployment among insured males in Wales peaked, the country was among the world's most depressed. By 1939, when the Ministry of Health reported on tuberculosis in Wales, the picture it painted of squalid living conditions, high death rates and children in parlous need made frightening reading. A proportion of 95.9 deaths per 1,000 births was recorded in Wrexham. In Mountain Ash, mothers were too malnourished to breastfeed their children. Infants did not necessarily survive their first year of life. This was a country made sick by want and fearful by hunger. No fewer than 17 tuberculosis sanatoria were opened throughout the country, but even then Wales topped the charts when it came to this killer disease. Diphtheria and scarlet fever were rife too.

At about the same time, at the height of the Depression, civil war broke out in Spain. Democratic forces loyal to the Spanish republic, which had been in existence for five years, clashed with the fascist army of General Franco. Many working people in Wales saw the struggle as a battle for the future of mankind, and 177 men from the country enlisted as members of the International Brigades set up to defend the republic. The men travelled to Spain and threw themselves into the fight. Of the 177 who went, 33 died. Among them was Sammy

Morris of Ammanford, who sent a letter home shortly before his death in which he succinctly summed up his philosophy: 'Share the wealth; share the land; share the rhubarb; share the tent.'

The apparent collapse of capitalism during the Depression increased support for socialists and communists in Wales, who were at the forefront of all protests. As one Swansea Liberal complained, 'Marx's *Kapital* has ejected the Bible from the minds of thousands of young Welshmen'.[5] Committed Marxists, such as S. O. Davies, the miners' agent for Merthyr and 'humble follower of Lenin', and Arthur Cook, a founding member of the Communist Party, introduced a new militancy and political ethos to the leadership of the coalfield. The community of Maerdy was so left-leaning that it was known as 'Little Moscow'.

The impoverishment of industrial Wales dealt a devastating blow to chapel culture and to the Welsh language. The number of Welsh speakers fell from 44.6 per cent in 1911 to 37.1 per cent ten years later. By 1931 a parlous decline in the language had begun. To try to staunch the haemorrhage, Ifan ab Owen Edwards established the youth movement Urdd Gobaith Cymru in 1922, and three years later saw the genesis of Plaid Genedlaethol Cymru, the National Party of Wales. Despite these efforts, English continued its growth as the majority language of the people.

Disagreement over support for the unemployed led to the collapse of the Labour government of 1929–31, and the subsequent National Government believed that little could be done apart from waiting for circumstances to improve. In 1937, however, the government began to provide assistance for companies by creating jobs in areas of high unemployment, which proved to be the foundation of regional economic policies to which Wales was to become much indebted.

In some areas in Wales there was economic progress. Advances in technology and the growth in man-made materials meant that Flintshire benefited from having the Courtaulds rayon factory, which employed a couple of thousand workers. The steelworks at Ebbw Vale opened in 1938, and the trading estate at Treforest saw 13 new factories open between 1932 and 1938. However, there was little real improvement in the Welsh economy, and for coal communities, such as Gresford and Rhosllannerchrugog, men found themselves mining misery.

There were some limited sources of optimism for the future in matters of education, with investment in public education at the elementary level, and a hike in university income of 91 per cent. A new university college was established at Swansea in 1920, and Coleg Harlech opened in 1927, with the visionary aim of educating adult workers. But a commitment to learning was most obvious at secondary school level: 37 new schools were opened between 1919 and 1938, while the number of pupils rose by over 80 per cent.

In the last month of peacetime, in August 1939, unemployment among uninsured males in Wales was 15.2 per cent. But by now many of the natural resources of the country were dwindling: coal and slate were no longer quite so bountiful, and industrialization could no longer promise improvements in living standards. For the economy, at least, war came as something of a relief.

CHAPTER TWENTY-TWO

RAINING BOMBS

In terms of naked statistics, Wales suffered much less in the Second World War (1939–45) than during the First World War, but the loss of 15,000 Welsh people in the armed forces still cut deep into the national psyche.

If the First World War was a soldiers' war, the Second World War was a civilians' war, since they faced as much danger as serving troops. It was a war that had implications for every individual, each of whom had to contend with rationing books, blackouts and air-raid precautions, but collectively these trials and challenges bound people together into defiant communities. A sense of humour helped as well, not to mention a certain stoicism: in Canton, Cardiff, a man ushering a neighbour into an air-raid shelter was told she had to find her false teeth first, to which he replied, 'Never mind those, Hitler's dropping bombs not sandwiches.'[1]

The people of Wales had known that war was coming. The news had been full of accounts of the rise of fascism in countries such as Spain, Italy and Germany. Now the front pages of newspapers detailing Adolf Hitler's arrogant annexations of neighbouring countries stoked popular anger. It was easy to rally support for such a clear-cut and morally justified cause.

The invasion of Czechoslovakia in September 1938 prompted 20 Welsh MPs to vote against the agreement that Prime Minister Neville Chamberlain had struck with Hitler in Munich, and that had led him confidently to proclaim 'Peace for our time'. Ironically, this was such a peaceful time that every man, woman and child in the land had just been issued with a gas mask, while air-raid shelters were being swiftly constructed almost everywhere. As a local resident from Cardiff Bernard Parsons revealed:

The government supplied these Anderson Shelters. They came up on a wagon and the council workers decided where each one was going. And they dug this big hole to take it. They put the pieces of the shelter into the hole, then bolted it all together – both sides, then top and bottom with a big square for a door …[2]

Not everyone rallied to the cause: the Welsh Nationalist Party, formed in 1925, objected to the war on the grounds that the British state didn't have the right to declare war on behalf of Wales. In the end, however, Wales played its part.

No fewer than a million and a half mothers and children were evacuated from cities such as Birmingham, Liverpool and London, and Wales welcomed a great many of them, having been designated a 'reception area'. Aberdare took in all the pupils of the Ilford and Essex mixed grammar schools, and 19,000 evacuees found themselves in Flintshire.

The influx of English children served to dilute Welshness and the Welsh language, but the war itself, with its sense of 'we're all in this together', promoted a sense of Britishness that flew like a defiant Union Jack in the face of nationalism and national identity.

During the second year of the conflict, in 1940, the whole of Britain was edgy about the prospect of an invasion by Germany, especially after the devastations of Dunkirk that year, when a third of a million Allied soldiers had to be rescued from the beaches of France by a fleet of 850 small boats. Leaflets were issued in Welsh giving advice about what to do should the Germans come. There were even some distributed via post offices, explaining how to wage guerrilla warfare should that be necessary:

> *If you happen to be standing in a ditch or behind a tree or some other position of safety, and you have some kind of grenade or bomb in your hand, and a car comes along with enemy officers, driven even by your best friend, you must let them have it. It is what your friend would want you to do.*[3]

Requiring land on which to train the legions of new recruits at the start of the war, the military started to appropriate large tracts, such as the Stackpole estate in Pembrokeshire. The requisition of 40,000 acres and the forced expulsion of 219 Welsh speakers from 54 homes on the Epynt Mountain was seen by some as nothing short of a cultural clearance. The poet and scholar Iorwerth C. Peate, who visited the area just before the expulsions, described how one old woman had spoken of her deep roots in the area and of how her family had farmed there for generations. In tears, she put it starkly: 'It is the end of the world here.'[4]

With much of the war fought in and from the skies, some of Wales's towns bore the brunt of bombing raids. Junkers and Dorniers of the Luftwaffe concentrated on industrial and transport hubs, dropping great tonnages of bombs on places such as Pembroke Dock, Cardiff and Swansea. Butetown in Cardiff was badly hit, and Newport too. Death rained down from the skies.

Swansea, in particular, suffered massively. The whole of the city centre, along with outlying districts, such as Townhill, Manselton and Brynhyfryd, was obliterated by consecutive raids over three days in February 1941. 'Every searchlight goes up, a glade of magnesium waning to a distant hill which we know to be Swansea,' wrote the poet Lynette Roberts from her home in Llan-y-bri in Carmarthenshire, some 30 miles away. She noted how in the 'Himmel blue sky ... the pillars of smoke writhe and the astringent sky lies pale at her side.'[5]

She had known that the devastation was coming: the 'elbow-drone of Jerries burden the sky and our sailing planes tack in and out with their fine metallic hum ... Swansea's sure to be bad; look at those flares like a swarm of orange bees.' The poet was right: Swansea was badly hit, the town demonically lit up as 70 German aircraft dropped some 35,000 incendiaries and 800 high-explosive bombs on the place. The burning town was clearly visible from Devon on the other side of the Bristol Channel.

A grim tally of 230 people were killed in Swansea, and more than 400 were injured, leaving a town 'split in two', as poet John Ormond described it, having himself witnessed the buildings that 'flowered red in the air' and the dead, their 'arms outstretched to embrace the fire'.[6]

A total of about a thousand people were killed in air raids in 1941 alone, with buildings such as Llandaff Cathedral and Cardiff castle being substantially damaged. Cardiff's populace cowered under a rain of bombs: 165 people alone were killed in January 1941, and streets lay in complete and utter ruin.

But there were other devastations wrought by German planes jettisoning their payload before heading for home: on 30 April 1941, 20 people were killed in Cwm-parc in the Rhondda, while 800 were made homeless.

Because so much of the course of the war was decided up in the clouds, it meant that there was a burgeoning industry in Wales making aeroplanes and related equipment. In Llanberis and Caernarfon the North East Coast Aircraft Company employed 3,000 staff to make parts for bombers, while just across the Menai Straits, the 200 workers in the Saunders Roe Company manufactured seaplanes. In the northeast of the country, at the aircraft factory at Broughton, strenuous efforts by staff enabled the production of 5,540 Wellington bombers, and in one famous instance they were filmed for propaganda purposes making one from scratch in 24 hours.

It was a war in which everyone mucked in, be it by maintaining the blackout, observing strict rationing of food, or 'keeping the home fires burning'. Men too old for active service could join the Local Defence Volunteers, commonly known as the 'Home Guard' or latterly as 'Dad's Army', while one in ten men who were conscripted became 'Bevin Boys', replacing the colliers who had gone off to fight.

Experienced miners took a dim view of the Bevin Boys, the brainchild of Labour MP Ernest Bevin. With a new demand for their labour, the miners regained some of their former power, and staged a series of unofficial wartime strikes. Some of these were extremely well supported: no fewer than 100,000 men went on strike on 2 March 1944 in protest against a plan to do away with distinctions in pay between the skilled and unskilled. In many of the traditional heavy industries, such as tin and steel, there was a shortage of labour, and the

Essential Work Order of 1941 designated coal mining as a 'reserved occupation'.

As was the case in the First World War, women bore more than their fair share of the work, as the eight Royal Ordnance Factories established throughout the country testified. Seven new ones at Bridgend, Hirwaun, Llanishen, Glas-coed (in Monmouthshire), Newport, Marchwiel (near Wrexham), and Rhyd-y-mwyn were created to bolster the efforts of Pembrey, where the manufacture of TNT built on a long history of munitions manufacture at the site, having been initially owned by the Nobel company.

Bridgend became, by reputation, the biggest factory in Britain, and in its heyday the workforce numbered a staggering 35,000 people, the majority being women who came from a wide catchment area, travelling from as far away as Carmarthen, Barry and Merthyr. At Hirwaun 14,000 workers made small arms. It could be dirty and dangerous work. A woman from Aberdare, Gwen Obern, was blinded and had both her hands blown off in her first week at Bridgend. Making the pellets of explosives for use in detonators turned the workers' hair and skin yellow, and blonde hair green, so munitions workers were nicknamed 'canaries'.

Women worked in the countryside too, where the Women's Land Army (WLA) laboured on the land. Initially, farmers paid low wages until they were forced to increase them. But as demand for food rose, and new land had to be cultivated, armed with plough and spade, the WLA was better appreciated. By 1941 there were 2,000 land girls working in Denbighshire alone, undertaking a wide range of tasks, from tilling the soil to harvesting the crops. In 1942 the specialist Women's Timber Corps was established, with bases in places such as

Brechfa and Crickhowell, where trees were felled and timber trimmed for use as pit props and telegraph poles.

The number of women in the workplace constituted a striking socio-cultural shift. As the *Aberdare Leader* noted on 9 October 1943:

> *Women and girls of all ages, married and unmarried, wearing turbans and 'slacks', smoking, laughing, haversacks slung on their shoulders, or little attaché cases in their hands – contrasting rather incongruously with 'permed' hair and lipstick – hurrying in large numbers to the bus or railway station, or, at the end of their day, pouring out of them in a swarm, tired, work-stained, but still laughing and cracking a joke. An unfamiliar sight surely in Wales, where women's place was always regarded as being in the home.*[7]

Elsewhere, factories in places such as Trefforest were requisitioned by the Ministry of Aircraft Production. Work had returned to places that had been starved of it, and the people took to it with alacrity. And so the waging of war had filled the valleys with work and wages. Boys swaggered in the streets with pockets full of money. Omnibuses crowded with women and girls went to and fro between the scattered mining villages and the concentrated munitions factories.

The little houses of the hospitable miners were filled with English children from the 'blitzed' towns over the border. The Welsh economy was in robust good health, and the workforce had been trained because of the exigencies of war production, which had also led to many new factories being built, making anything from torpedoes to trucks, radar gear to artillery shells. The expulsive power of a new experience had dimmed the memories of the 1930s' Depression. The sufferings of enforced idleness had given way to the horrors of bombing and burning.

During the course of the war, the Liberal Party had undergone a change of fortune and was in decline by the 1940s. Lloyd George, now Earl Lloyd George of Dwyfor, died on 26 March 1945. Clement Davies from Montgomeryshire became leader of the Liberal Parliamentary Party, but the party was losing votes, and by 1951 there were only half a dozen Liberal MPs. Although there were localized successes in the south, the Liberal years in Wales were well and truly over.

The Labour Representation Committee, meanwhile, had officially changed its name to the 'Labour Party' in 1906, the year it had gained only one seat in Wales. After the war's end, the party's prospects were much more favourable, and Labour captured 25 seats out of a total of 36. This post-war vote represented almost 60 per cent of the vote, which was some ten per cent more than the rest of Britain.

The Tories were consigned to four seats: Monmouthshire, Flintshire, Denbighshire and the Caernarfon Boroughs, which had been Lloyd George's old seat. The Liberals, for their part, were left with seven seats, with Lloyd George's daughter Megan keeping Anglesey and his son Gwilym retaining Pembrokeshire, but only just. The Plaid Cymru candidates might as well have stayed at home since all eight of them lost their deposits.

CHAPTER TWENTY-THREE

LABOUR DAYS

The Second World War transformed Wales, switching poles of negativity into positivity. The victory of the Allies over the dark forces of fascism led to an upsurge of confidence in the future, all a very far remove from the deprivations, suffering and starvation that the country had faced before 1939.

There was a new workforce, and new factories to engage that force, but there were new allegiances too. The miners who went on strike in the 1940s in the south Wales coalfields weren't looking elsewhere *in Wales* for comrades to join their fight for better conditions, equality and dignity of labour. Their natural allies were people *of the same class* – that is, the industrialized working class – who laboured as they did in heavy industry all over Britain. The Welsh colliers had much more in common with miners in the north of England or the west of Scotland than they did with farmers in north or west Wales. So it was to Westminster that Wales looked in the first post-war election of July 1945.

There had been a slow build-up of support for Labour over the years. Four MPs were supported by the Miners' Federation of Great Britain in 1908; ten MPs won seats in a party with a more avowedly socialist agenda, and by 1922 Labour had captured half the total number of seats. It was a steady trajectory.

The relationship between Labour and the workers of the industrial heartlands burgeoned, so that there was not only political representation at a Westminster level, but a strong display at a local level too: every local authority in the coalfields of the south was under Labour control by the 1920s.

The 1930s had seen a party riven with dissent between Labour's moderate leaders and its more militant and left-leaning bodies, such as the South Wales Miners' Federation. Links with communists led to some members being disaffiliated. There were gains in the northern coalfield too, and even, briefly, in the slate-quarrying northwest.

The post-war win in 1945 not only consolidated these advances, it dwarfed them. In individual towns the Labour landslide most resembled an avalanche: in the steel and tin town of Llanelli, Labour MP James Griffiths claimed a totally overwhelming majority of 34,000 over his nearest rival. In Abertillery, despite the Labour majority of 24,000, the local agent and secretary of the Welsh regional council of Labour, Cliff Prothero, insisted on a recount just to see if he could ensure that the Conservative candidate would lose his deposit! In the event, the poor man just managed to hold onto it, with 200 votes. Change was stalking the land and recolouring the political map. Even Liberal strongholds, such as Merioneth and Anglesey, were seriously challenged.

Labour was about to have six highly significant years of power in which they would transform society. In the decade or so after the war, working-class horizons expanded. 'You've never had it so good' was a believable slogan in the late 1950s. Such social reforms were not only attractive to the Welsh populace, they were seen as the bedrock of a new social order with fairness at its core. The decisive reason for

Labour's overwhelming victory at the ballot box in 1945 was its commitment to create a welfare state.

Labour won because of its talk of better housing, support for the unemployed, a national health service that would provide free health-care for all, and the proposition that heavy industry should be owned by the people rather than being greedily driven by private profit. Talk soon translated into action, and the first day of January 1947 marked the nationalization of the coal industry.

At the heart of these big changes was a scheme pioneered in the Sirhowy valley, driven by a local hero, Labour politician Aneurin Bevan. Its slogan: 'Free health for all'.

Aneurin Bevan had been born in Tredegar in 1897, and at the age of 13 started his working life down the pit. By the time he was 21 he was running a club that provided medical care for the local commu-nity, funded by contributions made by the miners themselves, and five years later he became leader of Tredegar Urban District Council.

Bevan was a both a warm personality and political firebrand. An avowed Marxist, he had been expelled from the Labour Party in 1939 for supporting the Spanish Popular Front, which had been battling the dictator General Franco. Bevan was MP for Ebbw Vale from 1929, when he was just 32 years of age, and soon he was clashing with both Lloyd George and Winston Churchill on their policies for health. During the war he maintained a steady stream of criticism of Churchill, who had become prime minister, not least through the pages of *Tribune* magazine, which he edited.

After the Labour landslide in 1945, Bevan became the minister for health in Clement Attlee's cabinet. In the same cabinet, Welsh MP James Griffiths was beavering away to produce a system of national insurance, which was delivered via three major bills between 1946 and 1948. This was a period of pronounced social change, and Bevan was swift to capitalize on his opportunity to apply what he had pioneered in Tredegar during the 1920s. He was determined to 'Tredegarize' the rest of Britain.

Bevan was able to make these changes because there was a real smell of prosperity in the air, which meant access to ready money from the Treasury to improve health and education. His plan was bolstered by his own great powers of oratory, nourished by a love of words and European literature. Bevan's legislative masterwork, the product of heated and meticulously detailed negotiations with doctors and other health workers, resulted in the setting up of the National Health Service (NHS), which is still viewed as the greatest legislative achievement of any Labour government. His was a Welsh contribution to a great British project. Indeed, one that would be, and is still, claimed as one of the pillars of British society.

Bevan later resigned his cabinet post in the 1950s over Hugh Gaitskell's imposition of prescription charges, and established an oppositional faction within Westminster known as the Bevanites. Whatever one makes of Bevan's politics and record in government, there's no doubt that he deserves his place amongst the political greats as the architect of a truly ground-breaking scheme. The NHS is a monumental achievement, an institution that's still cherished and fought over today, and it showed that changes pioneered in Wales could significantly improve the lives of people throughout Britain.

With Labour's agenda expressly designed for the whole of Britain, there was little room for separatism or nationalism. While Bevan wanted to 'Tredegarize' Britain, he was also clear that Wales was very much a part of Britain. Calls to establish a secretary of state for Wales went unheeded; indeed, Bevan was immensely hostile to the idea, as he demonstrated in a speech to the House of Commons on 28 October 1946:

> There has been too great a tendency to identify Welsh culture with Welsh speaking ... What some of us are afraid of is that, if this psychosis is developed too far, we shall see in some of the English-speaking parts of Wales a vast majority tyrannized over by a few Welsh-speaking people in Cardiganshire ... The whole of the Civil Service of Wales would be eventually provided from those small pockets of Welsh-speaking, Welsh-writing zealots and the vast majority of Welshmen would be denied participation in the government of their own country.[1]

Despite this attitude, there had been efforts to view Wales through a different lens. James Griffiths tried to get Wales recognized as a place apart during discussions over the newly nationalized electricity industry in 1946, but he failed in his efforts. A Council for Wales and Monmouthshire was set up by way of a sop in 1948 under Labour prime minister Clement Attlee. It had no cabinet minister as chair and was simply an advisory body, but it did advise the establishment of a Welsh Office and a secretary of state for Wales, both of which came into being in 1964.*

Labour's six years of power came to end with the election in 1950, which saw their majority slump from 150 to just six, although Wales stood apart from this, with 27 out of 36 seats still held by Labour.

---

* The veteran Labour MP for Llanelli Jim Griffiths became the first-ever secretary of state for Wales in 1964, in Harold Wilson's cabinet.

Under the Conservatives, the 1950s were a decade of boom, with better wages, full employment, growing home- and car-ownership, and an increasing trend for travel abroad in the form of package holidays. They also saw the growth of new kinds of industry: traditional heavy industries were joined by 'advance factories' – factories built to encourage local economic development – and lighter technologies. The people of Wales were once again asked to prove their adaptability.

Like other parts of Britain, work in Wales was still dominated by the old heavy industries, and the post-war boom gave fresh impetus to the coal industry. The mines had been nationalized in 1947, along with a clutch of other industries and utilities, such as railways, docks, electricity, gas, road haulage, and iron- and steel-making.

In that same year, the Steel Company of Wales began draining and clearing lakes and marshland in Port Talbot, repositioning sand dunes and raising the level of the whole site by 3 metres in order to build the most modern steelworks in the world. This opened in 1951, followed by the same company's new plants at Trostre in Llanelli and Felindre on the outskirts of Swansea.

With the Baglan Bay petrochemical complex and the Llandarcy oil refinery just down the road, Port Talbot was poised to become a modern industrial hub. The integrated Margam and Abbey Works employed thousands of men whose families were housed on the specially built new Sandfields Estate. There was good money to be made in the coking ovens and furnaces, and the housing conditions of the workers was far superior to the old valley terraces where many members of this workforce used to live. Here the slogan 'We've never had it so good' didn't sound in the least bit hollow.

Another huge steel production facility, the RTB/Spencer steel plant went into production at Llanwern near Newport in 1962, with new peripheral housing estates springing up to house the workers and their families. Investment wasn't confined to the south of the country: Shotton in Flintshire fired up its new blast furnaces to make steel; in west Wales the Esso oil refinery, adjoining the deep harbour at Milford Haven, went into production and eventually became the most important oil port in Britain.

With affluence came the consumer society. The first supermarket advertisements suggested that Welsh housewives could share the creature comforts of their American counterparts, not to mention the same washing powder. People wanted vacuum cleaners and washing machines, so Hoover built a factory in Merthyr in 1948, which, in its prime, employed 5,000 men and women in a town of 20,000 people. This joined other new factories, such as Hotpoint in Llandudno, Prestcold refrigerators in Swansea, and British Nylon Spinners at Pontypool, in feeding the ever-open maw of the consumer age. The new products were often made from new materials, setting in train new factories making plastic in Barry and nylon in Pontypool.

State intervention was crucial to this economic advance. The whole of south Wales was declared a development area. The Bridgend ordnance factory became the nucleus of a trading estate employing 30,000 people, while advance factories were set up, including Imperial Metals at Gowerton, and Girling car components at Cwmbrân. This diversification and modernization of industry created much greater opportunities for the employment of women, and industrial Wales became a place of two-income families. Steel towns, such as Ebbw Vale and Port Talbot, thrived, partly due to demand for domestic consumer durables and partly from the thriving car industry.

The 1960s brought international companies, such as Sony and Ford Motors, to Bridgend and Swansea respectively. The car industry started to entrench itself in the Welsh economy, as vehicles started to roll off the production lines at the Rover works in Cardiff, while 50 miles to the west, the Fisher-Ludlow body-press works at Llanelli opened to greet the beginning of the 1960s. Government work, moving from London, brought the Passport Office to Newport, Companies House to Cardiff, the Driver Vehicle Licensing Centre and Land Registry to Swansea, and the Royal Mint to Llantrisant.

The concentration of development growth on the south coast of Wales and Deeside (the area along the river Dee in Clwyd) became very evident, and Cardiff and Newport expanded their populations by 40 per cent in the 1950s and 1960s.

Transport infrastructure, notably the opening of the Severn Bridge in 1966, the Heads of the Valleys Road, and the extension of the M4 in the early 1970s, all helped to drive and consolidate this growth. The closure of many railway lines by Lord Beeching in 1963 also played its part in accelerating the growth of roads and emphasis on road haulage.

Even hard-pressed Welsh agriculture saw some improvements. From 1947 minimum prices were guaranteed for most farm products, and subsidies were provided for hill farmers. Grants for farm improvement expanded through to the 1960s, and agricultural co-operatives proved so popular in Wales that they quickly made up a fifth of the entire membership in the UK.

This government-led boom was a remarkable transformation, but much of the capital came from outside Britain, which left Wales extremely vulnerable to global economic changes.

Fear of 'The Bomb' and of a communist threat during the Cold War undermined the security of the new affluence. RAF bases in Wales were considered prime targets, as was Brecon, which was a possible centre for regional government in the event of a nuclear attack. The very emptiness of large parts of Wales meant that it was seen as a place of refuge. The campaigns of CND tried to counteract the fear of the Soviet threat and championed the benefits of disarmament. The Welsh had a strong pacifist tradition and philosopher Bertrand Russell and Plaid politician Gwynfor Evans were notable among Wales-based public figures who were important to the Campaign for Nuclear Disarmament.

Missiles had their advocates as well, being viewed as a counter-balance to the threat of the Soviet Bear and the silos of trans-continental ballistic missiles. A cold wind seemingly blew in over the Carpathians, or from Siberia, and the popular imagination was full of images of James Bond tackling fiendish Russians. Unsurprisingly, Cold War attitudes were as chilly in Wales as elsewhere in Britain.

This period even saw the first stirrings of a 'green' awareness, of the need to redeem landscapes devastated by heavy industry and to conserve nature, which, it was realized, was not a boundless resource. The first reclamation project began in the lower Swansea valley on soil poisoned by copper-working. Swansea's people were amazed to see Kilvey Hill transformed from a bare mountain into a forest, even though the Forestry Commission's rows of alien sitka pines were not popular throughout Wales.

Despite the anxieties about nuclear war, it's hard not to look back wistfully to a time when young people left school on a Friday and found employment down the works the following Monday. Full employment and free health care, courtesy of the National Health Service, fuelled well-being and self-belief.

Leisure became an important adjunct of work, and new pastimes, such as rambling, emerged. After centuries of smog and smoke from factory chimneys, people claimed the right to fresh air: open-air exercise and enjoyment of the countryside came in the form of the new National Parks, such as Snowdonia and the Pembrokeshire Coast. These were opened in the early 1950s, capitalizing on the spirit of optimism that prevailed after the Second World War, and were followed by the designation of the Brecon Beacons National Park in 1957.

If there is one symbol of the success of that green movement in Wales, it is the red kite, a bird of prey driven to the very edge of extinction, but zealously protected by conservationists and farmers during the longest bird species rescue story anywhere in the world. Not only did the kite remain in its upland habitats, but it also spread its wings into the lowlands, and became an unofficial national bird for a country now considerably more at ease with itself.

CHAPTER TWENTY-FOUR

A NATIONALIST SPIRIT

By the middle of the twentieth century changes in the pattern and distribution of work had led to profound challenges for the Welsh language. The classic transition of people from village to city applied to Wales just as surely as any other modern country, as young people left the countryside in droves to look for better futures. Welsh became a language in geographical retreat: areas where it had been the majority language contracted into ever-diminishing concentric circles, leaving increasingly smaller pockets, such as central Anglesey, Arfon and Dwyfor.

The language held strong in some rural areas, particularly in the north and west of the country, but these were often hilly and sparsely populated, with the speakers themselves tending to be older. In urban strongholds of the language, such as east Carmarthenshire and west Glamorgan, industries such as coal and tin were in steep decline, with only a quarter of the number of colliers employed in Carmarthenshire in the early 1920s still employed in the county 50 years later. Other industries even more intimately connected with the language, such as slate in the northwest and agriculture, were similarly haemorrhaging jobs.

A language spoken by close on a million people in 1911 had become a minority language a decade later because of the war: a generation of young men had been lost, perhaps as many as 20,000 of them, mown down on the battlefield. By the census of 1951, numbers of Welsh speakers were down to 714,686, and the downward trend was alarmingly apparent.

One of the pillars of Welsh language culture, the chapel, was itself crumbling: from the 1960s onwards, middle-class Welsh speakers were no longer attending the chapels built by their forebears. And with important decisions about the language – including means of safeguarding it, such as education and broadcasting – being made in Westminster, there was a feeling of powerlessness coupled with resentment.

During the 1950s and 1960s, Welsh radicalism was most apparent in the language campaigns that drew inspiration from civil disobedience in support of civil rights in the USA, and the peaceful demonstrations against the Vietnam War.

Campaigners responded to the multiple pressures on a language under threat in its traditional heartlands from Gwynedd to Ceredigion. The countryside, indeed, was slowly emptying, and a new wave of in-migration from England saw English-speakers buying up housing, a foretaste of much larger incursions in the 1980s, which were direct threats to the cohesion and well-being of Welsh-language communities.

Organized religion was in retreat. This was a period that saw Wales, which had been one of the most religious countries on Earth, become one of the most secular. Not that there was a revolt against Christianity – it was more of a gradual drift away from the pulpit, the deacons, and hymns in the minor key. As the old Nonconformist Wales began to wither, new nationalist politics emerged, based on cultural concerns. Even Sundays, traditionally days when no one dared do any work other than walk to chapel, were set to become a lot less sacred.

In 1961 Wales held a referendum on Sunday opening for pubs. It was at heart an administrative procedure, yet it tells us a good deal about what kind of place Wales was becoming. The country had been dry on the Sabbath since 1881, when legislation curtailing the sale of alcohol on Sundays in Wales had been passed after much campaigning by John Roberts, MP for Flint Boroughs. Pembrokeshire, Merionethshire, Anglesey, Caernarfon, Denbighshire, Cardiganshire, Ceredigion and Flintshire all voted to stay dry. The decision by the other, more urbanized counties to allow drinking on Sunday reflected the demise of Nonconformist Wales.

As these referenda were held every seven years, support for the sanctity of Sunday slowly eroded with each of these public votes. A royal commission found that the law was properly upheld in rural areas, whereas workers in the industrial heartlands flouted it widely in order to slake their thirsts. After the 1989 referendum on the issue, only Dwyfor in the northwest remained dry.

The perception of the Welsh way of life as being under threat due to erosion of the language, religion and culture was certainly exacerbated by the British government's approach to the Welsh countryside. Great swathes of rural Wales were redesigned as villages were turned into reservoirs in order to supply growing urban areas in England and Wales with a reliable water supply.

The drowning of the farming community of Capel Celyn and the planned drowning of the Tryweryn valley near Bala in 1965 were, ironically, incendiary acts. Eight hundred acres of land, comprising 12 complete farms and land belonging to another four, were to be drowned in order to supply water to the city of Liverpool.

This was not the first time Liverpool had ridden roughshod over people in regard to water supplies: the tactics they employed over Tryweryn pretty much mirrored those of the 1880s, when the village of Llanwddyn in Montgomeryshire was inundated to create a reservoir at Lake Vyrnwy.

The Tryweryn valley scheme was opposed by all but one of the Welsh MPs, but they were powerless to stop the development because the government was determined to push the Bill through Parliament. The local authorities had no voice in the decision either, and this caused great resentment. The political parties in Wales were united in their opposition to the scheme because it was considered an affront to Wales that valuable resources were being taken away from the country.

In 1956 the Tryweryn Defence Committee was formed and it included some of Wales's most prominent and revered personalities, including Ifan ab Owen Edwards, Megan Lloyd George, T. I. Ellis, and Lord Ogmore. Many branches were formed, including the Capel Celyn Defence Committee and even a Liverpool branch of the Tryweryn Defence Committee, shored up by the presence of so many Welsh people in the city.

The Tryweryn cause inspired Plaid Cymru and provided an impetus to its campaigns. In September 1956 the party held a Save Tryweryn Rally in Bala, leading a procession of protesters through the centre of the town.

The Lord Mayor of Cardiff, Alderman J. H. Morgan, called a Save Tryweryn meeting in October 1956, at which 300 representatives from local government and trade unions, and ten MPs were present. Alderman Huw T. Edwards was appointed chair, and it was decided to send a delegation from the conference to Liverpool to appeal for a change of heart.

In November 1956 a procession led by Plaid Cymru representative Gwynfor Evans, and including 70 of the villagers, was held in Liverpool. In August 1957 Evans proposed an alternative, that Merionnydd County Council could build a reservoir in Cwm Croes, where only one farm would be affected, and sell the water from the reservoir to Liverpool Corporation. He argued that the flooding of Tryweryn 'hammered home the fact that one of the richest Welsh natural resources was being exploited without benefit to the Welsh people and that this was possible because of the nation's complete lack of political freedom'.[1]

Despite these suggestions, the Tryweryn Bill was endorsed by Parliament on 1 August 1957. This was a private measure, sponsored by Liverpool City Council and passed by Harold Macmillan's Conservative government, with the support of Henry Brooke, minister for Welsh affairs. The measure allowed for the compulsory purchase of land to build the reservoir.

The scheme at Tryweryn went ahead in the face of huge public and political opposition, and the town's school, post office, chapel and cemetery all disappeared under the standing water of Llyn Celyn reservoir. A total of 48 people were robbed of their homes. New roads had to be built, since the road from Bala to Ffestiniog was drowned, and the total cost of the project was £20 million. Llyn Celyn, which lay behind the biggest dam in Wales, held a huge capacity of water. Today there is a memorial garden on the side of the lake to which the gravestones from Capel Celyn cemetery have been removed.

As if to add insult to injury, the Lord Mayor of Liverpool attended the ceremony to open the reservoir on 28 October 1965. Also present at the event were young members of the Free Wales Army (FWA), a group of young nationalists intent on making enough noise to attract the attention of the national press. Dressed in military uniform and carrying Welsh dragon flags, the FWA had been actively recruiting, mainly in mid-Wales, since 1963, and probably never had as many as a hundred members, but this was the first time they had stepped out of the shadows.

In 1969 the ringleaders and founder members of FWA, Julian Cayo Evans (who has a Cardiff pub named after him) and Dennis Coslett were found guilty of conspiracy to cause explosions and were eventually sentenced to 15 months' imprisonment after a 53-day trial, which, by strange coincidence, concluded on the very day of the investiture of Prince Charles as Prince of Wales.

Legitimate debate and legal protest were augmented by more extreme action. On three occasions between 1962 and 1963 there were attempts to sabotage the building of the reservoir. On 10 February 1963 a transmitter exploded on the site and a 22-year-old Aberystwyth student, Emyr Llywelyn Jones, was sentenced to 12 months in prison for his part in the act. In response to his sentence, two other members of MAC (Mudiad Amddiffyn Cymru, the Movement for the Defence of Wales, a secret nationalist organization), namely Owain Williams and John Albert Jones, blew up a pylon at Gellilydan.

The village of Tryweryn had been drowned, but the publicity surrounding the event had raised the profile of the national political party. Plaid Genedlaethol Cymru was founded in 1925 by Saunders Lewis, a highly politicized intellectual writer, who was later dismissed from his post at Swansea University because of his role in the burning of the Penyberth Bombing School (to train RAF bombers) on the Llŷn Peninsula in 1936. His fellow academic Ambrose Bebb outlined what he believed to be the overwhelming cultural needs of Wales in an essay entitled 'Achub y Cymraeg; Achub Cymru' (Save the Welsh, Save Wales):

> A Welsh Government is the only thing that will give us a wholly
> Welsh society, with a Welsh civilization, Welsh literature, and
> Welsh life, with the language blossoming in the security that will
> come from a government which will defend it. Indeed, here, ultimately is the strongest argument: there is no civilization without
> politics. Conclusion? Let us work for home rule. For the time
> being, politics first.[2]

Plaid Cymru made little electoral progress, but fears for the future of the Welsh language and public outrage over the Tryweryn affair prompted Saunders Lewis to choose 'Tynged yr Iaith' (The Fate of the Language) as the title of his BBC radio lecture in 1962.

There had been detrimental factors affecting the language before the twentieth century, of course, not least the excoriation of the Blue Books, but factors such as the coming of the railways in the nineteenth century and the burgeoning of the British Empire also played their parts. Even Darwinian ideas about the survival of the fittest were harnessed by some to suggest that the demise of Welsh was inevitable since it was unfit for purpose in the modern age.

It was against this complicated background, not to mention the decline evidenced in census after census, that Saunders Lewis advocated revolutionary tactics to safeguard the Welsh language. He urged young people to abandon their electoral campaigning and concentrate instead on making it 'impossible for the business of local and central government to continue without using Welsh'. In the absence of such efforts, he predicted the death of the language, without which an independent Wales would be worthless.

It touched a nerve. The doomsday scenario depicted in 'Tynged yr Iaith' led directly to the foundation of Cymdeithas yr Iaith Cymraeg, the Welsh Language Society, at Plaid Cymru's annual conference at Pontarddulais in August 1962. Saunders Lewis's call to action was particularly heeded by younger members, who embarked on a succession of campaigns calling for Welsh language road tax forms and an improved status for the language, embracing over the years a range of language-related issues in fields such as housing, broadcasting, planning and education.

The movement avoided violence, but refusals to pay taxes and damage to public property resulted in over 200 members being sent to jail. The society's activities eventually resulted in language provision in the fields of Welsh education and Welsh-language broadcasting. TV and radio started to contribute to a sense of Welsh identity, with the formation of a separate BBC Wales and the creation of the commercial channel TWW.

Plaid Cymru also made some political headway. While people such as Saunders Lewis were at pains to ensure that it didn't become a cultural pressure group, the existence and energies of Cymdeithas yr Iaith left Plaid Cymru to concentrate on issues other than the language. MP Gwynfor Evans's indefatigable campaigning over Tryweryn fed into his famous 1966 win over Labour's candidate,

Gwilym Prys Davies, for the Carmarthen seat, which Evans won by a majority of 2,436. This was the seventh time he had fought parliamentary elections, and the scenes of jubilation at the count constituted a watershed in Welsh politics.

Gwynfor Evans and Plaid Cymru had come from nowhere to steal a historic victory, and in so doing entered the mainstream of Welsh political life. It stunned the Labour Party in particular, who realized that nationalism was not a force to be casually dismissed.

A highly significant litmus test for national allegiance came in 1969. Despite the presence of Welsh-language protestors, thousands cheered as Prince Charles was invested as Prince of Wales at Caernarfon castle in 1969. But for some the investiture ceremony, with its 4,000 guests, was a flagrant reminder of both royal privilege and Welsh subjugation, and popular songs by singers such as Dafydd Iwan gave vent to a simmering anger.

Edward I had very pointedly crowned his son Edward as Prince of Wales in 1301 at Caernarfon castle, where he had also been born. At a stroke, the English king was underlining both the death of Llywelyn and the final severance of any princely line in Wales. During the centuries that had elapsed since then, the title Prince of Wales had been given to a total of 21 heirs to the English throne, but most of these princes paid little or no heed to Wales, its people or their collective wishes. The long-forgotten ceremony of investiture was resurrected for Prince Edward in 1911, and again at the tail end of the 'swinging sixties'.

Threats were made against Prince Charles, and early on the morning of the Investiture, two members of Mudiad Amddiffyn Cymru were killed in the coastal town of Abergele when the bomb they were carrying exploded before they could plant it on a railway line along which the royal train would run. Some days after the investiture, a young boy was disabled by a bomb that had been left in the town and failed to explode on time.

Some criticized the press and broadcasters for giving too much coverage to the views of a small minority of people who opposed the event. There were 90,000 people on the streets of one of the most comprehensively Welsh-speaking towns in Wales, all enthusiastically waving Union Jacks. The event was even more a paradox because on the day of the investiture itself, 71 per cent of those polled by the *Western Mail* newspaper supported a Wales with its own parliament and law-making powers, but an even higher proportion of 74 per cent were glad that the investiture was taking place and that Charles was to be Prince of Wales. A colossal TV audience of 500 million people watched the event worldwide, with 19 million tuning in around the UK.

CHAPTER TWENTY-FIVE

NATIONAL PRIDE

The beginning of the twentieth century had great days of self-assertion, with the building of new national institutions such as the National Museum in Cardiff and the National Library of Wales in Aberystwyth. The evolving debate about independence, fuelled by Plaid Cymru, considered possible models for devolution or even eventual independence. Yet while this evolving sense of nationalism was being represented in new architecture and political debate, perhaps the real spirit of the nation was being expressed elsewhere, on muddy playing fields and in popular song, places where the bulk of the populace could express its allegiances.

Four months before his investiture, Prince Charles had attended the Wales v. Ireland Rugby Union international at Cardiff Arms Park. This was part of a wider campaign to ingratiate him with the Welsh public, which included his attending university at Aberystwyth.

Wales won the Triple Crown* that year, the beginning of a golden era for the game. But the crowds had stopped singing 'God Save the Queen'. According to *The Times*, Welshmen expressed 'their tribal loyalty and some of their identity and surface nationalism' through

---

* A tournament contested by the four national teams of the British Isles. The team that beats all three of the opposing teams wins the Triple Crown.

the game. And the national team gave plenty of reasons for loyalty and enthusiasm.

The first rugby clubs in Wales, such as Neath, Llanelli, Swansea, Newport and Cardiff, were all established in the 1870s by men who usually received a privileged education and played rugby in private schools in England. The sport was soon embraced by the working class, who found it a perfect expression for local pride and an invigorating means of physical recreation. The Welsh Rugby Union itself had been established in Neath in March 1881 by Richard Mallick, who also masterminded the first game between Wales and England.

Rugby spread through south Wales like wildfire and interest grew exponentially with the success of the international side, which won the Triple Crown in 1893. The combination of players who were already hardened by work underground or in the heat of tinplate works, coupled with the adoption of adventurous playing formations, planted the seeds of what would be seen as the first golden age of rugby. During the first 11 years of the twentieth century, Wales won a total of six further Triple Crowns, due in large measure to the combination of working-class forwards and middle-class backs. The latter, nimble and mercurial, were often able to make the more muscular opposition look like stumbling dolts and neutralize any physical advantages they might have had. Questions were raised about the rather cavalier attitude of the Welsh with regard to paying amateurs, but a quiet stream of payments to players continued.

A pinnacle of triumph in the early years was the win against the New Zealand All Blacks on 16 December 1905, the only success of any team against them in a 32-match series. The game came to represent the zenith of Edwardian high hopes and optimism. The captain,

Gwyn Nicholls, and winger Teddy Morgan, who between them scored the game-winning try, became household names, along with Dickie Owen, who invented the game plan. Also securing himself a place in history was lock forward, Dai 'Tarw' Jones, a towering Treherbert collier and former policeman who showed, in his rampant charging play, precisely why they nicknamed him 'The Bull'.

The team soon seemed to truly represent the nation, a conflation that meant that Wales's fortunes off the pitch were often intimately interlinked with the team's success. The 1905 win was described in the press in terms equivalent to the lavishing of laurel wreaths, and with seeming references to the native princes:

> When you consider for a moment what Wales had to do, and when you think of how she did it, there arises in every man the feeling of highest admiration for qualities that find the most popular expression … 'Gallant Little Wales' has produced sons of strong determination, invincible stamina, resolute, mentally keen, physically sound. It needs no imaginative power to perceive that the qualities that conquered on Saturday have found another expression in the history of Welsh education: that long struggle against the odds that has given the Principality her great schools and her progressive colleges. The national traits are equally apparent in both contexts.[1]

The drain of people away from Wales, especially young men, led to the closure of 12 rugby clubs in the 1930s. The number of both players and supporters was already dwindling. The international side found itself in the doldrums and stayed there. Even exceptional players, such as Albert Jenkins, were sometimes left on the bench, subject to the vagaries of selection. As if to compound the woes of the Welsh Rugby Union, between 1919 and 1939 there was a mass defection to the north of England to play Rugby League. A total of 48 international players accepted professional terms, knowing full well that they would face a lifetime ban from the Rugby Union for being turncoats.

Some sort of salvation came in the form of players who had come up through the university sides, be they Oxford and Cambridge 'Blues' (sportsmen who had represented their university) such as Cliff Jones, or the products of Welsh universities, such as Watcyn Thomas and Haydn Tanner. The innate strength of workers in heavy industry could create packs with the forward momentum of a Panzer division. Such a side could set up the necessary try-scoring platforms for the Welsh team to claim such historic wins as those against England in 1933 and New Zealand again in 1935.

Post-war rugby picked up just as the economy did, and there were Triple Crown-winning runs in 1950 and 1952, when stars such as Bleddyn Williams and the world's greatest fly-half, Cliff Morgan, shone, not least when the latter travelled with the British Lions to maul South Africa in 1955.

Rugby has had few passages of play to match the dazzlingly intuitive tries scored by Gareth Edwards in the 1970s. This instinctive scrum-half, backed by the mercurial skills of Barry John, the side-stepping genius of Phil Bennett, as well as the free-flowing attacking style of fullback J. P. R. Williams, can properly take his place in the loftiest pantheon of rugby players. This was also the era of Carwyn James, who coached Welsh club rugby – leading Llanelli to repeated success – and the British Lions. Yet, mystifyingly, James, who brought a razor-sharp intellect to the game, was never given the job of coaching Wales.

The captain of the Lions team, John Dawes, played for London Welsh, a squad full of talent. Collectively they forced the Welsh Rugby Union to invest in a bigger prize cabinet as they amassed a total of three Grand Slam wins and six Triple Crowns between 1969 and 1979, with four of those won in successive years. Rugby had come a long way since it first arrived in Wales less than a century earlier.

Success on the rugby pitch, coupled with the camaraderie of local clubs, from Ammanford to Abercarn, served to shore up the evolving national awareness. There was also a burgeoning confidence amongst the working class, both socially and at work; in 1972, for instance, the miners went on strike and won a whopping 45 per cent pay rise.

If the defiant and mercurial spirit of the Welsh nation was captured by its rugby team, its football squad, during its chequered history, barely managed to make it into the top 100 in the world rankings. Yet Association Football was very popular and remains so, not least because of Swansea's entry into the Premiership in 2011.

While rugby was played mainly in south Wales, with pockets of enthusiasm elsewhere, football was played right throughout the land. Indeed, there were four times as many Association Football clubs as rugby clubs, and enthusiastic fans paid close attention to the exploits of teams in England, such as Liverpool and Everton, which had obvious appeal for fans in north Wales because of their geographical and cultural proximity. Other big teams attracted fans throughout Wales: these included Arsenal, Chelsea, Manchester United and Manchester City, where former Morriston tinplate worker Billy Meredith excelled as an outside-right, a genuine early football star. As an international side, Wales gained real prominence for a brief period in 1958 when it qualified for the World Cup. But it was a star set to wane rather than continuously shine.

The game of football had its genesis in public schools, before spreading in the 1860s and 1870s throughout places such as the Midlands and the north of England, when clubs appeared in Wrexham and Ruabon. The Football Association of Wales was created in 1876, with the Welsh Cup inaugurated a year later.

To begin with, Wrexham and its hinterland formed the heartland of the game, but missionary attempts were made to foster interest in the south of the country, such as staging a Welsh international fixture in Swansea in 1894 to drum up support for the sport in both Glamorgan and west Wales and in Cardiff two years later.

A seminal event in the development of football was the entry of Welsh clubs, such as Aberdare, Swansea and Ton Pentre, into the new English Southern League in 1909–10. In 1915 Swansea built on this structural advance and managed the totally unexpected defeat of the Football League Champions, Blackburn Rovers, giving a much-needed shot in the arm for south Walian football. This had a domino effect. Cardiff joined the Football League in 1920 and proved to be a very successful side. They gained promotion to the First Division in 1921, and almost managed to win the championship. A burgeoning Cardiff was soon joined in the league by five other clubs, namely Newport, Wrexham, Aberdare, Swansea and Merthyr.

With half a dozen teams therefore in the league, the interwar years were good ones for football in Wales, as evidenced by the fact that in 1926 Swansea Town netted £33,000 in gate receipts (the equivalent of

£1.1 million today), although the punishing depression of the 1930s made things much, much harder for such clubs. By 1935 Swansea's spiral of financial decline meant it had been forced to launch a campaign with the slogan 'Save the Club from Decline'. Luckily, loyal supporters rallied to the cause and saved it from extinction.

A main focus for support and excitement in these years was that soccer grail, the FA Cup, and Cardiff appeared in the Wembley final of 1925, while Swansea made it to the semi-final in 1926. Welsh hopes culminated in, and were ultimately vindicated by, Cardiff's win over Arsenal in 1927, the only time a non-English side had captured the cup. The winning goal was scored for Cardiff by a Scotsman called Ferguson and resulted from a mistake by the Arsenal goalkeeper, a Welshman, Dan Lewis. But it was a winning goal regardless. The glory days were soon over for Cardiff, who slid into the Third Division by the early 1930s.

The 1950s saw some glory returning: Cardiff had two periods in the First Division between 1952 and 1957, and non-league sides, such as Barry and Bangor, punched, or rather played, well above their weight. Stars were hotly pursued by rival clubs. Swansea-born John Charles, for example, was poached by Juventus from Leeds for a very healthy £65,000 transfer fee, while inside-forward Ivor Allchurch and striker John Toshack were both hailed as world class talents. By the end of the decade the Welsh team had made it into the World Cup Finals in Sweden, but there they had only a modicum of success, winning just one game out of the five they played.

There were certainly peaks and troughs in the years that followed. As a club, Swansea's star rose in the football firmament, and saw them in the First Division between 1981 and 1983, but the light was quickly extinguished as they disappeared into the depths. Newport dropped out of the Football League altogether in 1988. After the Home International series came to an end in 1984, qualification for the World Cup became increasingly important, not only as a barometer of talent, but also as an opportunity for players to further develop their abilities at an international level, and Wales did not fare well. The League of Wales was created in 1992, but some clubs, such as Cardiff and Wrexham, stuck with the English League.

A new stadium in Cardiff fostered hopes of Premiership entry for the city's club, but this ambition was consistently thwarted, while the national team failed to go far either in the European Championship or the 2006 World Cup qualifiers.

Association Football was a relative newcomer in comparison with boxing, which had a history predating the Industrial Revolution, even if it was more generally associated with the towns built on steel, iron and coal. While bare-knuckle contests for ready cash eventually gave way to the Queensbury rules – devised, in fact, by J. G. Chambers from Llanelli – these clandestine hillside contests continued even into an age when the south Wales valleys generated a run of professional champions equal to any other comparable place in the world, with the 'Tylorstown Terror' Jimmy Wilde and Freddie Welsh being just two of the luminaries of the ring. Wilde's economic moves, uncannily clever footwork and powerful right hand gave him the edge on his opponent, as a boxing correspondent noted in 1916:

> *You have seen those boxers who dance all over the ring, and you have heard them often described as artists in footwork ... Wilde's footwork is of a different calibre.*[2]

Cardiff produced another southpaw in 'Peerless' Jim Driscoll, who was born in the Irish quarter of the city and started his pugilist career in fairground boxing booths before becoming British featherweight champion. His popularity was well attested to at his life's end: his funeral at Cathays cemetery was attended by no fewer than 100,000 mourners. Later, in the 1930s, the same city produced the partly Danish heavyweight Jack Petersen, who won 22 professional bouts by the time he was 21 years of age, and whose fight against Heine Muller of Germany at Ninian Park on 15 May 1933 drew an enormous crowd of 53,000, suggesting it might be 'the largest crowd ever to attend a boxing match in Europe'. Meanwhile, the Rhondda fighter-factory kept on churning them out: Tonypandy produced Tommy Farr, who had been hugely toughened up by pit-fighting, where colliers stood in holes up to their waists only a few feet apart and aimed to knock the opponent unconscious. Famously, Farr went 15 rounds against Joe Louis in New York in 1937, and became a symbol of steely defiance, with a style of boxing well suited to close fighting.

After the war, Wales produced such fighters as Colin Jones of Gorseinon and Cardiff's Steve Robinson, who held the world featherweight title between 1993 and 1995. Newbridge's Joe Calzaghe and Swansea's Enzo Maccarinelli became world champions as the twentieth century drew to a close, at super middleweight and cruiserweight respectively. The factory of fighters that was south Wales just kept them coming.

If the bouts between Welsh boxers and their American counterparts in venues such as the Yankee Stadium and Madison Square Gardens drew huge, enthusiastic crowds, they were as nothing to the mass appeal of a new musical phenomenon that came out of cities such as Philadelphia and New York and crossed the Atlantic with ease.

In September 1956, Bill Haley's film *Rock Around the Clock* introduced a shocking new craze to Wales: rock'n'roll. For chapel-goers, brought up on the hymns of Pantycelyn, this was the devil's own music, and in English too. For everyone else it was an invitation to shake, rattle and roll.

The Haley film was nothing short of an outrage, according to a family doctor who, writing in the *South Wales Echo*, deplored the 'uncouth bedlam of sound' that depended on the 'abuse of decent musical instruments and the debasement of music itself'. Worse than the music itself, was its effect on the audience: 'They clapped, howled, hissed, yelled. They got out of their seats and performed horrid contortions all over the place. Not content with this, they smashed up seats, tore fire extinguishers from places and generally ran amok.'[4]

If the film caused such consternation and excitement, then Bill Haley's live concert in Wales generated much, much more, as was reported in the *Western Mail* on 19 January 1957: 'Requests from about 60,000 fans have flooded into Cardiff this week for seats at Bill Haley's two-and-a-half hour show of concentrated rock'n'roll. Thousands of people, mostly teenagers, formed a queue more than a quarter of a mile long yesterday morning outside the Capitol Theatre where the two performances of the show are to be held on 21 February. Some had stayed up all night.'[5]

The first blasts of rock'n'roll were shocking to Welsh ears much more accustomed to sol-fa and the solemnity of hymns and arias but, by now, industrialized Wales had been fully part of the modern world for three generations – the majority of people lived an urban life with dance-halls and cinemas and clubs of all kinds.

The soundtrack to the new Wales after the Second World War was supplied by performers such as Tom Jones and Shirley Bassey, singers who went on to attract and keep a loyal, global audience of fans from the 1960s to the present day. Former collier Jones, born Tommy Woodward in Pontypridd in 1940, became one of the hottest properties in the world, able to command huge sums for appearances at Caesar's Palace in Las Vegas. Bands such as the Manic Street Preachers, Catatonia, Super Furry Animals and the Stereophonics would later mirror his success sufficiently for the tag 'Cool Cymru' to be invented.

There were also parallel advances in Welsh-language pop music. BBC radio programmes such as *Noson Lawen*, promoted it, and offered a folksy alternative to swing, which was all the rage elsewhere, even as Welsh-language skiffle acts offered their take on music that was successful for the likes of Lonnie Donegan in English. The 1960s saw showcases for Welsh-language pop on television: singers such as Dafydd Iwan adapted songs by Arlo Guthrie to the Welsh situation, and others, such as Meic Stevens and Heather Jones, sang only in Welsh.

National pride was flourishing again, whether on the pitch, in the ring, on the radio, or at the ballot-box, and self-determination was in the air. There was disparate protest against a distant English government making decisions that impacted on Wales, then a more focused movement led by radical leaders, who demanded respect and recognition for Welsh culture and language, and called for a Welsh voice in politics.

Yet the Welsh economy still operated at the behest and under the influence of politicians in London, who were themselves in thrall to global events and forces. The Yom Kippur war between Israel and a coalition of Arab states, including Egypt and Syria, in October 1973 tripled the price of oil, thereby increasing the demand for coal.

Edward Heath's Conservative government decided to ration petrol and in March 1974 introduced a three-day week, when commercial users of electricity were limited to three specified days' consumption. Little wonder that the public, unhappy with Conservative policies, voted in a Labour government under Harold Wilson later that year.

When a punk band, the Sex Pistols, played a later famous gig in Caerphilly in 1976 and sang 'no future', it was in keeping with the mood in Wales. The frenetic screeching of lead singer Johnny Rotten seemed almost an anthem for a Wales mired in joblessness. There were more job losses in the coal industry, and other industries suffered too: the Ebbw Vale steelworks, for instance, was partially closed in 1975. In a brief few years, boom had been replaced by bust, and the dole offices started to fill.

In 1976 Britain faced nothing less than financial meltdown. The Labour government was forced to apply to the International Monetary Fund for a loan of nearly $4 billion. The elegantly besuited IMF negotiators insisted on deep cuts in public expenditure, greatly affecting economic and social policy. In Wales this translated into an enormous loss of 60,000 jobs between 1976 and 1979, while interest rates stood at a staggering 28 per cent. In such circumstances, something had to give.

Wales was by now a country riddled with discontent, especially in those areas that had grown like topsy around the coal mines. As the old industries declined so too did the communities that had accreted around them. But there was one long shadow yet to be cast over the coal field, a tragedy that would touch the hearts of the world.

CHAPTER TWENTY-SIX

ABERFAN

I was there for about an hour and a half until the fire brigade found me. I heard cries and screams, but I couldn't move. The desk was jammed into my stomach and my leg was under the radiator. The little girl next to me was dead and her head was on my shoulder.[1]

One of the barometers of economic change in Wales was the fate of the coalfields, which reflected both global trends and the domestic political agenda. The history of Welsh pits was also punctuated by appalling tragedies, such as the Universal colliery disaster at Senghennydd in 1913, which claimed the lives of 439 men while leaving only one survivor, an ostler found lying by the side of a dead horse. Sadly, this event, with its grim death toll, was far from unique. In 1934, when miners were campaigning for an extra two shillings a day to supplement their very meagre wages, an underground explosion in Gresford, near Wrexham, killed no fewer than 260 miners and three rescue workers, forcing the closure of the mine. It also served to attract public sympathy and widespread support for the colliers' demands, although the eventual pay increase was far from generous.

But there was one event that cast a greater shadow than any of the other tragedies caused by coal in Wales. At 9.15 a.m. on 21 October

1966, a waterlogged tip slid down the mountainside at Aberfan near Merthyr, engulfing a farm, houses and part of the school in an awful river of mud, slurry and coal waste. A total of 144 people were killed, 116 of whom were children. A generation was lost and there was no one in this close-knit community who was not directly affected by the tragedy.

The deaths seared themselves into the conscience of the day and into the collective memory. It was the Welsh equivalent to the Kennedy assassination: people remembered exactly where they were when they heard the news. In schools up and down the land, children stood quietly in remembrance without having to be told to. At least 50,000 letters of condolence were sent to the village that coal had destroyed.

In October 1966, after resolutions by both Houses of Parliament, the secretary of state for Wales, Cledwyn Hughes, appointed a tribunal to inquire into the causes of the disaster. It was chaired by Sir Herbert Edmund Davies, a barrister who knew his mining law. The tribunal sat for over two months, calling a total of 136 witnesses, examining 300 exhibits and amassing testimony totalling two and a half million words. Local fears about the tip, long held, were expressed. Fingers of blame were pointed.

Lord Robens, chairman of the National Coal Board (NCB), appeared dramatically in the final days of the tribunal to give evidence, and admitted that the NCB had been at fault. Had this admission been made at the beginning of the inquiry, much of what followed at the tribunal would have been unnecessary. The tribunal retired on the 28 April 1967 to consider its verdict.

When the report was published on 3 August 1967, it knew exactly where to apportion blame:

... the Aberfan Disaster is a terrifying tale of bungling ineptitude by many men charged with tasks for which they were totally unfitted, of failure to heed clear warnings, and of total lack of direction from above. Not villains but decent men, led astray by foolishness or by ignorance or by both in combination, are responsible for what happened at Aberfan.

The report concluded:

Blame for the disaster rests upon the National Coal Board. This is shared, though in varying degrees, among the NCB headquarters, the South Western Divisional Board, and certain individuals. ... The legal liability of the NCB to pay compensation of the personal injuries, fatal or otherwise, and damage to property, is incontestable and uncontested.[2]

The tragedy engendered a series of campaigns to persuade the Welsh Office to remove some of the larger tips and level off some of the others. For decades the earthmovers and excavators reclaimed land, getting rid of the huge industrial scars, resculpting the artificial mountains of slag and spoil, and thereby erasing the past.

Aberfan was a unique tragedy. It is impossible to stand before the serried, quiet ranks of children's graves that cling to the small hillside cemetery and not be moved beyond measure by the simple, heartfelt epitaphs: 'In memory of our darling little maid' and 'Richard Goldsworthy, Aged 10, who loved Light, Freedom and Animals'.

The novelist Laurie Lee was commissioned by the American magazine *Redbook* to visit Aberfan a year after the disaster. Lee's resulting piece is both poignant and precise: 'This must once have been a trim little working-class terrace, staidly Victorian but specially Welsh ... until the wave of slag broke against it, smashed the doors and windows, and squeezed through the rooms like toothpaste ..."[3]

The story of Aberfan was a tragic instance of a disaster resulting from the intensity of the coal industry; yet it was also a telling part of the story of the decline of coal and the project of nationalization.

Because of that sense of catastrophe and desertion, Aberfan became a byword for the tragic human cost of coal extraction. But the industry in Wales was also in crisis, not least because of the availability of alternative fuel sources, such as oil.

In 1959, there were 141 NCB collieries in south Wales, employing 93,000 people. By 1969, there were just 55 collieries and 40,000 employees. The North Wales Coalfield also lost half its workforce in the decade after 1962, leaving just two pits in the area. More pits were closed during the 1960s than at any time in the history of the industry in Wales.

Coal had become a tragic story in itself. An industry that had employed over a quarter of a million men was reduced to a handful of pits, and the National Union of Mineworkers (NUM) became a shadow of its former self. But if economic forces and newer fuels had conspired against the coal industry, there was one other factor that would play a pivotal role in its demise: a female prime minister who had her ideological heart set on dismantling heavy industry.

CHAPTER TWENTY-SEVEN

MARGARET THATCHER AND THE MINERS

Change in Wales in the 1980s came as a result of the neo-liberal policies of a remarkably determined woman. As the election results of 1979 amply demonstrated, Wales embraced the Grantham shopkeeper's daughter, the 'Iron Lady' Margaret Thatcher, if not Thatcherism, to a demonstrably high degree. This was an amazing turnaround.

In 1945 Wales was second only to the East End of London when it came to its lack of support for the Tories, who that year received only a quarter of Welsh votes. Six years later, in 1951, the Conservatives were able to claim six Parliamentary seats and had overtaken the Liberals. In 1979, coinciding with the rejection of devolution in the referendum that spring, 11 seats were won by the Tories in Wales, their best result since the 1860s. There were record numbers of Tory MPs in 1983, when they claimed 14 of the 38 Welsh seats available. They capitalized on the formation of the SDP-Liberal Alliance, which, in turn, stole traditional Labour votes.

One of the key moments of Mrs Thatcher's premiership was her decision to defy Argentina's annexation of the Falkland Islands in 1982. Britain dispatched warships to the South Atlantic in April to oust the invaders from the islands, which the Argentinians called the

Malvinas. Mrs Thatcher's battle was widely seen as an international diversion from domestic discontent and difficulty, and Wales felt the effects directly. Thirty-two members of the Welsh Guards lost their lives when the ship *Sir Galahad* was attacked by jets at Bluff Cove.

The Thatcher government lost further Welsh support when it looked poised to renege on promises made prior to their election to establish a Welsh-language television channel. But a threat by the honorary president of Plaid Cymru, Gwynfor Evans, to fast to death unless such a broadcast service materialized, pressurized the Conservatives into fulfilling their promise: in November 1982, Sianel Pedwar Cymru (S4C) took to the airwaves.

Despite some concessions, and judging by the frequency of graffiti on Welsh walls proclaiming a desire to see 'Thatcher Out', the Iron Lady's policies soon became deeply unpopular in Wales. The fact that she appointed secretaries of state for Wales who came from English constituencies exacerbated the situation even further. The Conservatives polled only eight Welsh seats in 1987, and in the elections of May 1997 and June 2001 they failed to win a single one. The first elections to the Assembly for Wales provided little solace when they polled a little under 16 per cent of the vote – enough to give them one seat in Monmouthshire, and, by dint of proportional representation – which gave each party extra members according to its general support – a further eight seats.

While many were made anxious by the effects of Thatcherism, one group of Welsh women viewed nuclear disarmament as their paramount concern. 'Women for Life on Earth' grew out of the Campaign for Nuclear Disarmament, and its members were galvanized into action by the decision to site cruise missiles at Greenham Common airfield in Berkshire. A group of 36 women, four men and a handful of children, organized by Ann Pettit from Llanpumsaint in Carmarthenshire, marched from Cardiff to the air base.

These protesters, in turn, attracted other, mainly female, activists, who at one point numbered 30,000 and managed to link hands all the way around the perimeter fence. Some women went to prison because of their actions and one, Helen Thomas, a 23-year-old from Newcastle Emlyn, died at Greenham Common after she was struck by the wing mirror of a police vehicle. Other protests were organized in Wales, such as the 'peace camp' at Porth, and at the oceanographic research station at Brawdy in Pembrokeshire, which was used to track Russian nuclear submarines. When the nuclear accident at Chernobyl in Russia in April 1986 led to the fall of radioactive rain on Welsh hills, there was some vindication for such concern about the effects of the nuclear age, especially when the movement of sheep in north Wales had to be restricted for many years afterwards.

The Thatcher era saw advances in individualism, such as the decision that five million council-house tenants in the UK were to be given the right to buy their own homes. This meant that during the next 30 years, council estates in Wales would see over 135,000 homes sold off in this way. At the same time, the miners' strike of 1984 was a watershed moment for Wales.

The economic crises of the 1970s had resulted in miners' strikes in 1972 (the first time all the miners of the UK had downed tools at the same time since 1926) and again in 1974 – both supported by the Labour Party and both seen as pivotal in bringing down the Conservative government of Ted Heath.

In 1981, there was the threat of a further strike when pit closures were proposed, but the government backed down from these plans, feeling its position was not strong enough. The coal industry was thus poised for further confrontation between the NUM and the government. The miners showed which way the wind was blowing when various NUM regions resolved to strike should pits be closed for reasons other than geological or resource exhaustion. But the South Wales Coalfield was running at a titanic loss – over £2.5 million a week – and seemed to proffer a bare neck for the new axe to chop.

The unions were most certainly in the front line: Thatcher saw that if she broke the miners, then organized unionism wouldn't stand a chance, and she could further promote her project of strengthening private capitalism while reducing the role of the state. In the early 1980s, the National Union of Mineworkers was very strong, with a high membership and strong links to the Labour Party. It was also defiantly left wing and militant, with no qualms about threatening industrial action.

By the end of 1983, with the Falklands War won and a mandate from that year's general election, Thatcher felt far more secure in her position and was more than willing to tackle the unions. The struggle over the mining industry would pretty much come to define her premiership. Thatcher, now in her second term, showed that she meant business when she appointed Ian MacGregor as head of the National Coal Board, which oversaw the industry. MacGregor had a reputation as an industrial axeman who had plenty of experience of such matters, having overseen cutbacks and closures during his previous role at British Steel, when well over 100,000 jobs were shed.

In 1984, it was announced that 20 pits were to close, which would result in the loss of 20,000 jobs. It was later disclosed that the government, in preparation for the much-anticipated industrial action, had been stockpiling coal to take Britain through the winter.

Locally organized strikes across the UK soon consolidated as a national NUM strike in March 1984. But the union's leader, Arthur Scargill, suggested that NUM regions could decide whether or not to strike on an independent basis. In Wales support was weak, with only 10 out of 28 pits in south Wales voting to back the strike. Meanwhile, Margaret Thatcher ratcheted up the pressure by referring to striking miners as 'the enemy within' and to the action as 'the rule of the mob'.

Scargill, in turn, compared the government's techniques in crowd control to those of a 'Latin American state'. The dispute had little chance of ending amicably or quickly. As the strike continued, strains and stresses began to be felt. The workers earned no money and were ineligible for benefits as the strike was deemed illegal; they had to rely on scrimping, saving and handouts.

Observance of the strike within Wales differed from north to south. In the north, only 35 per cent of the 1,000 men employed went on strike, and this had dwindled to ten per cent by the end of the strike in 1985. By contrast, the South Wales Coalfield contained the staunchest supporters of industrial action. At the start of the strike, 99.6 per cent of the 21,500 workers joined the action. This reduced to 93 per cent by the end. No other area retained such a level.

In South Wales, although only 6 per cent of the miners went back to work, even that small percentage was sufficient to lead to personal relationships becoming strained, as the men who had decided to work through the strike were dubbed 'scabs' in the lacerating lexicon of industrial relations. On the picket lines of mines and steelworks, such as those at Port Talbot, buses carrying scabs were attacked, and other disturbances occurred. Miners repeatedly and fiercely clashed with massed ranks of police all over the UK.

With so many men unemployed across a swathe of South Wales, which was almost single-industry, the region suffered hugely from deprivation and community breakdown. Some communities became ghost villages.

One incident in South Wales accelerated the ending of the strike and turned some otherwise sympathetic members of the public against the miners. The killing of David Wilkie, a taxi driver, was a tragedy and a public relations disaster for the NUM. Wilkie had been driving David Williams, a working miner, to the Merthyr Vale mine with a police escort on 6 November 1984, when two striking miners dropped a concrete block from a bridge onto the car, killing Wilkie instantly. This coincided with a gradual slide in public and media support for the action, amid scandals and accusations. Families found it increasingly difficult to sustain themselves, and the NUM funds were running too low to pay for pickets' transport.

The official end of the strike came on 3 March 1985, when a vote was passed to return to work even without a new agreement with management. The pits closed rapidly over the next few years, and in 1994 the industry was finally privatized almost 50 years after it had been nationalized in 1946. It marked a very definite end of an era, as Kim Howells, the NUM's research officer, recalled:

One thing it did was drive out once and for all the ghosts of syndicalism which have never haunted anywhere more than they

have haunted South Wales; and I think we learnt that the days
of union picketing its way to victory are long gone and were prob-
ably long gone a decade ago.[1]

The long, and for some very profitable, saga of Welsh coal manufacture had reached its final chapter. There were, however, a few
unexpected pages yet to be written, and these would have a heroic
twist to them. In 1995 a group of miners famously bought the Tower
Colliery in the Cynon valley, which had originally opened in 1805, to
keep it as a going concern. It became Wales's only working deep mine,
and the oldest continuously worked deep-coal mine in the UK.

Tower Colliery would eventually close due to dwindling coal
seams. Although some small-scale mining and open-cast working
continued in places, such as the Vale of Neath, it was the end of an
industry that had once employed almost 300,000 men.

CHAPTER TWENTY-EIGHT

TWENTY-FIRST-CENTURY WALES

When the Welsh playwright Ed Thomas wrote 'So old Wales is dead and new Wales is already a possibility, an eclectic self-defined Wales with attitude'[1] for an *Observer* article in 1978, it was the eve of the Welsh devolution referendum, held on the suggested creation of a National assembly. The proposed assembly would be a democratically elected body able to make laws for Wales and represent the interests of Wales and its people. As the day of the momentous decision loomed, Thomas depicted a country once again on the brink of change, ready perhaps to shed the old skin of the past.

This attempt to move the country another step towards independence resonated with echoes of attempts down the centuries to unite the country and dissociate it from its powerful neighbour to the east. These were attempts often compromised by disunity and rivalry, or the arrival of new invaders or conquerors. Even the landscape was shaped as a series of hurdles to unity, where the relative equality of its many valleys meant there was no natural location on this corrugated map where a capital might grow. Even Cardiff had to make its case to be the home of the National Assembly, and that debate served to underline the differences between parts of the country, not least the north and the south, which didn't even have a decent road to link them both.

The post-war Labour government headed by Clem Attlee had been, at best, lukewarm towards any devolution prospects for Wales, even though there had been the consolation prize of establishing the Council for Wales and Monmouthshire. In 1950, however, the cross-party 'Parliament for Wales' campaign was established and there had been some momentum behind the idea of a measure of independence for the country.

The Conservatives appointed a minister for Welsh affairs in 1951. This, however, seemed to be the extent of progress in Welsh independence: S. O. Davies, MP for Merthyr, tabled a Government of Wales Bill, which was rejected. Meanwhile, although the Parliament for Wales campaign was able to marshal a quarter of a million signatures for a petition to give to Parliament, for all the good these did, they might as well have been written on sand.

Labour was getting nervous about the growth in nationalist sentiment, and in 1959 they promised to establish a secretary of state for Wales. Five years later, Labour set up the Welsh Office, and Llanelli's veteran MP, James Griffiths, who had held that seat since 1936, became the first to head it. Significant swings to Plaid Cymru in by-elections – Rhondda West in 1967 and Caerphilly in 1968 – brought them within a whisker of success, forcing Labour to commit ever more fully to devolution.

Devolution was now much discussed. In October 1973 a royal commission produced the Kilbrandon Report, which generally supported the idea of an elected Welsh assembly, although not all the members of the commission were in agreement. The Labour Party then started a long debate on the subject, leading eventually to the introduction of the Wales and Scotland Bill, which suggested a legislative assembly for Scotland and an executive assembly, that is one without law-making powers, for Wales. In July 1978 this formed the basis for the Wales Act, itself consequently debated to the point where it was felt that a referendum was needed to judge support for this measure of devolution.

The date for a referendum on the proposed Welsh assembly was set for St David's Day, 1 March 1979. Other than the Conservatives, all the Welsh parties were signed up to support the establishment of such an assembly. Despite this majority support, half a dozen high-profile Labour politicians, including Leo Abse, MP for Pontypool, and Neil Kinnock, MP for Bedwellty (later Islwyn), were already preparing for the vote to go against the formation of an assembly, and hoped it would.

These politicians claimed that a Welsh assembly would lead to a disunited kingdom, and that the assembly would favour Welsh speakers. There were also suggestions that north Wales would suffer, or be sidelined as a consequence of a Cardiff-centric assembly. Their joint document, called 'Facts to Beat the Fantasies', said that the devolution proposals 'would impose costs the people of Wales cannot afford to pay, risks they cannot afford to take, conflict with the rest of Britain and disharmony within Wales which they do not want'.[2]

In predicting the outcome of the vote, one might have looked back on the 'three Wales model' as posited by Sir Alfred Zimmern in 1921, and which was subsequently used by politicians, historians and political analysts such as Denis Balsom, who would reference it in the 1980s. It divided Wales into three parts: *Y Fro*, a Welsh-speaking northwest and west; the Welsh Wales of the industrial southeastern valleys, being a Socialist stretch of land pretty much coincident with the coalfield; and the coastal belts in the north and south, including areas such as south Pembrokeshire – this third part was noted as English-speaking, where people preferred to align themselves with Britain rather than Wales. This was clearly evident in the voting patterns of the May 1979 referendum.

The votes went the naysayers' way, with 956,330 voting against and 243,048 voting for the motion. Every Welsh county voted 'no', with the strongest negativity in Gwent, where the no-vote commanded over 75 per cent of the electorate, while in the Welsh-speaking heartlands of Gwynedd, a third of voters were against the notion of a representative assembly.

For now, it seemed, devolution was off the cards, and such proposals were put firmly on the back burner. Wales subsequently underwent a series of economic crises, not least when Thatcher's intentions to reduce manufacturing industry became a reality; heavy industry suffered huge job losses, of which the miners' were a highly visible proportion.

Unemployment rose and rose, and it was against this backdrop that the Campaign for a Welsh Assembly was re-established in 1982, but with a change in focus from the Parliament for Wales campaign that had been established in 1950. Its aim was to canvass votes for Welsh problems to be given Welsh solutions, and also challenged the increasing dominance of quangos (publicly funded private organizations) in Welsh life.

Bodies such as the Land Authority for Wales, the Welsh Development Agency and the Development Board for Rural Wales had multiplied rapidly – there were 40 quangos in Wales in 1979. This was a period that also saw the unions systematically challenged, and thoroughly right-wing thinking introduced into the Welsh Office under successive secretaries of state, such as Peter Walker and John Redwood.

By May 1995, the ongoing debate in the country had led to the Labour Party announcing proposals for a new referendum. In 1997, 18 years of Conservative rule came to an end and ushered a smiling, youthful Tony Blair into 10 Downing Street. Labour would honour the pledge made by its leader John Smith before his premature death: a referendum was announced and Ron Davies, secretary of state for Wales and MP for Caerphilly, promptly championed the 'yes' vote. He argued that 'through the Welsh National Assembly we can create a country that more fully embodies the values of social justice and equality which have long animated the people of Wales'.[3]

A joint campaign with the Liberals and Plaid Cymru in 1997 managed to turn the negative reaction of 1979 into a narrow margin of support, with 559,419 votes for and 552,698 against. The margin was tight, with a majority of 6,721 votes, but it also represented a swing of 30 per cent towards approving the notion of an assembly since the previous referendum. The 'yes' vote was most pronounced in those areas that had suffered most because of monetarism and Thatcherism.

This 'yes' vote precipitated a Wales-wide scramble to attract the new assembly, with Swansea, Wrexham and Machynlleth all vying for position, and Cardiff ultimately seeing the new 60-seat National Assembly for Wales housed in Cardiff Bay in 1999 on the eve of the new millennium.

Initially housed temporarily in Crickhowell House, the National Assembly was eventually given a glass, slate and steel home designed by the Richard Rogers partnership. The sleek lines and open glass frontage were sometimes marred by the plastic buckets on the floor catching rain from the leaking roof and lending some credence to the early view that it was merely a superannuated version of a county council. The building was officially opened by Queen Elizabeth II on St David's Day in 2006 and, perhaps in anticipation of further power gains, was named *Y Senedd*.*

The first elections were held in March 1999. Ron Davies was expected to run the show as the first minister, but media coverage of his self-described 'moment of madness' on Clapham Common led to the appointment of Alun Michael, a Blairite. Michael quickly yielded the job to a committed devolutionist Rhodri Morgan, who had been MP for Cardiff West since 1987. In February 2000 Morgan started to steer the new political craft through decidedly choppy seas.

The limitations of the assembly's powers were sometimes cruelly exposed – for example, its inability to influence decisions by multinational companies to close down plants or factories in Wales, including the closure of the plant owned by the steel company Corus in Ebbw Vale. The National Assembly also wrestled with the mechanics of redistributing wealth more equably. Affluent stretches, such as the M4 corridor and the A55 expressway across north Wales, were worlds apart from the social and economic ravages evident in communities sometimes only ten miles away.

In 1999 Labour held a minority position following the first elections for the National Assembly, in part because of proportional representation. Plaid Cymru won traditional Labour seats in Rhondda

---

* *Senedd* translates as 'senate' in English but, tellingly, means 'parliament' in Welsh.

and Islwyn, taking the highest share of the vote of any Wales-wide elections, and entering into a coalition partnership with the Liberals in October 2000. Interestingly, in the general election of 2001, Labour still enjoyed substantial support from Welsh voters.

In the next assembly elections in 2003, Labour won 30 seats and Rhodri Morgan, as first minister, decided to go it alone without a coalition partner: power was precarious, as the opposition, of all hues, could among them marshal 30 votes. It proved to be even more of a knife-edge contest when one member, Peter Law, left Labour in protest against the decision by the party to select candidates for the general election from shortlists made up entirely of women, an attempt to alter the gender imbalance in both the party and in Parliament. When Peter Law eventually won at Blaenau Gwent as an independent, it represented the loss of Labour's safest Welsh seat.

By the next election for the National Assembly in 2007, Labour had 26 seats, while Plaid Cymru had 15, but Labour had failed to create a coalition with the Liberal Democrats. The solution was a coalition with Plaid Cymru, a case of former enemies becoming bedfellows.

This coalition, coincidentally, came into being on 7 July 2007, which was the 700th anniversary of the death of Edward I, who had conquered Wales and built castles to reinforce the fears of a subjugated people. The coalition between Labour and Plaid Cymru saw these unlikely political partners draw up an agreement called 'One Wales', which committed the administration to move towards a Welsh parliament with full law-making powers.

The often-quoted logic from Ron Davies that 'devolution was a process rather than an event' became very clear as Labour politicians, such as Rhodri Morgan, pursued policies for Wales that were very different from those in Westminster. As he put it, 'clear red water' separated them. The policies included making all medical prescriptions free, as well as granting free entry to museums and galleries, abolishing health trusts and supporting higher education differently in Wales from the rest of the UK.

Matters would be taken further courtesy of the Government of Wales Act, which empowered the assembly to acquire law-making powers, subject to a referendum. Some saw this as nothing more than plain subterfuge. Journalist Martin Shipton suggested that 'We remain as subservient as we ever were to the Westminster parliament', and further that 'The devolution settlement imposed on Wales by the Government of Wales Act of 2006 amounts to nothing more than a conjuring trick designed to conceal an instrument of national humiliation.'[4] Conjuring trick or not, in some areas the new institution was becoming a world leader, not least when it came to the representation of women, who made up half the assembly membership.

Wales was increasingly finding its own way of doing things, in fields ranging from politics through healthcare to sport. This difference was very apparent on one sad day in 2007, when the country had its first 'state funeral', a coming together of Wales, when thousands of mourners paid their final tributes to international rugby star, popular broadcaster and actor Ray Gravell, at his funeral at Llanelli's Stradey Park. A flag-draped coffin was carried onto the field by six former and then-current Llanelli players while the scoreboard carried details in Welsh that reminded mourners of a great victory by Llanelli over the All Blacks on 31 October 1972, in which Gravell had played his part.

The coffin was placed on a stand on a red carpet on the pitch, and rugby player Robin McBryde, carrying the eisteddfod sword – which had been proudly borne by Gravell at numerous *eisteddfodau* – stood at its head. The sword, never completely unsheathed and thus a symbol of peace, is a key part of ceremonies at the annual festival of literature, music and performance.

Gravell's service, which included the Welsh hymns 'Calon Lân' and 'Cwm Rhondda', was conducted by the Reverend Meirion Evans, a former archdruid and friend, reflecting the fact that Gravell, known by all as Grav, had been the eisteddfod's herald, bearing the self-same sword that he used to bear aloft at its ceremonies.

The presence of these traditions at a modern funeral highlights the fact that Wales in the twenty-first century was a place of startling contradictions. Its confident, youthful capital city looks out over the area of standing water known as Cardiff Bay. The extreme ebb and flow of the tide, resulting in unattractive but ecologically rich mudflats at low tide, ceased with the creation of a barrage, completed in 1999. The idea was imported from the US city of Baltimore, as Cardiff's own stretch of water wasn't dissimilar to the Inner Harbor in Maryland.

Cardiff could also boast the Millennium Stadium, an architectural triumph ready for the staging of the rugby World Cup in 2000. The city's skyline was increasingly punctuated by building cranes, hard at work on new skyscrapers and tower blocks.

Yet despite the seemingly breakneck development of the capital, the country remained notably poor. While chill economic winds blew across the land, there was still real confidence in such fields as the arts, as evidenced by the distinctive 'golden armadillo-shaped' Wales Millennium Centre (WMC), opened in November 2004. Designed by

Jonathan Adams, this signature building housed the 2,000-seat Donald Gordon Theatre. Outside, slate brought from north Wales had been arranged to resemble the strata of rock at the coastal outcrops of Southern-down, and their polychromatic beauty echoed the music of the Welsh National Opera, which was given its first permanent home inside the building, also shared with an array of other arts bodies.

On the imposing façade of the WMC ran the world's largest poem, appearing in giant letters, by Wales's first national poet, Gwyneth Lewis. It seemingly bridged the worlds of industry and creativity, and did so in both Welsh and English:

Creu gwir fel gwydr o ffwrnais awen
In these stones horizons sing

The English line is not a translation of the Welsh words, which mean 'Creating truth, like glass, from the furnace of inspiration'. It brings to mind the night sky above that industrial dynamo town of Merthyr Tydfil in its heyday, lit up by the furnaces of the ironworks.

Another recent highlight in the Welsh arts was the totally transformative theatre event in Easter 2011, when Hollywood actor Michael Sheen returned home to the steelmaking town of Port Talbot to act in *The Passion*. This crowned the first year's activities of National Theatre Wales, a company born out of a decision not to replicate eras such as the Edwardian age, when institutions were as much about the grandness of their buildings as about the scale of their ambitions. Other works in the first year, such as Mike Pearson and Mike Brooke's staging of Kaite O'Reilly's translation of *The Persians* on Mynydd Epynt, underlined the ambition of the new company. Its sister theatre, *Theatr Genedlaethol Cymru*, worked on the same model, commissioning work without the need for expenditure on expensive bricks and mortar.

Despite these cultural achievements, recent times have been hard on Wales. The charity Save the Children revealed in 2011 that one in seven children in Wales is being brought up in severe poverty.[5] The cuts to the public sector by David Cameron's coalition government from 2010 onwards led to severe spending cuts with a subsequent loss of jobs. Wales was catapulted into more lean times, though not on the scale of the 1930s, when writer Alun Richards had felt the pain of his school chum forced to wear his sister's shoes.

By 2011, when a referendum was held about giving the assembly law-making powers in 20 subject areas, such as health, education, culture and economic development, more than 50 per cent of voters in all 22 counties, except Monmouthshire, backed change by voting 'yes'. Yet the margin in Monmouthshire was slender. The unanimity of the voting map encouraged First Minister Carwyn Jones to suggest that 'from the coast to the border, the north to the south, our country is united'.

The 2011 vote for greater assembly powers showed that the difference between Anglesey, where 50.9 per cent voted 'yes' and Torfaen, where the figure was 49.8 per cent, was nothing more than slight. The Torfaen votes were essential for the overall vote to favour more powers for the assembly, but so too were the 12,381 votes cast in Monmouthshire: 'but for three hundred or so votes cast in Monmouthshire, the voting map of Wales in the referendum might have been one colour'.[6]

Using the mechanism of democracy, Wales had edged towards the sort of political unity sought by Welsh princes, such as Llywelyn ab Iorwerth, Llywelyn ap Gruffudd and Owain Glyndŵr. Yet despite the fact that more people in Wales are comfortable with seeing themselves as Welsh, and trusting in uniquely Welsh institutions, Wales is still a country in which the people are heavily influenced by British broadcasting. Republican zeal on the part of some is tempered by old-fashioned royalism: on the streets of its youthful capital there were more requests for permits for street parties to celebrate the royal wedding of Prince William to Kate Middleton than in any other area of the UK apart from London.

Wales remains both a country and a conundrum, where British-ness and Welshness often tussle, or prove interchangeable. It is a nation small enough to hold out the promise of being understood, yet large enough to always have more to discover around every corner. It is a place where economic poverty and cultural ambition sit cheek by jowl.

The story of Wales is an ongoing project – a story that tells of accommodations with a powerful neighbour, that details various attempts at nation-building, that recounts sporting ambitions and dreams realized, that displays linguistic resurgence and attempts to realize the limitless potential of a diverse population. There are nowadays three million individual stories in Wales, each unique but collectively arresting.

> *Your house, Llywelyn, is today a hill, and out of that hill*
> *an oak rears, seismic with acorns: timber for ships, barrels,*
> > *dreams –*
> *for the hall you left us that's ours to complete.*[7]

TIMELINE

Italics are used for dates and events specific to Welsh history.

BCE

c. 40,000–10,000	Old Stone Age (Palaeolithic era)
c. 27,000	*Burial of the 'Red Lady of Paviland' in Goat's Hole Cave*
c. 9500–4000	Middle Stone Age (Mesolithic era)
c. 9000	The last ice age
c. 4000–2000	New Stone Age (Neolithic era)
c. 4000	Agriculture arrives in western Britain
c. 3500	*Bryn Celli Ddu constructed on Anglesey*
c. 2700	*Hindwell Palisade constructed in the Walton Basin in Radnorshire*
c. 2000–1000	Bronze Age
	Beaker Folk emerge in Wales
c. 2000	*Copper mined and cast at Great Orme, near Llandudno*
c. 1950–1550	*Gold and bronze Mold Cape crafted (discovered at Bryn-yr-ellyllon)*
c. 1300–1150	*Penard Period*

c. 650–43 CE	Iron Age
	Celtic language and Celts (Keltoi/Celtae) a fully formed people, span from Ireland to Turkey

CE

c. 43	The Romans arrive in Britain.
	Wales and England now called Britannia
c. 122	Work begins on Hadrian's Wall
c. 410	The Roman's leave Britannia, ushering in the Dark Ages or Heroic Age.
450–700	'Age of the Saints'
	Anglo-Saxons arrive on British shores
577	Battle at Dyrham leads to Anglo-Saxon conquest of Cornwall, severing Briton Wales from southwest England.
716–57	Aethelbald rules Mercia. Wat's Dyke is constructed.
757–96	*Offa rules the kingdom of Mercia. Offa's Dyke is constructed. Britons inhabit Wales.*
789	First Viking attacks begin in western Europe
793	Vikings longboats reach Lindisfarne on the northeast coast of England
844–78	*Rhodri the Great expands his territories from Gwynedd*

c. 852–77	*'Black Gentiles' from Dublin raid and loot Wales*
871–99	Reign of Alfred the Great
878	*Vikings overwinter for the first time in Dyfed*
910–50	*Hywel the Good expands his territories from Seisyllwg*
	The Laws of Hywel Dda compiled
925–39	Reign of Athelstan
978	*Vikings attack Anglesey and enslave 2,000 people*
1039–63	*Gruffudd ap Llywelyn conquers all of Wales*
1042–66	Edward the Confessor rules, followed briefly by Harold I
1066	The Normans arrive
	Battle of Hastings
	William the Conqueror takes English crown
	Normans name the Cymry people 'Welsh' (foreigners) and their country 'Wales' (foreign land)
1067	*Work begins on Chepstow castle*
1087–1100	Reign of William II
1100–35	Reign of Henry I
1093	*Rhys ap Tewdwr, leader of Deheubarth, is killed defending Brycheiniog against the Normans*
c. 1200	*Boundaries between Marchia Wallie and Pura Wallia now defined*

1105	*Henry I grants Flemish settlers permission to take land in south Pembrokeshire*
1135–54	Reign of Stephen I
1137–70	*Owain Gwynedd rules Gwynedd*
1154–89	Reign of Henry II, first Plantagenet king
	Henry II keen to bring Wales back into the control of the Crown.
1163	*Rhys ap Gruffudd swears oath of allegiance to Henry II at Woodstock*
1164	*Abbey at Strata Florida established*
1172	*Rhys ap Gruffudd, Lord Rhys, appointed 'Justice in all south Wales'*
1197	*Rhys ap Gruffudd dies*
1189	Reign of Richard I
1215–17	First Baron's War in England
1216–72	Reign of Henry III
1200–40	*Llywelyn the Great creates a unified Wales*
1247	*Treaty of Woodstock*
1255–82	*Llywelyn the Last*
1264–7	Second Barons' War in England
1267	*Treaty of Montgomery recognizes Llywelyn the Last as Prince of Wales*
1272–1307	Reign of Edward I
1277	*Edward I campaigns against Llywelyn the Last*

1282	*Llywelyn the Last killed; Wales becomes an English colony*
1284	*Statute of Rhuddlan*
1301	Edward II crowned Prince of Wales
1307–27	Reign of Edward II
1315–22	Famine ravages Europe
1327–30	Roger Mortimer rules England
1330–77	Reign of Edward III
1330–1	Famine returns
1346	Edward the Black Prince dies prematurely
1347–51	Black Death devastates Europe
1349	*Black Death first reaches Wales*
c.1350	White Book of Rhydderch *compiled, containing tales of the* Mabinogion
1377	Reign of Richard II
c. 1380	Red Book of Hergest *compiled, containing tales of the* Mabinogion
1399	Henry IV usurps English throne
1400–13	*Glyndŵr Rebellion*
1401–2	*The Lancastrian Penal Code*
1413	Henry V rules England
1455–87	War of the Roses
1483–5	Reign of Richard III

1485	Battle of Bosworth; Henry VII crowned king
1509–47	Reign of Henry VIII
c. 1533	Henry VIII breaks with Rome and becomes head of the Church of England
1536	*Act of Union; English law replaces Welsh law in Wales*
1542–3	*Second Act of Union*
1547–53	Reign of Edward VI; England and Wales become officially Protestant
1553–8	Reign of Mary I; England and Wales revert to Catholicism
1558–1603	Elizabeth I; England and Wales became Protestant again
1588	*William Morgan's Welsh edition of the Bible is published*
1603–25	Reign of James I
1625–49	Reign of Charles I
1630	*The Welsh Bible is published*
1642	First English Civil War begins
1648	Second English Civil War begins
1650	*The Commission for the Propagation of the Gospel in Wales is established*
1730s	*Methodism establishes itself in Wales*
1737	*Griffith Jones's travelling schools promote Welsh literacy*

1739	*Disastrous harvest*
1740	*Food riots*
1775–83	American War of Independence
1780	*Parys Mountain is the largest copper mine in the world*
1803–15	Napoleonic Wars
1811	*Cyfarthfa ironworks are the wealthiest in the world*
1823	William Buckland discovers 'Red Lady of Paviland' at Goat's Hole Cave
1837–1901	Reign of Victoria
1830	Wareham Riots
1837	*Working Men's Association is established*
1839	Chartist protests
1840s	*Welsh coal is the fuel of choice for the British Empire*
1841	*Taff Vale Railway opens, connecting Merthyr to the sea ports*
1846	*William Williams's Blue Books published*
1842	General Strike
1851	*Religious Census shows four-fifths of Welsh worshippers are Nonconformist*
1876	*Football Association of Wales created*
1881	*Welsh Rugby Union established in Neath*
1893	*The University of Wales is founded*

1905	*Cardiff becomes a city*
1907	*National Museum of Wales and National Library open*
1908	*Royal Commission on the Ancient and Historical Monuments of Wales established*
1913	*Senghennydd disaster*
1914–18	First World War
1920s	*Depression hits Wales*
1925	*Welsh Nationalist Party (Plaid Genedlaethol Cymru) founded by Saunders Lewis*
1939–45	Second World War
1945	Labour Party elected
1947	Nationalization of railways, docks, electricity and gas boards, road haulage, iron, steel and coal industries
1948	National Health Service established
1950	Conservative government elected
	Cross-party 'Parliament for Wales' campaign established
1951	*Conservative government appoints a minister of Welsh affairs*
1952–present	Reign of Elizabeth II
1955	*Cardiff becomes the capital of Wales*
1957	Brecon Beacons designated a national park

1961	*Referendum on Sunday opening hours for pubs in Wales*
1964	*Labour government establishes the Welsh Office*
1965	*Llyn Celyn reservoir opened*
1966	*Aberfan disaster*
	Severn Bridge opened
1969	*Prince Charles invested as Prince of Wales*
1972	UK miners' strike lasts seven weeks
1973	*Kilbrandon Report supports idea of an elected Welsh assembly*
1974	UK miners' strike lasts 16 weeks
	Three-day week introduced
1976	Britain applies to International Monetary Fund for a $4 billion loan
1976–79	Wales suffers 60,000 jobs losses
1978	*Wales Act*
1979	Conservative government elected, under leadership of Margaret Thatcher
1979	*Referendum on a National Assembly, majority vote 'no'*
1978–95	*Earliest human remains (230,000 years old) found at Pontnewydd Cave, Elwy valley.*
1982	*Sianel Pedwar Cymru (S4C) begins transmitting*
1984–5	UK miners' strike in response to pit closures

1986	Nuclear disaster at Chernobyl, Russia – radioactive rain falls on Welsh hills
1994	Coal industry privatized by Conservative government
1995	Tower Colliery in Cynon valley bought by miners
1997	Labour government elected, under leadership of Tony Blair
	Referendum on National Assembly, majority vote 'yes'
1999	*National Assembly for Wales established in Cardiff*
2000	Wales hosts Rugby World Cup at the Millennium Stadium
2004	Wales Millennium Centre opened
2006	*National Assembly moves to its permanent home*
2007	*Coalition between Labour Party and Plaid Cymru. One Wales agreement drawn up.*
2011	*Swansea City Football Club enters Premiership*
	Referendum on increased law-making powers for the National Assembly, majority vote 'yes'

NOTES

PART ONE: Before Wales

Chapter 1: The Red Lady of Paviland

1. Quoted in Professor Stephen Aldhouse-Green, 'Great Sites: Paviland Cave', *British Archaeology* (York: The Council of British Archaeology, October 2001), Issue 61.
2. Letter from Buckland to Lady Mary Cole (15 February 1823), quoted in Marianne Sommer, *Bones and Ochre: The Curious Afterlife of the Red Lady of Paviland* (Cambridge, Massachusetts and London: Harvard University Press, 2007), 29.

Chapter 2: The Stone Ages

1. Steve Burrow, *The Tomb Builders in Wales 4000–3000 BC* (Cardiff: National Museum Wales Books, 2006), 104.
2. Ibid., 12.
3. John Davies, *A History of Wales* (London: Penguin, 1994), 10.
4. Burrow, op. cit., 82.
5. Alex Gibson, *The Walton Basin, Powys, Wales: Survey at the Hindwell Neolithic Enclosure* (Welshpool: Clwyd-Powys Archaeological Trust, 1999).

Chapter 3: Bronze and Iron Ages

1. Neil McGregor, *A History of the World in 100 Objects* (BBC Audio Ltd, 2011).
2. Ibid.
3. Geraint H. Jenkins, *A Concise History of Wales* (Cambridge: Cambridge University Press, 2008), 15.
4. For more about the discoveries at Coygan see Russell Davies, *Carmarthenshire: A Concise History* (Cardiff: University of Wales Press, 2006), 2–5.
5. *Culhwch ac Olwen,* quoted in John Davies, *The Making of Wales* (Stroud: The History Press, 2009), 26.

Chapter 4: Edge of Empire

1. *Tacitus, The Annals,* quoted in Trevor Rowley, *The Welsh Border: Archaeology, History & Landscape* (Stroud: Tempus, 2001), 46.
2. Tacitus, *The Annals,* translated by A. J. Woodman (Indianapolis: Hackett Publishing, 2004).
3. Tacitus, quoted in Anne Ross, *Druids: Preachers of Immortality* (Stroud: Tempus, 2004), 40.
4. BBC News online, 23 August 2011 (http://www.bbc.co.uk/news/uk-wales-14628286).
5. Gildas, *The Ruin of Britain* (London: Phillimore, 1978), 18.
6. Gwyn A. Williams, *When Was Wales?* (Harmondsworth: Penguin, 1985), 20.

PART TWO: Invasion and Assimilation

Chapter 5: Anglo-Saxons and Britons

1. Meic Stephens, *The Oxford Companion to the Literature of Wales* (Oxford: Oxford University Press, 1986), 216.
2. John Davies, *The Making of Wales* (Stroud: The History Press, 2009), 35.
3. Taken from transcripts of Doctor Alan Lane's interview for the BBC series *The Story of Wales* (BBC ONE, 2011).

Chapter 6: The Vikings and Rhodri the Great

1. Anonymous, ninth-century Ireland, quoted in Neil Hegarty, *Story of Ireland* (London: BBC Books, 2011), 36.

Chapter 7: Law and Order

1. From the Laws of Hywel Dda, quoted in Alice Thomas Ellis, *Wales: An Anthology* (London: Collins, 1989), 63.
2. Ibid.
3. *Brenhinedd y Season,* quoted inMeic Stephens, *A Most Peculiar People* (Cardiff: University of Wales Press, 1992), 5.

Chapter 8: Norman Wales

1. Rhygyfarch, 'Lament', *c.* 1094.
2. Jan Morris, *The Matter of Wales: Epic Views of a Small Country* (Penguin: London, 1984), 300.
3. Extract from *Brut y Tywysogyon,* translated by Roger Turvey, *The Lord Rhys: Prince of Deheubarth* (Llandysul: Gomer Press, 1996), 118.

Chapter 9: Religious Awakening

1. This assessment of St Illtud was included in a seventh-century biography of St Samson, penned by a Breton monk.
2. *Vita Davidis*, quoted in A.W. Wade-Evans, *St David* (London: Society for the Promotion of Christian Knowledge, 1923), 1.
3. J. E. Lloyd, quoted in Meic Stephens, *The Oxford Companion to the Literature of Wales* (Oxford: Oxford University Press, 1986), 564.

Chapter 10: Llywelyn the Great and Llywelyn the Last

1. A. Owen (ed.), *Ancient Laws and Institutions of Wales; Comprising Laws Supposed to be Enacted by Howel The Good, Modified by Subsequent Regulations under the Native Princes Prior to the Conquest by Edward the First* (London: Eyre & Spottiswoode, 1841).
2. Quoted in R. R. Davies, *The Age of Conquest* (Oxford: Oxford University Press, 1987), 243.
3. Quoted in Thomas Tout, *The Collected Papers of Thomas Frederick Tout* (Manchester: Manchester University Press, 1932), 54.
4. Quoted in Davies, op.cit., 312.

PART THREE: Colonization and Rebellion

Chapter 11: Treason and Plague

1. Statute of Rhuddlan, quoted in Trevor Herbert and Gareth Elwyn Jones, *Edward I and Wales* (Cardiff: University of Wales Press, 1988), 75.
2. Robert S. Gottfried, *The Black Death: Natural and Human Disaster in Medieval Europe* (New York: The Free Press, 1983), xiii.
3. Quoted in Philip Ziegler, *The Black Death* (New York: Harper & Row, 1971), 190.
4. Quoted in Geraint H. Jenkins, *A Concise History of Wales* (Cambridge: Cambridge University Press, 2007), 98.
5. Sir John Wynn, *The History of the Gwydir Family*, quoted in Glanmor Williams, *Renewal and Reformation Wales c.1415–1642* (Oxford: Oxford University Press, 1993), 90.
6. William Rees, 'The Black Death in England and Wales, as exhibited in Manorial Documents,' *Journal of the Royal Society of Medicine* (Sect Hist Med, 1923), Vol. 16: 27–45.
7. Jenkins, op. cit., 100.

Chapter 12: A Last Revolt

1. Iolo Goch, 'Llys Swain Glyndŵr yol Sycharth, quotes in Gwynfor Evans, *Land of My Fathers: 2000 Years of Welsh History* (Talybont: Y Lolfa, 1998), 257.
2. Quoted in Christopher Snyder, *The Britons* (Hoboken, New Jersey: John Wiley & Sons, 2003), 246.
3. Quoted in Evans, op. cit., 262.
4. Quoted in Meic Stephens, *A Most Peculiar People* (Cardiff: University of Wales Press, 1992), 12.
5. Quoted in Dylan Rees, *Carmarthenshire* (Cardiff: University of Wales Press, 2006), 52.
6. J. E. Lloyd, quoted in R. R. Davies, *Owain Glyndŵr* (Talybont: Y Lolfa, 2010), 150.

Chapter 13: Tudor Wales

1. Hugh Holland, 'Epitaph on Henry, Prince of Wales' *c.* 1625.
2. Quoted in David Williams, *A History of Modern Wales* (London, John Murray, 1977), 21.
3. Quoted in David Williams, *A History of Modern Wales* (London: John Murray, 1977), 20.
4. Quoted in Gwyn A. Williams, *When Was Wales?* (Harmondsworth: Penguin, 1985), 114.
5. John Davies, *A History of Wales* (London: Penguin, 1994), 258.
6. Geraint H. Jenkins, *A Concise History of Wales* (Cambridge: Cambridge University Press, 2008), 129.
7. Geraint H. Jenkins, 'Taphy-land historians and the Union of England and Wales 1536–2007', *Journal of Irish and Scottish Studies* (March 2008), Vol. 1, Issue 2.
8. Siôn Brwynog (*c.* 1553), translated by W. Ambrose Bebb in *Cyfnod y Tuduriaid* (1939) and quoted in Trevor Herbert and Gareth Elwyn Jones, Tudor Wales (Cardiff: University of Wales Press, 1988), 122.
9. Quoted in Trevor Herbert and Gareth Elwyn Jones, *Tudor Wales* (Cardiff: University of Wales Press, 1988), 123.
10. 'The much-loved schoolmaster executed under Elizabeth I', *Catholic Herald* (13 October 2011).
11. Thomas Pennant, *Tours in Wales* (London: Wilkie & Robinson, 1810), 146.
12. Quoted in Chester Greenough, *Collected Studies* (Manchester, New Hampshire: Ayer Publishing, 1970), 225.

13. J. Evans, quoted in Marcus Tanner, *The Last of the Celts* (New Haven and London: Yale University Press, 2004), 161.
14. Ibid.

Chapter 14: Civil War
1. A London Puritan, quoted in Gwyn Alf Williams, *When was Wales?* (Harmondsworth: Penguin, 1985), 131.

PART FOUR: Industrial Wales
Chapter 15: A Flurry of Thought
1. Quoted in Ceri Lewis, *Iolo Morganwg* (Caernarfon: Gwasg Pantycelyn, 1995), 14.
2. Geraint H. Jenkins, *A Concise History of Wales* (Cambridge: Cambridge University Press, 2008), 217.
3. Quoted in Gwyneth Tyson Roberts, *The Language of the Blue Books* (Cardiff: University of Wales Press, 1998), 23.
4. Ibid., 3.
5. Ibid., 204.
6. Ibid., 171–2.

Chapter 16: The Golden Age
1. John Davies, *The Making of Wales* (Stroud: The History Press, 2009), 137.
2. The *Gloucester Journal* (14 August 1786).
3. Alun Withey, 'History of Disease in Wales', *Western Mail* (29 March 2011), also available online) www.WalesOnline.co.uk.
4. Quoted in the *Cambrian* (29 April 1809).
5. Ian Skidmore, *Gwynedd* (London: Robert Hale, 1986), 64.
6. A. H. Dodd, *A Short History of Wales* (Ruthin: John Jones, 1990), 121.

Chapter 17: The Reign of King Coal
1. John Davies, *A History of Wales* (London: Penguin, 1994), 469.
2. Quoted in John Davies, *Cardiff: A Pocket Guide* (Cardiff: University of Wales Press/*The Western Mail*, 2002), 67.

Chapter 18: Making Tracks
1. Quoted in W. J. Hughes, *Wales and the Welsh in English Literature* (Wrexham: Hughes and Son, 1924), 95.

2. Ibid., 146.
3. Earnest de Selincourt (ed.), 'Letter to Jane Pollard, July 1791' in *The Letters of William and Dorothy Wordsworth: The Early Years* (Oxford: Clarendon Press, 1967), Vol. 1, 51.
4. F. W. H. Myers, *Wordsworth* (Cambridge: Cambridge University Press, 2011), 33.

Chapter 19: Revolt and Unrest

1. For more on this 'rural Voltaire' see Geraint H. Jenkins, 'A Rank Republican (and) a Leveller', *Welsh History Review*, Vol. 17, No. 3 (June, 1995): 365–86.
2. Trevor Herbert and Gareth Elwyn Jones, *People and Protest: Wales 1815-1880* (Cardiff: University of Wales Press, 1990), 122.
3. Letter from Edward Crompton Lloyd Hall to Sir James Graham, quoted in ibid., 131.
4. Quoted in ibid., 152.
5. Quoted in Dave Reid, 'The Chartist March on Newport (1839) – A Workers' Rising', Socialist Party Wales archive (http://www.socialistpartywales.org.uk/theory1.shtml).

PART FIVE: The Making of Modern Wales

Chapter 20: A Liberal Wales

1. Kenneth O. Morgan, *Wales in British Politics: 1868–1922* (Cardiff: University of Wales Press, 1991), 26.
2. Quoted in Trevor Herbert and Gareth Elwyn Jones, *Wales Between the Wars* (Cardiff: University of Wales Press, 1988), 99.
3. Ibid., 145.
4. David Lloyd George, speech made as president of the Baptist Union at Treorchy in the Rhondda in 1909, quoted in Dai Smith, *Wales: A Question for History* (Bridgend: Seren, 1999), 90.
5. J.M. Keynes, quoted in Trevor Herbert and Gareth Elwyn Jones, *Wales 1880–1914* (Cardiff: University of Wales Press, 1988), 139.

Chapter 21: Depression Wales

1. Quoted in Trevor Herbert and Gareth Elwyn Jones, *Wales Between the Wars* (Cardiff: University of Wales Press, 1988), 52.
2. Quoted in Meic Stephens, *Artists in Wales* (Llandysul: Gomer, 1971), 58.

3. Quoted in Gareth Elwyn Jones and Dai Smith, *The People of Wales* (Llandysul: Gomer, 1999), 192.

4. Quoted in Meic Stephens, *Artists in Wales* (Llandysul: Gomer, 1971), 120.

5. Quoted in Kenneth O. Morgan, *Rebirth of a Nation: Wales 1880–1980* (Oxford: Oxford University Press, 1981), 193.

Chapter 22: Raining Bombs

1. Quoted in Prys Morgan, *The Tempus History of Wales* (Stroud: Tempus, 2001), 229.

2. Quoted in Phil Carradice, *Wales at War* (Llandysul: Gomer, 2003), 38.

3. Lynette Roberts, *Collected Poems*, ed. Patrick McGuinness (Manchester: Carcanet, 2005), xix.

4. Tony Curtis (ed.), 'The City Split in Two', *After the First Death: An Anthology of Wales and War in the Twentieth Century* (Bridgend: Seren Books, 2007), 142.

5. Quoted in Deirdre Beddoe, *Out of the Shadows: A History of Women in Twentieth Century Wales* (Cardiff: University of Wales Press, 2000), 117.

Chapter 23: Labour Days

1. Meic Stephens, *A Most Peculiar People* (Cardiff: University of Wales Press, 1992), 106.

Chapter 24: A Nationalist Spirit

1. Quoted in Laura McAllister, *Plaid Cymru: The Emergence of a Political Party* (Bridgend, Seren Books, 2001), 100.

2. Ambrose Bebb, 'Achub y Gymraeg; Achub Cymru', *Y Geninen* (May 1923), 124.

Chapter 25: National Pride

1. Quoted in Dai Smith, *Wales: A Question for History* (Bridgend: Seren Books, 1999), 78.

2. Quoted in Peter Stead and Gareth Williams (eds), *Wales and Its Boxers: The Fighting Tradition* (Cardiff: University of Wales Press, 2008), 59.

3. Ibid., 111.

4. Quoted in Trevor Herbert and Gareth Elwyn Jones (eds.), *Post-War Wales* (Cardiff: University of Wales Press, 1995), 125–7.

Chapter 26: Aberfan

1. Pupil, Pantglas Junior School, Aberfan (1966).
2. Iain McLean and Martin Johnes, *Aberfan: Disasters and Government* (Cardiff: Welsh Academic Press, 2000).
3. Ibid.

Chapter 27: Margaret Thatcher and the Miners

1. Kim Howells, 'After the Strike', *Planet* magazine (June/July 1985), No.51.

Chapter 28: Twenty-first-century Wales

1. Edward Thomas, 'A Land Fit for Heroes. (Max Boyce excluded)', *The Observer* (20 July 1997).
2. 'Anti-devolution Group say Assembly Poses Great Threats', *Western Mail* (7 February 1979).
3. Richard Wyn Jones and Roger Scully (eds), 'Devolution in Wales: What Does the Public Think?', *Findings from the Economic and Research Council's Research Programme on Devolution and Constitutional Change* (June 2004), briefing No. 7, 6.
4. Martin Shipton, speech at a conference on Welsh devolution, organized by the Bevan Foundation and Positif Politics (November 2008), quoted in Martin Shipton, *Poor Man's Parliament: Ten Years of the Welsh Assembly* (Bridgend: Seren Books, 2011), 276.
5. 'Child poverty in Wales exposed as UK's worst', *Western Mail* (23 February 2011).
6. Rhys Jones, 'Mapping Referenda', *Planet* magazine (May 2011), No. 202, 118.
7. Nigel Jenkins, 'Llywelyn ap Gruffudd Fychan', *Hotel Gwales* (Llandysul: Gomer, 2006).

FURTHER READING

A World of Welsh Copper, ESRC Global and Local Worlds of Welsh Copper Project (22 November 2011), www.welshcopper.org.uk/en/.

Aldhouse-Green, Professor Stephen, 'Great Sites: Paviland Cave', *British Archaeology* (York: The Council of British Archaeology, October 2001), Issue 61.

Beddoe, Deirdre, *Out of the Shadows: A History of Women in Twentieth Century Wales* (Cardiff: University of Wales Press, 2000).

Berry, Dave, *Wales and Cinema: The First Hundred Years* (Cardiff: University of Wales Press, 1994).

Black, Jeremy, *A New History of Wales* (London: Sutton, 2000).

Bowen, E. G., *Saints, Seaways and Settlements* (Cardiff: University of Wales Press, 1977).

Burgess, Colin and Lynch, Frances, *Prehistoric Man in Wales and the West* (Bath: Adams and Dart, 1972).

Burrow, Steve, *The Tomb Builders in Wales 4000 – 3000 BC* (Cardiff: National Museum Wales Books, 2006).

Carr, A. D., *Medieval Wales* (Basingstoke: Macmillan Press, 1995).

Carradice, Phil, *Wales at War* (Llandysul: Gomer, 2003).

Chadwick, Nora, *The Druids* (Cardiff: University of Wales Press, 1966).

Coombes, Bert, *These Poor Hands* (Cardiff: University of Wales Press, 2002).

Cunliffe, Barry, *Facing the Ocean: The Atlantic and Its Peoples, 8000BC–AD 1500* (Oxford: Oxford University Press, 2001).

Cunliffe, Barry. *Iron Age Communities in Britain* (London and New York: Routledge, 1991)

Curtis, Tony (ed.), *After the First Death: An Anthology of Wales and War in the Twentieth Century* (Bridgend: Seren Books, 2007).

Curtis, Tony (ed.), *Wales: the Imagined Nation: Essays in Cultural and National Identity* (Bridgend: Poetry Wales Press, 1986).

Davies, D. Hywel, *The Welsh Nationalist Party: 1925-1945: A Call to Nationhood* (Cardiff: University of Wales Press, 1983).

Davies, Grahame, *The Dragon and the Crescent: Nine Centuries of Welsh Contact with Islam* (Bridgend: Seren, 2011).

Davies, John, *A History of Wales* (London: Penguin, 1994).

Davies, John, *Cardiff: A Pocket Guide* (Cardiff: University of Wales Press/ Western Mail, 2002).

Davies, John, *The Making of Wales* (Stroud: The History Press, 2009).

Davies, John; Jenkins, Nigel; Baines, Menna and Lynch, Peredur (eds.), *The Welsh Academy Encyclopaedia of Wales* (Cardiff: University of Wales Press, 2008).

Davies, R. R., *The Age of Conquest: Wales 1063-1415* (Oxford: Oxford University Press, 1987).

Davies, R. R., *Owain Glyndŵr* (Talybont: Y Lolfa, 2010).

Davies, Russell, *Carmarthenshire: A Concise History* (Cardiff: University of Wales Press, 2006).

Davies, Sioned (trans.), *The Mabinogion* (Oxford: Oxford University Press, 2007).

Davies, Wendy, *Wales in the Early Middle Ages* (Leicester: Leicester University Press, 1982).

Dodd, A. H., *A Short History of Wales* (Ruthin: John Jones, 1998).

Ellis, Alice Thomas, *Wales: An Anthology* (London: Collins, 1989).

Eluere, Christiane, *The Celts: First Masters of Europe* (London: Thames & Hudson, 1995).

Evans, Gwynfor, *Land of My Fathers: 2000 Years of Welsh History* (Talybont: Y Lolfa, 1998).

Evans, Gwynfor, *Fighting for Wales* (Talybont: Y Lolfa, 1991).

Evans, J. Wyn and Wooding, Jonathan M., *St David of Wales: Cult, Church and Nation* (Woodbridge: Boydell Press, 2007).

Evans, J., *Pictures of the Welsh during the Tudor Period…with Some Account of the Translation of the Bible into Welsh by Bishop Morgan* (Liverpool: publisher, 1893)

Fox, Cyril, *Ancient Monuments: South Wales* (London: Her Majesty's Stationery Office, 1955).

Gerald of Wales, *The Journey Through Wales and The Description of Wales* (London: Penguin, 2004).

Gibson, Alex, *The Walton Basin, Powys, Wales: Survey at the Hindwell Neolithic Enclosure* (Welshpool: Clwyd-Powys Archaeological Trust, 1999).

Gildas, *The Ruin of Britain* (London: Phillimore, 1978).

Gilpin, William, Rev., *Observations on the River Wye, and Several Parts of South Wales, &c. Relative Chiefly to Picturesque Beauty; made in the Summer of the Year 1770* (London, 1782).

Gottfried, Robert, *The Black Death: Natural and Human Disaster in Medieval Europe* (New York: The Free Press, 1983).

Herbert, Trevor and Jones, Gareth Elwyn, *Edward I and Wales* (Cardiff: University of Wales Press, 1988).

Herbert, Trevor and Jones, Gareth Elwyn, *People & Protest: Wales 1815-1880* (Cardiff: University of Wales Press, 1990).

Herbert, Trevor and Jones, Gareth Elwyn, *Post-War Wales* (Cardiff: University of Wales Press, 1995).

Herbert, Trevor and Jones, Gareth Elwyn, *The Remaking of Wales in the Eighteenth Century* (Cardiff: University of Wales Press, 1988).

Herbert, Trevor and Jones, Gareth Elwyn, *Tudor Wales* (Cardiff: University of Wales Press, 1988).

Herbert, Trevor and Jones, Gareth Elwyn, *Wales 1880-1914* (Cardiff: University of Wales Press).

Herbert, Trevor and Jones, Gareth Elwyn, *Wales Between the Wars* (Cardiff: University of Wales Press, 1988).

Hilling, John, *The Historic Architecture of Wales* (Cardiff: University of Wales Press, 1976).

Hughes, W.J., *Wales and the Welsh in English Literature* (Wrexham: Hughes and Son, 1924).

Jankulak, Karen, *Geoffrey of Monmouth* (Cardiff: University of Wales Press, 2010).

Jenkins, H. Geraint, *A Concise History of Wales* (Cambridge: Cambridge University Press, 2007).

Jenkins, H. Geraint, 'Taphy-land historians' and the Union of England and Wales 1536 – 2007,' *Journal of Irish and Scottish Studies* (March 2008), Vol. 1: Issue 2.

Jenkins, H. Geraint, 'A Rank Republican (and) a Leveller,' *Welsh History Review*, Vol. 17, No. 3 (June, 1995): 365-386.

Jenkins, Nigel, *Real Swansea* (Bridgend: Seren, 2008).

Jenkins, Nigel, 'Llywelyn ap Gruffudd Fychan,' *Hotel Gwales* (Llandysul: Gomer, 2006).

Johnes, Martin, *A History of Wales Since 1939* (Stroud: Amberley Publishing, 2011).

Jones, Gareth Elwyn and Smith, Dai, *The People of Wales.* (Llandysul: Gomer, 1999).

Jones, Graham, J., *A Pocket Guide to The History of Wales* (Cardiff: University of Wales Press/ *Western Mail*, 1998).

Jones, Rhys, 'Mapping Referenda', *Planet* magazine (May 2011), No. 202.

Jones, Richard Wyn and Scully, Roger (eds.), 'Devolution in Wales: What Does the Public Think?' *Findings from the Economic and Research Council's Research Programme on Devolution and Constitutional Change* (June 2004), briefing No. 7.

Koch, John T., *Tartessian: Celtic in the South-west at the Dawn of History* (Aberystwyth: Celtic Studies Publications, 2009).

Lewis, Ceri, *Iolo Morganwg* (Caernarfon: Gwasg Pantycelyn, 1995).

Lord, Peter, *The Visual Culture of Wales: Industrial Society* (Cardiff: University of Wales Press, 1998).

Lord, Peter, *The Visual Culture of Wales: Medieval Vision* (Cardiff: University of Wales Press, 2003).

Lord, Peter, *Words with Pictures: Welsh Images and Images of Wales in the Popular Press, 1640-1860* (Cardiff: University of Wales Press, 1995).

McAllister, Laura, *Plaid Cymru: The Emergence of a Political Party* (Bridgend: Seren, 2001).

Maund, Kari, *The Welsh Kings: The Medieval Rulers of Wales* (Stroud: Tempus, 2000).

Morgan, Gerald, *A Brief History of Wales* (Talybont: Y Lolfa, 2008).

Morgan, Kenneth, O., *Rebirth of a Nation: Wales 1880-1980* (Oxford: Oxford University Press, 1981).

Morgan, Kenneth, O., *Wales in British Politics: 1868-1922* (Cardiff: University of Wales Press, 1991).

Morgan, Prys, *The Tempus History of Wales* (Stroud: Tempus, 2001).

Morris, Jan, *The Matter of Wales: Epic Views of a Small Country* (London: Penguin, 1994).

Newman, John, *The Buildings of Wales: Gwent/Monmouthshire* (London: Penguin, 2000).

Owen, A. (ed.), *Ancient Laws and Institutions of Wales; Comprising Laws Supposed to be Enacted by Howel The Good, Modified by Subsequent Regulations under the Native Princes prior to the Conquest by Edward the First* (London: Eyre and Spottiswoode, 1841).

Pennant, Thomas, *Tours in Wales* (London: Wilkie & Robinson, 1810).

Powell, T.G.E., *The Celts* (London: Thames & Hudson, 1959).

Redknap, Mark, *Vikings in Wales: An Archaeological Quest* (Cardiff: National Museums and Galleries of Wales, 2000).

Rees, Dylan, *Carmarthenshire* (Cardiff: University of Wales Press, 2006).

Rees, William, 'The Black Death in England and Wales, as exhibited in Manorial Documents,' *Journal of the Royal Society of Medicine* (1923), Vol. 16 (Sect Hist Med): 27—45.

Richards, John, *Maritime Wales* (Stroud: Tempus, 2007).

Rivet, A.L.F., *Town and Country in Roman Britain* (Hutchinson: London, 1958).

Roberts, Dewi (ed.), *Wales: A Celebration* (Llanrwst: Gwasg Carreg Gwalch, 2000).

Roberts, Gwyneth Tyson, *The Language of the Blue Books: The Perfect Instruments of Empire* (Cardiff: University of Wales Press, 1998).

Roderick, A.J., *Wales Through the Ages* (Llandybie: Christopher Davies, 1959).

Ross, Anne, *Druids: Preachers of Immortality* (Stroud: Tempus, 2004).

Rowley, Trevor, *The Welsh Border: Archaeology, History & Landscape* (Stroud, Tempus, 1986).

Shipton, Martin, *Poor Man's Parliament: Ten Years of the Welsh Assembly* (Bridgend: Seren, 2011).

Skidmore, Ian, *Gwynedd* (London: Robert Hale, 1986).

Smith, Dai, *A People and a Proletariat* (London: Pluto Press, 1980).

Smith, Dai, *Wales: A Question for History* (Bridgend: Seren, 1999).

Smith, J. Beverley, *Llywelyn ap Gruffudd: Prince of Wales* (Cardiff: University of Wales Press, 1998).

Somer, Marianne, *Bones & Ochre: The Curious Afterlife of the Red Lady of Paviland* (Cambridge, Mass. and London: Harvard University Press, 2007).

Stead, Peter, *Acting Wales: Stars of Stage and Screen* (Cardiff: University of Wales Press, 2002).

Stead, Peter and Williams, Gareth, *Wales and its Boxers: The Fighting Tradition* (Cardiff: University of Wales Press, 2008).

Stephens, Meic, *Artists in Wales* (Llandysul: Gomer, 1971).

Stephens, Meic, *Artists in Wales, Vol. 2* (Llandysul: Gomer, 1973).

Stephens, Meic, *A Most Peculiar People* (Cardiff: University of Wales Press, 1992).

Stephens, Meic, *The Oxford Companion to the Literature of Wales* (Oxford: Oxford University Press, 1986).

Tacitus, *The Annals*, translated by A. J. Woodman (Indianapolis: Hackett Publishing, 2004).

Tanner, Marcus, *The Last of the Celts* (New Haven: Yale University Press, 2004).

Thomas Tout, *The Collected Papers of Thomas Frederick Tout* (Manchester: Manchester University Press, 1932).

Turvey, Roger, *The Lord Rhys: Prince of Deheubarth* (Llandysul: Gomer, 1997).

Vaughan-Thomas, Wynford, *Wales* (New York: St. Martin's Press, 1981).

Wade-Evans, A. W., *Life of St. David* (New York: Society for the Promoting Christian Knowledge, 1923).

Walker, David. *Medieval Wales* (Cambridge: Cambridge University Press, 1990).

Williams, David, *A History of Modern Wales* (London: John Murray, 1977).

Williams, Glanmor, *Renewal and Reformation Wales c.1415 – 1642* (Oxford: Oxford University Press, 1993).

Williams, Gwyn A., *When Was Wales?* (Harmondsworth: Penguin, 1985).

Williams, Mark, *Fiery Shapes: Celestial Portents and Astrology in Ireland and Wales, 700–1700* (Oxford: Oxford University Press, 2010).

Withey, Alun, 'History of Disease in Wales,' *Western Mail* and *WalesOnline.co.uk* (29 March 2011), www.walesonline.co.uk.

Ziegler, Philip, *The Black Death*, (New York: Harper & Row, 1971).

INDEX

Entries in *italics* indicate maps.

PICTURE CREDITS

ACKNOWLEDGEMENTS

Many historians have fed insight and information into the research process for the TV series and some of their interviews have supplied details found between the pages of this book.

In recent decades Wales has been blessed by successive flowerings of historians and I have been the beneficiary of the work of people such as Gwyn Alf Williams, Dai Smith and John Davies. I've been lucky to spend time in pubs with all three of them. John, in particular, turned the back room of the Halfway into a veritable university and I feel privileged to call him a friend. Something seeped in.

Huge thanks to my fellow writer Nigel Jenkins for allowing me to conclude the book with an excerpt from his elegy to Llywelyn ap Gruffydd Fychan from his collection *Hotel Gwales*.

I should like to thank Phil George from Green Bay Media for persuading me to write the book and to Albert DePetrillo at BBC Books for commissioning it.

I am also grateful to Huw Edwards for his typically clear-eyed, insightful and passionate introduction. *Diolch yn fawr, gyfaill.*

My single, biggest debt of thanks goes to my wonderful editor, Laura Higginson who thoroughly improved the text and gave its wide panorama her meticulous attention. Working with her was a 'sincere sensation', to quote Woody Allen.

Professor Geraint H. Jenkins kindly read the manuscript and made a great many useful suggestions and corrections. Needless to say, any faults that remain are entirely my own.

Last but certainly not least I'd like to thank my wife Sarah for putting up with my irritating refusals to come outside and enjoy the California sunshine: this history was written in Oakland, and there were too many occasions when my daughters, Elena and Onwy – not to mention the hummingbirds in the garden – were overlooked because 'dad was with his books'. Hopefully there'll be something in it for them to enjoy when they're older. It is certainly dedicated to them with love. *Gyda chariad hollol.*

Jon Gower